ESCAPING HITLER

MONTY HALLS is an ex-Royal Marine, marine biologist,
documentary broadcaster, expedition leader and writer.
He is best known for his Great Escapes series on BBC2 but has
presented series for Channel 4, Channel 5, the History Channel
and National Geographic. He is also a speaker and corporate
trainer in the area of leadership and team building. He has
written several books including *The Fisherman's Apprentice*
and the Monty Halls' Great Escape series, and is a regular
contributor to magazines and newspapers.

Also by Monty Halls

The Fisherman's Apprentice

Monty Halls' Great Irish Escape

The Great Escape: Adventures on the Wild West Coast

Monty Halls' Great Escape: Beachcomber's Cottage

Great Ocean Adventures

Dive: The Ultimate Guide to Sixty of the World's Top Dive Locations

ESCAPING HITLER

Heroic True Stories of
Great Escapes in Nazi Europe

MONTY HALLS

PAN BOOKS

First published 2017 by Sidgwick & Jackson

First published in paperback 2017 by Sidgwick & Jackson

This edition first published 2018 by Pan Books
an imprint of Pan Macmillan
20 New Wharf Road, London N1 9RR
Associated companies throughout the world
www.panmacmillan.com

ISBN 978-1-5098-6601-4

Copyright © Sea Dog TV and Film Productions Ltd 2017

The right of Monty Halls to be identified as the
author of this work has been asserted by him in accordance
with the Copyright, Designs and Patents Act 1988.

The picture acknowledgements on page 307 constitute
an extension of this copyright page.

7 9 8 6

A CIP catalogue record for this book is available from the British Library.

Map artwork by ML Design
Typeset by Palimpsest Book Production Limited, Falkirk, Stirlingshire
Printed and bound by CPI Group (UK) Ltd, Croydon, CR0 4YY

Visit **www.panmacmillan.com** to read more about all our books
and to buy them. You will also find features, author interviews and
news of any author events, and you can sign up for e-newsletters
so that you're always first to hear about our new releases.

To my dad,
who served his country,

and to Isla and Molly,
who I pray never have to witness
the horrors of conflict

CONTENTS

PART FOUR *The Crow's Flight, Slovenia*

PREFACE

It is not unreasonable to assume that the desire for freedom is universal, something fundamental to us all. Surely, when faced with a choice between imprisonment and liberty, simple human nature means that we would do whatever it takes to slip the bonds of captivity. But in researching this book, it became apparent that such decisions are seldom simple.

Time and time again, when I met the few remaining survivors of the Freedom Trails of the Second World War, I recognized an indomitable spirit which meant that they often defied logic, the enemy, the elements, and even their companions to take their fate into their own hands. It is only in trekking the trails that one realizes the physical challenge involved (and for most I only did key sections of the entire routes). Frequently, the escapees would arrive at the start of the main Freedom Trail – for example over the mountains of the Pyrenees – having already been on the run for several hundred kilometres over the course of many months. They were so often pitifully ill-equipped, malnourished and under immense mental strain, and yet they still had what it took to take on formidable natural features that required the skills and endurance of mountaineers.

Such independence of thought and action has also been readily apparent in the people who helped them on their way – the vast majority of escapers fully acknowledge that without local assistance and support, they would not have had the slightest chance of regaining their freedom. The courage of the local people who did offer this assistance is beyond debate, as they invariably faced brutal reprisals if captured. Despite the huge risk to themselves, they still gave everything they had in order to help complete strangers. To a large degree, they are the heroes of these stories.

They are old men and women now, those who remain to tell their own tales of escape or defiance of their enemy in an occupied land. But despite the passage of time, this crystal spirit still shines brightly. Although invariably modest and unassuming ('Anyone would have done it' is a recurring theme in most interviews), they do speak proudly of their deeds, wearing them as a badge of honour and a defining moment in their lives. Under the most pressing of circumstances, they weren't found wanting. How many of us – faced with similar, near impossible choices – would have shown the same strength of character?

Although such individual qualities are a continual theme in this book, the four main escape stories present contrasting circumstances and environments. The SAS raid in the Rossano Valley in Italy tells the tale of an extraordinary group of men exfiltrating through a benighted and stricken landscape (the SAS never retreat, they exfiltrate. I was reminded of this with some vigour by a modern Special Forces contact!). By stark contrast, the exploits of a young man from Hackney – one who had never left England before the war began – in not only living covertly in the midst of the German occupiers, but then making a heroic bid for freedom over the immense white wastes of Monte Amaro, represent a monument to an indefatigable will to survive as well as great personal initiative and drive. The Crow's Flight in Slovenia is truly one of the most remarkable escape stories of the entire war – the largest successful escape by Allied POWs during the conflict, and a feat of leadership by one man that rings through the ages. And finally, there are the Pyrenees escape lines – immense in their scale, both logistically and geographically. One in particular, the Pat O'Leary line, was run by a man who was truly a colossus in the annals of escape and evasion. These are routes that the Nazis never truly conquered, operating with a local support network that they never fully subdued.

As a former Royal Marine myself, it was absolutely fascinating to investigate the physical, moral and mental challenges that faced the individuals who moved along these trails. Like so many of my generation, I have never been pursued, harried and hunted by a relentless and well-equipped enemy. I have never lived in fear of my life through a simple accident of time and place, of ethnicity and of culture. To walk these trails through some of the most dramatic landscapes in Europe is all about perspective – we are indeed blessed, with so much of what we have today owed to the sacrifices of those who have gone before. I felt dwarfed by the immensity of the scenery around me and awestruck at the stoicism and bravery of the people who played out their roles against the backdrop of the Second World War. I urge you to attempt some of these walks yourself, to follow the stories, and to experience just how far we have come as a continent since those dark days. In this new age of mass migration, of the movement of desperate groups of people into unknown lands, the stories of the Freedom Trails truly resonate. They offer a template for the very best, and the very worst, of human nature.

I will finish with my own small tribute to the men and women who used these trails, as well as those who bravely maintained the networks and infrastructure around them. Your stories are truly inspirational, it has been my pleasure to meet you, and my great privilege to walk in your footsteps.

Monty Halls

PART ONE

The Promise of Freedom
Pyrenees, France

'Freedom is not a gift from heaven –
one must fight for it every day'

Simon Wiesenthal

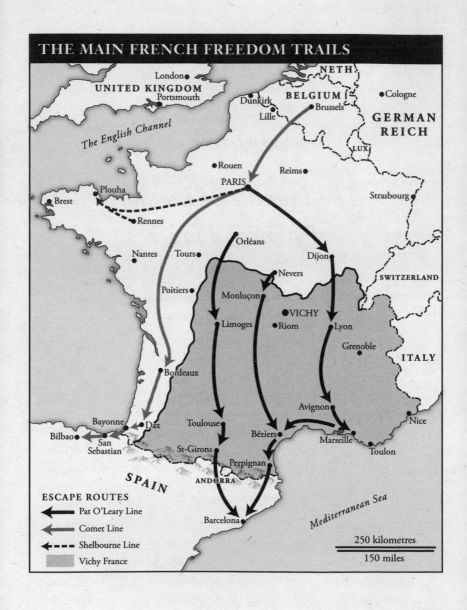

THE MAIN FRENCH FREEDOM TRAILS

UNITED KINGDOM

London

Portsmouth

The English Channel

NETH.

BELGIUM

Cologne

GERMAN REICH

Dunkirk

Lille

Brussels

LUX.

Rouen

Reims

Strasbourg

PARIS

Brest

Plouha

Rennes

Nantes

Tours

Orléans

Dijon

SWITZERLAND

Nevers

Poitiers

Monluçon

Bordeaux

Limoges

VICHY

Riom

Lyon

Grenoble

ITALY

Avignon

Bayonne

Dax

Toulouse

Béziers

Marseille

Nice

Bilbao

San Sebastian

St-Girons

Perpignan

Toulon

SPAIN

ANDORRA

Barcelona

Mediterranean Sea

ESCAPE ROUTES

→ Pat O'Leary Line

→ Comet Line

-→ Shelbourne Line

Vichy France

250 kilometres

150 miles

CHAPTER ONE

Escapers and Evaders

Per Ardua Libertas

'Through Hard Work, Liberty'

The title of a photographic survey of MI9's work,
produced by Christopher Clayton Hutton, and issued to
MI5 and MI6 (SIS) in an edition of fewer than
one hundred in 1942

In war, ordinary people are called upon to do extraordinary things, and are thrown into situations and circumstances so totally unfamiliar that they must learn fast if they are to survive. In the case of prisoners of war, they may have had virtually all of their rights removed, and their rank, honour and dignity stripped away by incarceration. But they could still maintain a flicker of hope – they could plan their escape. As Viktor Frankl notes in *Man's Search for Meaning*: 'Everything can be taken from a man but one thing: the last of the human freedoms – to choose one's attitude in any given set of circumstances, to choose one's own way.'

During the war, many prisoners exercised this right, but not as many as one might expect. Although there was an unspoken code amongst Allied soldiers that they should always seek a means of returning home and from there go back to the battle, for some, incarceration offered a way of seeing out the war in relative safety. Many men simply did not have the heart for an escape attempt. Others had skills which were indispensable in aiding other escapers, and therefore remained in the camps to assist their compatriots: the forgers of passports and other documents, the coders, the organizers and creators of escape aids. There were also those few who actively collaborated with the enemy, such as the traitor Harold Cole – a key character in one of the more compelling stories of the freedom trails. Indeed, there were occasions where POWs were actively discouraged from escaping – for example after the Italian surrender of September 1943, senior officers ordered prisoners to stay put in their camps until the Allied advance could liberate them.

But there were many, many POWs who did decide to make a run for it, and their stories are some of the most compelling of the entire war. They overcame overwhelming odds to escape, and once beyond the wire almost all of them relied heavily on civilian assistance and support. Networks sprang up throughout Europe to assist escapees, and were notable for the presence of a large number of women. Their stories are quite remarkable – almost invariably they were young, and operated with great courage in organizing and running the escape routes. Their names deserve to echo through the ages. Virginia d'Albert Lake, Marie Dissard, Lisa Fittko, Andrée ('Dédée') de Jongh, Elsie Maréchal, Nancy Wake (Fiocca) and Mary Lindell – all were titanic figures in the smooth running of the lines.

It's especially important to acknowledge the civilian contribution because so few received any recognition at all after the war. Instead, they were left to pick up the ruins of their lives, having paid a horrendous price for helping the strangers in their midst.

They knew the risks they were running, and still chose to do the right thing, to defy their enemies and to help their friends, albeit ones from distant lands who – on the whole – did not even speak their language. It should be remembered that while, for the most part, recaptured POWs could expect no more punishment than a return to camp and a spell in solitary confinement, the same did not apply to the civilians who helped them. If they were caught, they might face not only execution, but the killing of their families and the destruction of their homes. Their heroism was – on the whole – consistent and inspiring.

Which, of course, is not to say that everyone could be trusted: M. R. D. Foot, who served with Combined Operations HQ and the SAS during the war, was seriously wounded when he was run through with a pitchfork by a French farmer during one of his escape attempts. The escape lines' managers had to be constantly on the alert for Nazi double-agents posing as escapers or evaders, as well as direct intervention by German forces as the result of betrayal. There were traitors within their own ranks, such as the Dutchman Christiaan 'King Kong' Lindemans, and the French gangster and ardent Gestapo collaborator and torturer Abel 'Mammouth' Danos. Even Mary Lindell, the wealthy Surrey woman who married the Comte de Milleville and set up her own escape route, the Marie-Claire Line, has been accused in recent years of operating as a double agent.

And to this mix may be added the disagreements, rivalries and conflicts of interest which arose between the various secret service departments, often over budgets. MI6 (the Secret Intelligence Service, founded in 1916 out of the original 1909 Secret Service Bureau) was often wary of MI9, which was established in 1939 to aid POW escapees, and certainly resented the actions and interventions of the SOE (Special Operations Executive, formed in 1940 to conduct sabotage and subversion in occupied Europe).

But despite the many hazards and obstacles, the escape lines continued to run, and as the war progressed more and more prisoners slipped from captivity and into established local support networks. In turn, the Germans redoubled their efforts at infiltration, surveillance and intimidation. This cat-and-mouse game, played for the highest stakes imaginable, lasted throughout the war, with the tides of fortune favouring first one side and then the other. To prevail required an ability to adapt and evolve, as well as genuine courage. At stake was the fate of the escapees themselves – the 'packages', as they were known.

Prisoners of war were of varying value to their captors. Captured aircrew and elite troops were of more value than ordinary infantry. In Britain, for example, Axis POWs were divided into three categories, white, grey and black. 'White' meant infantry, repatriated as soon as possible after hostilities ended. 'Grey' indicated aircrew, U-boat crew and other elite troops, such as paratroopers and Waffen-SS, who were only sent back after debriefing. For some this was as late as 1948 – they were kept in open prisons and used as farm labourers for the intervening period. Finally, there was 'black', which denoted Nazis, who were retained for thorough interrogation and – if possible – a 'denazification' procedure.

This tiered system is why the famous Great Escape from Stalag-Luft III (Sagan) in March 1944 – about six months after the Wooden Horse escape from the same camp – caused such annoyance to the Germans, and such an extreme reaction from them. All the escapers were aircrew – and whether Britain had enough aircrew to take the fight to the Germans hung in the balance throughout the war.

It was not just POWs who used the escape lines – as the intensity and number of air raids increased, so did the number of aircraft shot down and crews forced to bail out. Indeed, the RAF has calculated that, during the Second World War, of every one hundred aircrew, fifty-five would die in action, thirty-one would survive the war, but of those three would receive life-altering injuries, and the remaining fourteen would parachute into occupied territory (a distinctly hazardous thing to do – it wasn't unusual for them to be killed out of hand by locals whose families had been the victims of air raids, as Len Deighton so vividly describes in his novel *Bomber*). Of those fourteen men, twelve would be taken prisoner. But two – that's 2 per cent of all RAF aircrew involved in the conflict, still a substantial figure – would go on the run. For the fight to be continued, it was crucial that these men made their way back home safely.

It's no surprise that both the escapes from Stalag-Luft III were made into feature films after the war, in 1950 and 1963. The earlier film, *The Wooden Horse*, conveys succinctly what life in the camps and on the run must have been like. Successful escapes had a positive effect on morale, both in and out of the camps, though even among belligerents who were signatories to the Geneva Convention there could be fear of reprisal. But this was no deterrent, and although certain privileges in the camp would often be withdrawn following an escape, it was still seen as the right thing to do. Certain rules applied as well: to kill, wound or even hit an enemy soldier or a civilian who attempted to obstruct an escape, was accounted criminal by many a Senior British Officer (SBO) in the camps. From a practical point of view, such actions, especially the first two, would also be sure to result in severe reprisals for fellow prisoners left behind. Escape proposals were also vetted by each camp's Escape Committee before being given the go-ahead by the camp's senior British or American officer.

The servicemen most likely to try to escape were those who had already shown promise, bravery and initiative as active combatants – those, too, who could least endure the deadly *ennui* of life in the camps. Some command of French, German or Italian would certainly help, but the Third Reich was so full of displaced persons and foreign labourers that it was easier to blend in than might be imagined – all that was required was the right kind of confidence, and ideally some local support.

Many thousands of prisoners, agents, refugees and downed airmen did successfully escape – 33,000 over the Pyrenees alone – including some of the most legendary figures of the entire war.

One of them is – if I may briefly indulge here – a personal hero of mine. Herbert 'Blondie' Hasler (1914–1987) was the leader of Operation Frankton, a covert attack by Royal Marines in six two-man collapsible kayaks to attach limpet mines to German ships in Bordeaux harbour in November 1942. The plan was for the commandos, who had been transported by submarine, to make their way overland to Spain after the operation. In the event, only Hasler and his partner, William Sparks, made it, after a march of 160 kilometres through enemy-held territory. They arrived at a friendly farm and were guided across the Pyrenees by locals using the Marie-Claire Line – after which Mary Lindell sent a secret message to Britain reporting their safe arrival in neutral territory. Hasler finally arrived back in Britain in April 1943. The mission he commanded was also the subject of a feature film, *Cockleshell Heroes*, in 1955.

For the modern walker such as myself, embarking on these routes for the first time and following the remarkable tales of those who used them, the freedom trails were irresistible. They make their way through some of the most glorious scenery in Europe, and along the way the paths, huts and caves which sheltered the escapers and their guides can still be seen, a poignant reminder of a none-too-distant and violent past which has directly affected all of us in modern society. I had proper equipment – windproof and waterproof jackets, mountain boots, trekking poles. Those who trod these paths as escapers had none of those things. They might have had nothing more on their feet than espadrilles, nothing more on their backs than a hand-me-down raincoat, and they'd be travelling at night, with little to eat or drink, through rain and snow. Even for a fully and properly equipped traveller, prepared and in training, these trails are no picnic. But they remain more or less intact to this day, a monument to the courage and endurance of those who used them in grim earnest. To walk the trails is to realize just how brightly the human spirit can burn, and how indefatigable people can be when the odds seem so impossibly stacked against them. And that brings me to the most important thing about the trails: many of these remarkable people are still alive, though now in their nineties. We are the fortunate – and final – generation who can have our own travels along the freedom trails vividly illuminated by the people who actually created and used them.

During the Second World War, particularly in its latter stages, Europe was criss-crossed with escape lines – routes created by local people, using local knowledge, and supported by individuals and communities along their length. They existed with one purpose alone, to provide a means of escape from occupied territories and into neutral or Allied controlled zones. Some were well known, both to the Allies and indeed the Axis powers, who did everything possible to disrupt and destroy them. Others were less prominent, involving boat crossings on moonless nights using muffled oars, or walking less conventional trails through obscure terrain. But – in the broadest terms – there were three main routes in western Europe.

The Comet Line was organized by a Belgian countess, Andrée de Jongh, and ran from Brussels and Paris down to Bayonne and over the western end of the Pyrenees to San Sebastian and Bilbao. From there, escapers would make their way to Madrid and thence to Gibraltar.

The Pat O'Leary Line or the Pat Line, as it was known unofficially, or PAO, to give it its formal appellation, took various routes to the Pyrenees, and became a network of great complexity and scope. Its story, as we shall see, is one of intrigue, betrayal, courage, and – ultimately – great humanity.

The Shelburne Line was the shortest of the three, and the one which involved no seriously difficult terrain. It was also the only one never to be infiltrated by the Germans. It ran from Paris and Rennes to Plouha in Brittany, whence escapers and evaders were taken by a British motor gun boat to safety at Falmouth.

There were of course many other, lesser known freedom trails. In Italy, there were numerous routes from what, after September 1943, became the Axis-occupied north to the Allied-occupied south. From Germany itself there were also routes into Switzerland and Sweden. One famous route, the scene of the largest of all prisoner breakouts, crossed Slovenia. And then there were the many escapers and evaders who took their own highways to liberty, with varying degrees of success. Of course, the first point on any escape, no matter how elaborate the network and sophisticated the infrastructure to support it, is the simple decision of an individual to go on the run. Making such a decision was influenced by timing, the right circumstances, and – crucially – the right frame of mind.

The psychological state of captured prisoners wasn't something taken into account until relatively late in military history. To be captured had been regarded as dishonourable and disgraceful in earlier conflicts, and during the Second World War it still was in the eyes of one combatant, Japan – which partly accounts for that country's treatment of POWs. Russia too was slow to change its views, and the fact that it was not a signatory of the Geneva Convention was one of the reasons why Soviet troops received much worse treatment in the camps than other nationalities.

Between the end of the First World War and the start of the second, the pace of technological development in warfare meant that capture carried less and less of a stigma. The speed at which an army could move, outflanking an opponent and bringing devastating fire down upon them, had increased dramatically (typified by the Blitzkreig tactics deployed by the Germans at the start of the War). Aircraft and tanks, longer range artillery, machine guns, mortars – all were developed to a point where surrender was often the only option available to a vanquished opponent. Submarine attacks became a new method of combat, paratroopers and commandos were introduced, and cost-effective, small-scale strike forces such as the SAS came into being, sweeping aside old rules of warfare and encouraging individual thought and initiative in fighting men. Indeed, one of the trails covered in this book follows the remarkable exfiltration by a small SAS patrol from the Rossano Valley in northern Italy, through the Marble Mountains and westwards to the Mediterranean coast and the safety of the Allied lines. The training, initiative and expertise of that patrol cannot be overstated – it is hard to imagine that only thirty years earlier generals had still been sending men into set-piece battles along the lines of Waterloo.

For the vast majority of captured troops, life in the prison camps was unutterably dull. Though sometimes a small number of books were available, and there may have been limited sporting facilities and various clubs and societies, these were hardly enough to pass the time – especially if none of those activities appealed to you. For many captives, young men in the prime of life and especially active, there was an urgent desire to get out, not just to re-join the fighting, but to escape the claustrophobia, to walk down streets, through a wood, to go to a movie, sleep in a proper bed, have a proper bath, wear clothes that didn't itch, get away from unmitigated male company and date a girl. And of course, despite everything, there was for some of them an element of personal shame at having been captured, however irrational that feeling may have been.

Once we take all these factors into account, it is unsurprising that as soon as the trauma of capture had receded, thoughts of escape grew in the minds of many. There was a psychological bonus to this: planning and organizing an escape, especially if you knew there were those outside willing to help you, alleviated the debilitating boredom of camp life. The act of planning stimulated the intellect and gave you a reason for living. Perhaps the worst element of being a prisoner of war was that your term of incarceration was indefinite. It would last as long as hostilities lasted, and that might mean decades, for all anyone knew. It could be argued that those whose skills made it essential for them to remain prisoners in order to help escapees had their own sense of purpose, but nonetheless the depressive effects of incarceration could be fatal. One poignant story is that of Malcolm Sinclair, the 'Red Fox', as the Germans called him. After two unsuccessful attempts to escape Colditz – in 1943 and early 1944 – on 25 September 1944 he suddenly made a run for the wire and was shot dead as he ignored warnings and tried to climb it. The Red Cross identified this as an 'act of despair'. Many inmates of the concentration camps sought death in this way – taking a considered, suicidal path to freedom of a sort. They had, at least, exercised Frankl's right to 'choose their own way'.

By 1942, all sections of the Allied military knew that capture could happen to anyone, and wasn't necessarily the result of cowardice or misjudgement. In their history of MI9, M. R. D. Foot and J. M. Langley note that in the overall course of the Second

World War about fifteen million people were taken prisoner. Escapers and evaders represent a very small percentage of that number. Although in the European theatre a larger percentage went on the run than in the global context of POWs, they still did not represent a substantial percentage of the total who were incarcerated. But even that small percentage of a percentage could cause great disruption to enemy infrastructure by tying up manpower which could be more usefully deployed elsewhere, and for some that was reason enough at least to try to get away from the camps.

Escape attempts were helped by the termination of the Molotov–Ribbentrop Pact in summer 1941, after which the vast majority of German forces were deployed on the Eastern Front. Guards in the camps, therefore, tended to be either very young, unfit, or too old for active service. Commandants were generally regular forces officers pulled out of retirement, and thus 'old school', in the positive sense of the expression – they abided by an honourable code from a more chivalrous time. Service for service, the guards had a degree of respect for the prisoners, despite 'goon-baiting' being one of the skills taught at the MI9 escape facility in Highgate – taunting guards was a small act of defiance that maintained morale, and might disrupt camp routine. The Wehrmacht officers also had little time for the SS and indeed Nazism, meaning that Jewish POWs were more often than not protected from transportation to the concentration camps.

Escape bids came most frequently from the officers' camps, the *Oflager*. This is not to say that Other Ranks did not attempt to escape or that they were not successful. Around one hundred Distinguished Service Medals were awarded to Other Ranks for escape or evasion activity or services while in captivity. But POWs of officer rank were not required to do any kind of work – in itself a double-edged sword, for inmates on work detail might at least see the outside of a camp, and people other than fellow prisoners.

Confined to camp, the officers had leisure to think, plan and to organize. Most officers were still recruited from middle- and upper-class backgrounds, and had gone through systems of education which not only reinforced the idea of a male society, but inculcated ideas of personal integrity and self-confidence coupled with a sense of duty and an ability to engage in teamwork – all perfect qualities to deal with the problems they would encounter as POWs.

They were also reared on books and stories which emphasized a spirit of adventure and derring-do, from *Boy's Own* magazine to the novels of H. Rider Haggard. From 1921 they were able to read a true-life adventure involving escape from the Germans – a volume that was to light the blue touch paper for so many escape bids during the Second World War.

The book was *The Escaping Club*, by Winchester-educated Squadron Leader Alfred John – 'Johnny' – Evans (1899–1960). Evans was shot down over the Somme on 16 July 1916 during an early morning reconnaissance flight. He didn't take happily to a POW's life, and quickly managed to escape. Recaptured, and sent to Fort 9 at Ingolstadt (the Great War's equivalent of Colditz), he escaped again and made his way, with Lieutenant Sidney Buckley, 160 kilometres to Switzerland. He arrived at the Schaffhausen Salient, west of the Bodensee, at 12.30 a.m. on 9 June 1917, after eighteen days on the run. His immensely readable book, which ran to five reprints in its year of publication, was both an adventure story and a prototype escaper's manual, containing clear and concise details of every aspect of camp life and escape procedure. The club he refers to was real: recaptured escapers shared their experiences with other prisoners and pooled knowledge to improve future attempts. Outside help was there too: maps and compasses were smuggled in with clothing and food parcels, and Evans' mother sent him home-made cakes which contained maps. Bags of flour, bottles of pickled prunes and jars of Gentleman's Relish all served as hiding places for escape aids.

Evans noted in his book that the possibility of escape was highest when being transported between facilities or camps, a fact vividly illustrated in his own audacious escape. Hearing that they were to be transferred from Fort 9 to a camp further from the Swiss border, Evans and Buckley decided to jump off their transport train:

> We had this in our favour, that we both talked German fairly fluently and well enough, with luck, to pass for Germans if only a few words were needed. Against us was the fact that, as we were going officially by train, we had to be in almost full uniform. By dint of continually wearing grey flannels, the English had induced the Germans to believe that grey flannels were part of the English uniform. I struck a bargain with a Frenchman for a Tyrolese hat, and Buckley very ingeniously made himself a very German-looking hat out of an old straw hat and some cloth. For food, we both stuffed the pockets of our tunics full of chocolate and condensed foods. Besides this I carried a home-made haversack full of biscuits and raw bacon, and Buckley had a small dispatch-case in which he had mainly condensed food – Oxo cubes, Horlick's malted milk, meat lozenges, etc. Thus equipped, and with Burberrys to cover our uniforms, we thought we should pass as Germans in the dark.

An escaper's manual indeed. In terms of how to manage food and smuggled-in kit, among many other things, *The Escaping Club* is the model and springboard for much of the thinking which inspired MI9 when it was formed eighteen years after the book's publication; and Johnny Evans was one of the department's key figures and ablest lecturers. With great foresight, and as an experienced Intelligence officer, he had returned to Schaffhausen before the outbreak of war in 1939, photographing the border area and making notes. His observations, together with detailed maps of the area, facilitated many escapes from Nazi Germany into Switzerland during the second conflict.

But the musings of a successful escapee from the First World War were not enough. The volume of POWs taken, and the impact this had on the war effort, meant that more formal measures were required. And this is where Winston Churchill stepped in. Churchill was himself an escaper in the Boer War, and as such he gave his blessing to the creation of a special department – MI9 – set up on 23 December 1939 to aid and promote escape and evasion, and offer moral and practical support to prisoners of war. It was formed at precisely the right moment, as six months later the Dunkirk debacle saw many thousands of members of the British Expeditionary Force in captivity. As early as August 1940, MI6 proposed to MI9 the setting-up of an escape line from Marseilles to Spain.

As its name suggests, MI9 existed within the new Directorate of Military Intelligence. It wasn't an easy birth, and the fact that it came under the same wing as MI6 and was not controlled by the Foreign Office (as Foreign Secretary Anthony Eden had hoped) led to friction between the two sub-departments which might otherwise have been avoided.

Nonetheless, MI9's mandate was clear, as outlined in its initial charter:

1. A new section of the Intelligence Directorate at the War Office has been formed. It will be called M. I. 9. It will work in close connection with and act as agent for the Admiralty and Air Ministry.

2. The Section is responsible for:
   (a) The preparation and execution of plans for facilitating the escape of British Prisoners of War of all three services in Germany or elsewhere.
   (b) Arranging instruction in connection with above.
   (c) Making other advance provision, as considered necessary.
   (d) Collection and dissemination of information obtained from British Prisoners of War.
   (e) Advising on counter-escape measures for German Prisoners of War in Great Britain, if requested to do so.

The new sub-department was to be housed in Room 424 of the Metropole Hotel in Northumberland Avenue, London. MI9 would be concerned with providing active aid to escapers and evaders, and facilitating their repatriation, as well as hindering any enemy action in guarding and preventing the escape of prisoners of war. It would also provide escape training, and recruit suitable military personnel to train in the use of codes, so they could send and receive information from MI9 through letters between home and the camps. Army doctors and chaplains were favourite trainees, as they had greater freedom of movement within the camps. The maintenance of morale through correspondence went hand-in-hand with the transmission of information relating to escape planning. Communication could also be two-way. As such the prisoners of war who'd been taught the codes could use them to request specific items which might be needed in advance of a planned escape. Recaptured POWs who had gleaned information while on the run which might be of use to the Allies could communicate this home by the same means.

MI9's head for the duration of its existence was Major, later Colonel and later still Brigadier Norman Crockatt DSO, MC (1894–1956), who had seen distinguished service in the First World War but who had never been a POW himself . He was a level-headed organizer, a flexible thinker and an able diplomat on the interdepartmental and office–political fronts. Room 424 of the Metropole was a vast room, but it quickly became too small to contain all of MI9's staff and activities, and it was a little too close to Whitehall for Crockatt's comfort. As such, he ultimately moved his centre of operations to Wilton Park, near Beaconsfield, though the original base was not relinquished.

A training school, designated Section D, was set up in Highgate, where servicemen would attend lectures on escape and evasion techniques. Section W dealt with the interrogation and debriefing of returning escapers and evaders (and weeding out possible fifth-columnists and other enemy agents). Section X dealt with the actual planning and organization of escapes. Section Y devised codes and secret communication, and finally Section Z supplied escape equipment – some of which it devised itself. Development took time – Crockatt's starting budget was £2,000, about £100,000 in today's money, and that had to cover all of these various subsections of MI9.

Crockatt's first task was to recruit his staff, and he was not altogether conventional in his choices. We have already encountered Johnny Evans. There was also Lieutenant Colonel James Langley (1916–83), educated at Uppingham and Trinity Hall, Cambridge. Langley, together with M. R. D. Foot, would publish MI9's official history in 1979. He was himself a successful escaper, having been left behind, wounded, at Dunkirk. As an illustration of the bedlam of that operation, he had been abandoned because the space his stretcher would have taken up could accommodate four men retreating by sea. He was captured and taken to Lille, where surgeons amputated his left arm – which didn't prevent him from escaping with a still-suppurating stump and, with the help of local French families, making his way home via Marseilles and Spain. He'd navigated by using the maps displayed in telephone kiosks (Evans' book had already emphasized the importance of maps for escapers). He liaised between the two sub-departments at MI9 and oversaw the escape lines which were already being established in Europe. He met his future wife, Peggy van Lier, a Belgian national who worked for the Resistance on the Comet Line, after she was compromised and brought to Britain for her own safety. They went on to have five children.

Langley and Evans were later joined by Airey Neave who – as a Conservative politician – was to die at the hands of the Irish National Liberation Army in a targeted bomb attack at the Houses of Parliament on 30 March 1979. Neave was a Royal Artillery lieutenant when he was captured in Calais in May 1940. He was ultimately sent to Colditz, from which he escaped – the first British officer to do so successfully – on 5 January 1942. He managed to reach Switzerland, and from there made his way home courtesy of the Pat O'Leary line. He joined MI9 that May, bringing priceless first-hand experience to his work for them, with a special emphasis on the importance of maps as escape tools.

One of Crockatt's other early appointees, on 22 February 1940, was perhaps the most interesting. This was Christopher Clayton Hutton – 'Clutty'. He'd served as a pilot with the Royal Flying Corps during the First World War, and had tried to enlist after the outbreak of hostilities in 1939 when he was already forty-six years old, but both the RAF and the Army turned him down. He then bombarded the War Office with letters and as a result found himself under Crockatt's command. He was ingenious, inventive and had a passion for the conjuror's art: as a young man, he had tried to outwit Houdini (and failed). Hutton was an eccentric and no respecter of rules and regulations. He was given to wearing loud jackets and had something of a moody and depressive demeanour. He was, however, touched by genius when it came to the creation of gadgetry – some people have identified him as the model for Ian Fleming's 'Q'. In Crockatt's opinion, he was a natural choice to run Section Z. 'Old ideas are no good,' he is said to have told Hutton, 'we want new ones.'

It was a challenge that Clutty took up with some gusto. Hutton's contribution to the war effort cannot be overstated. This flawed, irascible figure was possibly Crockatt's most inspired recruitment, with a restless desire to invent, explore and constantly develop new equipment to aid escape. His application to the task bordered on the maniacal, with perhaps his most superlative moment being his invention of the silk map.

Although he had previously perfected printing onto silk by adding pectin – a type of wax – into the ink, he faced a problem in that silk itself was in short supply, with most of it being used for the manufacture of parachutes. Such silk maps that did exist were given to aircrew as a priority, but Clutty felt that they should be made available to every potential escapee. Casting about restlessly for alternative materials, he heard about a shipment of mulberry leaf pulp en route to Japan (used there – extraordinarily – to make lightweight balloons to lift bombs into the jet stream). He intercepted the shipment, and 'jigged about like an excited schoolboy as I watched test after test with the new material. The results were sensational.'

The new maps could take seven different colours, did not rustle, could be dipped in water, and yet were thin enough to see through. Clutty now needed to get them into the hands of the men and women who needed them most, a task he approached with characteristic enthusiasm.

He started with flight boots, worn by all airmen for missions over occupied territory. The maps – silk and otherwise – went in the heel with a small compass. The boots were also equipped with laces that doubled as wire saws, and had a small knife within them that could be used to cut away marked sections of the boot themselves, so they would look like normal walking shoes.

But Clutty's real challenge was getting the maps to POWs in the camps, the people who needed them the most. MI9 had set up a number of fake organizations to supply materials permitted to all prisoners under the Geneva Convention. Frequently, the addresses of these organizations were in fact the ruins of houses destroyed in the Blitz. Using relentless ingenuity and drive, Clutty concealed maps in sporting equipment, in board games, and even in gramophone records (to release them, the prisoners had to break the records, and as such Clutty named this particular initiative 'Operation Smash Hit'). He would even cut maps into fifty-two pieces and conceal them within playing cards – the joker provided the key.

By a happy coincidence, the company that printed the silk maps – John Waddington Ltd – also made every Monopoly board in the UK. Soon boards sent to a prison camp not only contained a map, but also tiny tools secreted in minute compartments. This was done in a secret room at the factory by a select group of employees, and only came to light when the relevant documents were declassified in 1985.

A month into Clutty's concerted attempt to get as many maps and tools to POWs as possible (which he dubbed 'Operation Post Box'), escape bids by Allied prisoners had tripled. Maps, once inside the camps, were copied and thus proliferated. In addition to maps, the creation and delivery of escape aids amounted to a cottage industry.

Clutty's inventiveness seemed to know no bounds. He magnetized razor blades, so that when they were placed on still water

– for example a puddle – they would point north. He devised a more conventional miniature compass that was could be hidden in buttons, cufflinks, toothbrushes and pipes.

Such objects must have been fascinating and exciting for all who encountered them. Indeed, Clutty himself noted in his book *Official Secret – The Remarkable Story of Escape Aids*, published in 1960, that one of the greatest threats to the security of his devices was his own colleagues taking them home to show to their friends.

It is impossible to accurately estimate just how much of an impact Clayton Hutton made in terms of actual escapes, but the volume of his creations that made it into the hands of POWs, and conventional and Special Forces, is in itself a monument to his genius. By the end of the war it is estimated that 3.5 million silk maps had been printed – indeed there were so many that in the post-war years they were made into dresses, many of them with the maps still upon them. Historian Philip E. Orbanes notes that at least 744 captured airmen had freed themselves using materials designed by Hutton – the equivalent of the entire crew of 150 Wellington bombers.

With Hutton producing escape equipment at a frenetic rate, Clackett now needed to turn his attention to training the wider armed forces community. To do so he created an education pro-gramme on a truly mass scale. Lecturers at Highgate were paid two guineas a talk, plus expenses. MI9 at first had a tough job stimulating interest in its work from the Army and the Navy, but by 1944, 3,250 lectures had been delivered to 290,000 members of the RAF, 346,000 members of the Army, and 110,000 Royal Navy personnel. (Naval prisoners were fewer than those of the other forces, for the simple and sad reason that more were lost in action than saved.)

Not all lecturers came from the forces. Among them was

Jasper Maskelyne, who, like his father and his father's father, was a highly successful professional stage magician. He'd joined the Royal Engineers in the hope of using his skills to perfect the art of camouflage, and there is even a story – never fully substantiated – that he won round sceptical staff by creating the illusion of a German warship on the Thames through the use of mirrors and a model. After the war he published a book, *Magic, Top Secret*, which, while very entertaining, has since been shown to be rather a smoke-and-mirrors affair itself. He was posted to Egypt, where MI9's man there, Colonel Tony Simonds, recruited him in 1942, with the agreement of the Head of Deception, Dudley Clarke.

Maskelyne claimed to be the inventor of several escape devices and aids, though many of them were actually devised by Hutton; but he was brilliant at lectures, making them as diverting as they were instructive, and in a sense popularizing the idea of escape. Camouflage and deception remained his main fields of interest, but between 1942 and the end of the war he spoke to around 200,000 men, mostly British and American aircrew, travelling 170,000 kilometres to do so.

Maskelyne's greatest attribute was his ability to *sell* the idea of escaping. Norman Crockatt saw the instigation of 'escape-mindedness' in fighting men as of paramount importance. It was so successful that, as we'll see later, when the infamous Stay Put order was issued to POWs in camps in Italy, many prisoners found it impossible to obey. By then it had been made crystal clear to every POW that it was his duty to attempt escape. The American counterpart of MI9, MIS-X, drummed into its captive forces that being prisoners did not mean that they need not be active: they still had an indirect combative role to play, in information-gathering and in making it impossible for the Germans or the Italians to reduce the manpower used to guard them.

All Allied prisoners were encouraged to feel that they had not been forgotten or written off, and discipline among POWs was still conducted along military lines within the camps. This was another important factor in the maintenance of morale.

The will to escape was one thing, but confidence, teamwork, and above all luck were the elements required to pull it off. The Germans were well aware of the escape ethos and did as much as they could to stifle it. They were also aware of the existence of escape aids, in particular maps, but evidently not to the extent that they could intercept them as a matter of course. By 1944, they had uncovered nine escape maps, out of a total of 200 originals and 750,000 copies.

MI9 also produced a bulletin, marked 'MOST SECRET − KEEP UNDER LOCK AND KEY WHEN NOT IN USE', which was issued to Intelligence Officers attending courses at Highgate to aid them in instructing others. It detailed all the escape measures and devices developed to date (the bulletin was updated regularly), and began with a preface describing how Churchill, when escaping from the Boers, had found himself on the outside of a wall before he realized that his escape aids (such as they were in 1900) were still on the inside. The moral of this was, 'always carry your escape aids with you'. All information in the bulletin had to be memorized: it was forbidden to take notes. The briefings the bulletin contained were copious and detailed, right down to comportment − some of which sounds obvious, but in such circumstances the obvious needed to be stated:

- Do not march in a military fashion, but adopt a tired slouch.
- Try and 'collect' a bicycle.

- Sling your haversack: French peasants commonly carry one in this way, but never as a pack on their backs.
- Do not use a cane or walking-stick: it is a British custom.
- Get rid of army boots and adopt a paired of rope-soled shoes as worn by peasants, if procurable.
- French peasants are generally clean-shaven . . .
- Village priests are likely to be helpful . . .

. . . and so on. One deeply memorable line concerned sourcing food when on the run, and spoke volumes for MI9's desire to keep things as straightforward as possible for any escapee:

Every large animal in Europe is edible.

Despite such sweeping statements, every *i* had to be dotted and every *t* crossed. MI9 never lost sight of its humanitarian duty, or the value of a successful escaper or evader as a source of information on the enemy.

As Hutton and his team got into their stride, they found new and ever more ingenious ways of smuggling maps and other aids to POWs. (Evaders, of course, unless they were already equipped at the outset of their missions, were much more on their own. To them the value of the freedom trails and local support cannot be overstated.) Local currency was smuggled into camps, as were small hacksaw blades (which were magnetized to double as compasses). Compasses and maps could be concealed in cigars; plain cotton handkerchiefs, when soaked in simple chemical solutions, would reveal maps or instructions; miniature compasses and watches hid behind uniform buttons, cap badges and collar studs. Hutton even devised a miniature camera, disguised as a cigarette lighter. Key items, such as a miniature compass, a watch, a tiny but effective telescope and even multi-bladed pocket-knives (screwdriver, hacksaw blade, lock-breaker, knife blade, wire-cutter), could be concealed in, for example, chess set boxes. MI9 also sent blankets with concealed cutting patterns, so that they could be converted into makeshift civilian overcoats. Pencils, tobacco pouches and even Christmas crackers were utilized, all subtly marked to indicate their hidden contents. Their recipients were instructed on how to recognize these markings through coded messages woven into innocent letters from (often imaginary) family and loved ones. MI9 Y, the coding sub-section, had to concentrate hard when concocting the imaginary letters, as sometimes attention slipped and a German censor might notice that letters from a fond mother and an ardent girlfriend were written in the same handwriting on the same kind of paper. MI9 even had to be careful they didn't use the same typewriter for two different correspondents. Sometimes an indiscretion meant that genuine wives at home agonized over husbands' actually entirely fictitious girlfriends.

Parcels in which escape aids were smuggled were either from putative families or from fake charitable organizations, whose names provided a key for their recipients: the Lancashire Penny Fund; the Licensed Victuallers' Sports Association, and, perhaps best of all, the Old Ladies' Knitting Committee. Sometimes parcels were entirely innocent or contained 'good' as well as 'naughty' items; as the war progressed, some parcels were filled exclusively with naughty items, and had to be taken off the delivery trucks by the prisoners before they could be passed to the censor's office. Over time, the system developed so that it ran like clockwork, and was even aided by the Germans' efficiency and predictable logic. For example, if a 'naughty' deck of cards was discovered, the Germans would then inspect *only* decks of cards for a succeeding period. Coded messages home would warn MI9 to send no doctored packs for a while, while other items could continue unhindered. German efficiency also meant that post in and out of the camps – prisoners were allowed to send and receive a small number of letters and postcards monthly – was regular. It was far harder for POWs in Italian camps, where post was irregularly delivered and adherence to the protocols of the Geneva Convention less stringent.

Wirelesses and crystal sets were either smuggled in or cobbled together by the prisoners themselves, but MI9 forbade the use of them to send signals. As such, they were to be used just to listen in to BBC broadcasts, which also occasionally transmitted coded messages, as was sometimes the case in the regular Wednesday evening Forces broadcasts by the 'Radio Padre' – the Rt Revd Ronald Selby Wright.

Norman Crockatt also forbade the use of Red Cross parcels as cover for 'naughty' items. To have compromised their delivery would have been to deny a lifeline, in the most literal sense, to many thousands of prisoners who depended on them to supplement a less-than-meagre diet.

Apart from maps and escape aids, food was an essential part of the escaper's kit – Johnny Evans had been recommending its inclusion from the first. He had himself depended on condensed and concentrated foodstuffs for his own escape almost thirty years earlier. It left the deep impression on him that only genuine hunger can: 'The escaper's enemy is hunger. When a man is starving, he very soon becomes reckless and insensitive.'

Hutton came up with the idea of the escape pack – it was refined over time, but was originally a flat fifty-cigarette tin. Hutton duly acquired the tins from W. D. & H. O. Wills in Bristol. The kits contained malted milk tablets, liver toffee (essentially Bovril, but liver-flavoured and with the consistency of toffee), matches, chewing gum, fishing line, boiled sweets, compass, needle and thread, razor and soap (as neat an appearance as possible helped the escaper), water-purifying tablets (Halazone) and Benzedrine (to combat weariness). Later versions of the container were made of transparent plastic and, when emptied, could double as a water bottle. A bottle cap was attached, in which a watch and a compass were secreted. These later versions were curved so that they'd fit more comfortably against the wearer's body. Each version slotted neatly into a flying jacket or a battledress trouser map pocket. These escape packs became standard issue for RAF crews operating over mainland Europe.

Food and other supplies played another vital role in making life easier for POWs and facilitating their escape. As the war turned against Germany and conditions for Germans and their Allies worsened, it was increasingly easy to bribe the demoralized, underfed and elderly guards with chocolate and cigarettes, both useful and easily transferable currencies sent to the POWs in numbers by MI9 for precisely that purpose. Ralph Churches – leader of the Crow's Flight mass escape in Slovenia – used such bribery of his guards to devastating effect.

Between 1942 and 1945, MI9 organized the delivery of some 423,000 escape packs, over 1,700,000 compasses, watches and telescopes, and some 434,000 other items, such as 'undoctored' records, board games and so forth.

In doing so, MI9 provided much of the hardware required for escaping, but as an organization they had done so much more. Crockett and his band of mavericks and renegades provided inspiration and motivation for those incarcerated behind the wire of the camps – they not only facilitated many escapes, they also let the men who had been captured know that they were not alone and not forgotten. One can only speculate on the impact this had on their mental welfare – most planned escapes never took place, and so many that did were unsuccessful, but even the process of organizing them gave back some pride, dignity and purpose to the prisoners involved. Perhaps the one thing that MI9 really provided for all Allied POWs was hope.

By the end of the war, and before the POW camps were liberated, almost 36,000 men had made their way back to the UK. That is the equivalent of over three Army divisions. MI9, a group of eccentrics ridiculed and underfunded in the early days of their formation, had more than proved their worth.

CHAPTER TWO

Defying the Enemy

As I looked at the Col de la Core mountain pass, it struck me that there is a fine line between awe-inspiring and terrifying, between magnificent and menacing. The path ahead of me meandered up through green foothills, gentle and undulating, heading into the precipitous granite slopes of the mountains beyond, where it would become a twisting artery of dust and stone leading into a wilder, starker world. It was a path that had offered a tantalizing promise of freedom for so many.

The Pyrenees are an uncompromising natural feature, an unbroken barrier that demands a heavy toll from anyone wishing to cross it. Nowadays that means well-equipped hiking groups, picking their routes and their times, climbing while encased in Gore-Tex, fuelled by energy bars, guided by the unblinking eye of GPS and advised throughout by well-trained local guides.

For those making the same crossing in the Second World War, the contrast could not have been greater. For them this was a potentially lethal gamble, mountaineering with hopelessly inadequate clothing and equipment, every step taken while malnourished and desperate, all the while driven into a pitiless wilderness by a guide who himself was in fear of his life. Although the sun was on my back and a gentle summer breeze was in my face, I felt, for a brief moment, the long shadow of another time. I imagined myself in the same spot, as part of a stricken group of escapees and refugees, with the wind whistling and howling, the night settling in, about to take the first steps on a life or death journey that would mean walking into the darkness towards an entirely unknown fate.

The word 'legendary' is used with some abandon in modern life, but everything about the escape lines through the Pyrenees is Herculean in scale. The sheer number of people who crossed from occupied Europe into the freedom of Spain dwarfs any other escape route in the European theatre of war. The scale of the obstacle itself – with the border represented by wind-blasted peaks and ridges at heights of up to 3,400 metres – is equally unparalleled. And then there was the vast network of men and women throughout France and Belgium – numbering many hundreds – who trained and hid escapees and refugees prior to spiriting them to the base of the mountains before the crossing itself. These selfless servants of the escape routes ensured that these passages to liberty, lifelines in an occupied and subdued continent, were never truly conquered by the Nazis, and remained a beacon of hope for many millions of civilians and thousands of servicemen and women.

Everything here is on the grandest of scales, and as such there is only one way to really tell this story, and that is to head into the heart of the mountains themselves, to walk in the footsteps of the men and women who made this crossing. I tightened the straps on my rucksack, nodded to my guide, and took my first strides on the *Chemin de la Liberté* – starting out along perhaps the greatest of all the Freedom Trails, and onwards and upwards into the immense theatre of the Pyrenees.

*

As we've seen, in the Second World War, for the first time, vast numbers of combatants were taken prisoner. This posed a logistical and administrative challenge for the captors, but for the nations that saw their armed forces at first defeated, and then found their fighting men in the hands of the enemy, there was a simple, pressing need to facilitate their escape and repatriation. Nowhere was this issue more apparent than in France, and from the first stages of the war MI9 and SOE were alive to the need for escape routes for British POWs in the European theatre.

For more than eight months after the outbreak of war on 3 September 1939, about four and a half million French and British soldiers were massed along the Maginot Line and the Belgian frontier, there to hold back the German army if Hitler invaded. The Germans had already used their Blitzkrieg technique in Poland, Denmark and Norway, with Heinz Guderian deploying their tanks in a manner based on military strategies developed by Mongol Empire cavalry in the thirteenth century. Between 10 and 14 May 1940, they swept through Holland, Belgium and Luxembourg. The Belgian, French and British armies were no match for the highly trained, well-equipped Germans, and the small British Expeditionary Force had to conduct a fighting retreat to the northern coast, where they massed on the beaches at Dunkirk. Over 300,000 men were rescued by the Royal Navy, but not all got away. On 12 June 1940, at Saint-Valery-en-Caux, a town on the French coast about sixty kilometres north-east of Le Havre, a large British and French force surrendered in some confusion to the Germans, having failed to escape by sea. It was a notable battle not only because of the considerable number of prisoners taken, but also because French cavalry, following the example of their Polish counterparts a little earlier in the war, had actually charged German tanks. Despite such undeniable heroism – and within it the defiant death knell of another type of conflict – thousands were taken prisoner at a stroke.

The main military outfit caught up in the action at Saint-Valery-en-Caux was the 51st (Highland) Division. They fought a desperate rearguard action, together with the French 9th Army Corps, against the German 7th Panzer Division, which had ve-hicle and infantry support. As was so often the case at this stage of the war, the French and the British were under-equipped and lacked both training and combat experience. Their objective – to recapture Abbeville – proved to be an impossible one. Major-General Victor Morven Fortune, the officer commanding the 51st, requested permission to evacuate on 11 June 1940, but could not contact any Allied ships. The German Panzer division were implacable in pushing home their advantage, not wishing to let the British get away as they had done at Dunkirk. The 51st were pinned down, under constant assault, and all attempts to counter-attack were in vain. On the night of the 11th, while Fortune was still fighting the German tanks, the French surren-dered. Realizing that his position was now hopeless, Fortune had no option but to do likewise the following day. He spent the rest of the war as a POW.

The fighting prior to surrender is vividly described in the diaries of Peter Scott Janes, a young private of the 51st at the time. He neatly summarizes the varying personal reactions within a military formation in disarray, one entirely at the mercy of the enemy:

The bombs fell all the time, some of them ten yards away. Naylor was scared but was sticking it well. Heywood was panicky but he also did his best to keep cool. I was actually happy and got out of the trench and got a couple of blankets to make it more comfortable. I did not see a German at all and did not fire a single shot. The French machine-guns were firing continuously in bursts of about twenty rounds. They have a beautiful crack crack crack sound to them and it is very easy to distinguish from the Brens' roaring chatter or the big Vickers bellow. Then things got too hot and we got the order to retreat.

Once again, there was the misery and humiliation of capture. Janes gives a telling description:

A Major of our lot was crying as he burnt his papers and one fellow put his rifle muzzle onto his forehead and shot himself. The bugler came up to the Major and one of the corporals asked 'Shall we have the bugler blow retreat?' and the Major only nodded. I don't think I shall ever forget my own feelings when that bugle call rang out. Prisoner of War, something that none of us had ever dreamt of; it is something stunning, which strikes at one's very soul to find oneself a prisoner. I lay down with my face on the wet ground, my brain would not work at all for a few minutes. Around me I could hear some of the others as they smashed up the machine guns and other arms.

Even amid the despair and the disarray, some managed to evade capture, or to escape early in their imprisonment – indeed, modern escape training in the armed forces emphasizes that the early moments of capture are the optimum time to make a break for freedom. One of those who escaped was Janes himself – he was actually pulled out of a marching column of POWs by a French girl at Division, about fifty kilometres south-west of Lille in the Pas-de-Calais, when the Germans were looking the other way. Escapers and evaders either hid out with friendly French locals – some for quite a long time – until they could find a means of getting away altogether, or made their way south on their own initiative.

The German army took Paris on 14 June. Eight days later, France signed an armistice with Germany at Rethondes, the location chosen by Hitler for its symbolic value – on that spot Germany had signed an armistice in 1918. France undertook to pay a massive indemnity to Germany of 400 million francs a day and agreed that Germany would occupy the north and west of the country. The rest of the country became a 'free' French state. The French referred to the occupied North and West as 'la zone ja ja', and to Vichy France as 'la zone no no'. The line of demarcation, from south-west to east, passed close to Angoulême, Poitiers, Tours, Vierzon, Bourges, Nevers, Moulins, Châlons-sur Sâone, Poligny and Gex. This became known as the État Français, and was established under the government of First World War hero Maréchal Philippe Pétain (1856–1951), who turned eighty-four in 1940. His government was based at Vichy, under his principal prime minister, the lawyer and investor Pierre Laval (1883–1945).

The Vichy state was recognized by every country in the world except the United Kingdom. As Lenin had noted at the height of the Russian revolution: 'For decades nothing happens. Then, in a few days, decades happen.' In a matter of weeks Western Europe had been transformed, entire armies were under lock and key, and the scene was set for a new type of war.

The Vichy state was right-wing, traditionalist and dictatorial. Anti-British sentiment enjoyed a moment of popularity, especially when the British sank a French fleet to neutralize it at Mers-el-Kébir on 3 July (Operation Catapult). Feelings polarized and hardened over the next two years, with France divided not simply in geographical terms, but politically too.

It's difficult for the British to imagine what it's like to live in an occupied country, and impossible to imagine the kind of choices people in such a situation had to make. Initially, the Germans were less harsh in the imposition of their rule in France and some Frenchmen and women were, at least to begin with, even enthusiastic about their arrival. The Vichy government worked in close collaboration with the Germans. Their involvement in the deportation of Jews is notorious and Laval's own policy was pro-Nazi. He envisioned a Spanish–Italian–French–German axis, isolating Britain. He effectively controlled Vichy, since Pétain, an old man and by now frail, was little more than a figurehead.

But there remained an element within France that sought to defy their occupiers. Inspired by the stance taken by General de Gaulle, in London and at the head of a Free French government in exile (and indeed a Free French armed force initially active in France's African colonies), a resistance movement steadily grew in the home country. Given existing pre-war links between Britain and France, MI9 and SOE made it their business to establish contacts with representatives of this Resistance.

Within the SOE, RF section worked with de Gaulle's Free French, and many of its agents were French. DF section was given the responsibility of setting up escape lines. F section – controlled entirely by SOE – was headed by Colonel Maurice Buckmaster, and was kept so secret that de Gaulle didn't know about it, mainly because the British were not yet convinced that they wanted him to have too much control. In the nature of things, de Gaulle did discover F's existence, amidst much diplomatic embarrassment. Between these various sections, SOE established 102 operations across France between 1941 and 1944.

As the war progressed, Germany became increasingly concerned about Allied operations in North Africa – attacks could be launched directly from there into mainland Europe, and vital shipping lanes through the Mediterranean could be compromised. Add to this the rising tide of resistance in the southern regions of France, where rebellion had found fertile soil to grow and prosper, and it was clear to the Nazis that they needed to regain control from what they viewed as a weak and ineffective Vichy regime. The Reich officially annexed the État Français in November 1942. In response, in a last act of defiance and pride, the French Navy scuttled its own fleet at Toulon at the end of the same month.

Although the Vichy regime remained in place after annexation, its role was nominal. It did put some measures in place to protect Jews who held French citizenship, but Laval waived the German exemption for deportation of Jews aged sixteen or under. As a result, Vichy France handed over some 40,000 Jews to the Nazis.

The worsening political situation meant that the escape routes rapidly being established by SOE, MI9, the Resistance and the Free French became ever more important. They were not only a means for Allied servicemen and women to be spirited out of the country, but also a vital lifeline for Jewish refugees fleeing persecution. They were a means of survival for so many – for some the only way to avoid the concentration camps – and as such their maintenance and continued effective operation became absolutely key to the war effort in Europe.

Meanwhile, there was a clear hardening of resolve among the Vichy government in response to evidence of escalating resistance, with the French Milice (militia) founded at the end of January 1943. The Milice's job was unequivocal – to combat the Resistance by any means possible. Its titular Commander-in-Chief was the arch-collaborator Pierre Laval, but its actual leader was the French ultra-right-winger Joseph Darnand, who actually held the SS rank of *Sturmbannführer*, roughly equivalent to major. As well as the Milice, the Légion des Volontaires Français was established: this was a French fighting unit of the Wehrmacht, the German Army, although it was ultimately absorbed into the Waffen-SS.

Despite the best efforts of the Milice, there began to be a significant switch of attitude towards the Resistance in France among the wider population, especially in the light of Britain's holding firm against Germany. Also of importance was the USA's sympathetic attitude towards France (it entered the war in December 1941), and Hitler's decision to turn against Russia, with practical support coming from the Communists after the collapse of the Molotov–Ribbentrop pact in June 1941. The Western Allies were never comfortable with Communist influence, especially in France, Greece and Italy, but for the time being they took a pragmatic line. However, those whom the DF section of SOE worked with in France were neither Communists nor financially supported by them.

With the decisive victories over the Germans towards the end of 1942 and the beginning of 1943 in North Africa and at Stalingrad, the French knew that hope of liberation was no longer a chimera. People began to take heart, and in turn the Freedom Trails took on a more established shape.

A groundswell of anti-Pétain feeling gathered momentum – although sections of the French population remained loyal to him and his regime – and de Gaulle's Free French attracted more and more followers. But despite this flourishing of long-latent patriotism, ordinary French citizens still had incredibly difficult choices to make. Food, clothing and fuel were all controlled by the Germans, in concert with a flourishing and extortionate collaborationist black market. The Germans also exploited and undermined the value of the franc. About 1.6 million Frenchmen were prisoners of war, and at least half of them had left wives alone at home. These women enjoyed a small allowance from the Germans to live on, but about 10 per cent of them were reduced to such poverty that they were forced into prostitution in order to support their children. There were also the bombing raids of the Allied forces to contend with.

This was the background against which the Resistance and those who ran the French Freedom Trails worked. In this atmosphere, resistance continued to grow, but did so alongside collaboration, and as such bitter rifts grew between sections of the population.

There were three main escape lines through France actively organized by British undercover agencies in collaboration with the French Resistance – the Pat O'Leary Line, the Comet Line and the Shelburne Line. Principal gathering centres for POWs were established at Brussels, Lille, Amiens, Mons, Rheims and Rouen, with smaller ones at Rennes, and Plouha on the Breton coast. With the exception of the last two, these centres moved escapees and downed airmen on to Paris, which served as a clearing house for routes south, although some individuals were also sent west to Plouha.

The Shelburne Line, which was set up by Ray Labrosse and Lucien Dumais, ran from Paris and Rennes to Plouha. It was not just the shortest in length but worked for a relatively short period, from the end of 1943 until September 1944, and was mainly used by aircrew, who were guided by French *passeurs* and *passeuses* – as the male and female guides assisting them were called. Among those who made their getaway through the Shelburne was Guy Hamilton, then a naval officer and later a successful film director, whose credits included *An Inspector Calls*, *The Colditz Story*, and four of the early James Bond movies.

The other two evasion routes were of greater importance in terms of volume and longevity. The Comet Line ran from Brussels to Paris and then through western and south-western France via Bordeaux and Dax to Bayonne. From there it ran across the western end of the Pyrenees in the Basque country to San Sebastián and Bilbao in Spain, from where the 'parcels' travelled to Madrid and thence to Gibraltar.

The Comet Line (*Le Réseau Comète*) was the brainchild of a remarkable Belgian woman in her early twenties called Andrée de Jongh. Inspired by the story of the First World War nurse Edith Cavell, who was executed by firing squad in 1915 for helping British soldiers escape from occupied Belgium, de Jongh trained as a nurse. Following the German invasion of Belgium in 1940, she joined the Red Cross and became involved in sheltering British escapers and evaders following the debacle at Saint-Valery-en-Caux. This seminal experience led to her organizing, with her father's help, her own escape route. In August 1941, she travelled to Bilbao to persuade the British Consul there to arrange support for her work, and this in turn led to MI9's involvement.

One of the men she helped remembered her as 'tough, intelligent, brave – you'd take orders from her without question. She used to tease the Germans in a way that'd make your blood run cold. We were all in love with her and when we told her, she just scoffed.' Comet would grow to cover most of north-eastern France and southern Holland, as well as Belgium, becoming officially recognized as an important cog in the war machine. What's more, it was run with tremendous courage and integrity.

The Comet Line ran successfully over a 1,900-kilometre route even after the annexation of Vichy France, when Vichy police and the Milice were joined by members of the Abwehr (German military intelligence) and the *Geheime Feldpolizei* (the secret military police), as well as German specialist mountain troops who were deployed in the Pyrenees range itself. At this stage, the dangers became much greater, and many agents working on the line were arrested. They invariably faced torture and execution, or immediate deportation to the concentration camps. Nevertheless, the line became increasingly important to shot-down aircrew as raids over France intensified, and was responsible for the liberation of over a thousand escapers and evaders. One such evader was RAF tail gunner Bob Frost.

There was one, overriding emotion for Frost as he hung beneath his parachute in the cold night air, falling away from his crippled Wellington bomber as it turned in the dark sky above to begin its final, fatal dive.

'I was furious!' he says with a smile. 'It was a Wednesday night, and I was due to go on leave on Friday. As I floated down all I could think was *Well, there goes my leave!*'

Bob had taken off a few hours earlier, at 8.38 p.m. on 16 September 1942, from RAF Snaith, in East Yorkshire, little knowing that this was going to be his last flight. He was a tail gunner in a Wellington bomber that was to come down in Occupied Belgium after a night bombing raid over Germany.

'At that time,' says Bob, 'we lost thirty-six aircraft from one squadron in four months. It wasn't *if* you were shot down, it was when.'

Bob's commendable sense of detachment from his perilous situation may actually have been fuelled by a considerable sense of relief. In the Second World War, the decision to bail out of a stricken bomber did not in itself mean salvation – to make it out of the aircraft in one piece was in its own way a small triumph.

Bailing out from a Wellington was by no means easy, although (in stark contrast to a Lancaster) the tail gunner had it easier than most. In his case, he could simply turn his turret ninety degrees and roll out of the door hatches. The remainder of the crew had to retrieve their chutes from a storage compartment, then bail out through a hatch in the fuselage. With a crew of six men, each in a different position within the aircraft, this required a co-ordinated effort by all concerned, and not inconsiderable physicality.

There was also the split-second timing of the decision itself – different in every case, and made under the pressure of being in a stricken aircraft. Crew training emphasized the importance of going about the business of bailing out in an orderly and disciplined manner, with the aim of everyone being clear of the aircraft within thirty seconds. But of course to do so meant that the crew was deciding to take their chances in the night, on the wind, and in the hazardous and hostile world that awaited them on landing.

Assuming the crew survived the bailing out process itself, there was the prospect of landing among a murderous populace (one they'd been dropping 5,000 pounds of bombs on only moments before). This danger frequently led pilots to fly their aircraft until the very last moment and sometimes, tragically, beyond that moment. The mortality of aircrew in Bomber Command has been well documented – the survival rate was worse than that of an infantry officer in the First Word War – but there is every chance that many of those would not have been killed had the decision to abandon their aircraft come sooner.

There was also considerable variation in survival rates between aircraft types. From the moment a bomber was shot down, it has been calculated that only 13.2 per cent of aircrew survived from the Lancaster, 21.9 per cent from the Halifax and 24 per cent from the Stirling. There are many factors influencing these figures but the Lancaster's small escape hatch (22 inches wide by 26 inches long) and the need to move through a constricted fuselage, with a supporting spar to negotiate, may have been significant factors. By stark contrast the survival rate from USAAF B-17s abandoned in the air (i.e. excluding forced landings) was over 70 per cent. The latter may have been due to the more robust nature of the B-17, and that large numbers of USAAF raids took place in daylight, thus avoiding the confusion of a pitch-black fuselage and allowing the ability to pick a parachute landing site. Nonetheless the figures make stark reading.

And so there were powerful incentives to keep flying as long as possible. Added to the dangers of bailing out was the fact that a series of emergency landing strips had been established on the east coast of Britain that could take crippled aircraft. One of them – RAF Woodbridge in Suffolk – received 4,100 landings of this kind throughout the duration of the war. Limping home across the North Sea made real sense in a stricken bomber, but the pressure on the pilots was intense – an appalling dilemma between the lives of their crews, the state of their disintegrating aircraft, and the tantalizing glimmer of hope offered by a distant, friendly airfield.

As such, bailing out was always a last option, made when crashing was a certainty. It represented a moment when the crew gave up any semblance of control of their own destiny, and abandoned themselves to the vagaries of fate.

For Bob, the decision seemed strangely pre-ordained.

'A "tour" consisted of thirty trips,' said Bob, sitting in his front room in Kent seventy-five years later. 'The chances of getting through that many raids seemed non-existent. If you got to fourteen you were on borrowed time, and we'd made it to twenty-two by the time I got shot down. So I'd always thought – the same way we all did – about what I'd do if I had to bail out.'

The survival statistics of Bomber Command back up Bob's testimony entirely. During the war 8,325 bombers were lost in action, flying 364,514 operational sorties in the process. By 1943, one in six aircrew survived their first tour intact, and one in forty their second. By the end of the war, 55,573 aircrew had been killed out of a total strength of 125,000. In the entire Second World War theatre, only U-boat crews sustained higher casualty rates. Huge losses could be sustained in a single raid, with perhaps the nadir coming in a raid on Nuremberg involving 800 aircraft on 30 March 1944. Almost a hundred of those aircraft – sixty-four Lancasters and thirty-one Halifaxes – did not return, with 545 aircrew killed in a matter of hours by the fighter squadrons that descended on the vast formation in the glare of a full moon.

As part of 150 Squadron, Bob's Wellington had been flying a raid over the German industrial city of Essen when it was mortally hit.

'We actually had a single bomb on board,' he notes, 'a huge 4,000 pound blockbuster called a "Cookie". The idea was that we would be in the first wave, drop these huge bombs that blew the roofs off the buildings below, then a second wave of bombers with incendiaries would fly in after us to burn the place.'

Bob's Wellington had been struck by flak in the port engine during the raid, and the aircraft had lost all hydraulics. The undercarriage and gun turrets were not functioning and it was plain that the aircraft itself was struggling to stay airborne. The decision was finally made for the crew when the starboard engine spluttered and coughed, and then settled into stillness, enveloping the aircraft in an eerie hush broken only by the rush of the wind and the groan of the superstructure as the Wellington went into its death throes. This was a critical moment, with the pilot fighting for control to prevent the aircraft diving. Going into a dive was greatly feared by all aircrew, as the resultant centrifugal forces pinned them in their positions and meant almost certain death as the bomber hurtled towards the ground.

'There was no choice,' said Bob, 'it was "Jump for it, or else."'

Because he could not rotate his turret due to the loss of hydraulics, Bob exited the Wellington through a large hole in the side of the fuselage.

'The radio operator – Norman – had already gone through it, so I thought I might as well do the same. There was one thing I recall – we'd been given a pigeon in a box before taking off, and told to tie a message to its leg if we got shot down. I had to stuff this poor thing down my smock just before jumping out, and between the 13,000 feet where I bailed out, and the landing, it must have got out. I've no idea where it went – it's probably still flying home right now.'

Bob clearly recalls the moment of the landing.

'It didn't seem that I went to the ground, the ground came up to me, and there I was lying in the middle of a field, a ploughed field, with this damn great white parachute and I thought *everybody in the kingdom is going to see it*, so I gathered it in, and got to the side of the field.

'We all landed over a radius of about twenty-five miles. I had absolutely no idea where anybody else was. I worked out that there was only one place to go, and that was Gibraltar. So, using the Pole Star as a navigation point, I set off, all of nineteen years of age, to get to Gibraltar!'

He chuckles wryly at the memory of his own naivety – setting out on a thousand-mile trek, alone, lost, armed only with the optimism of youth.

Bob was to get lucky, stumbling across a farmhouse in the darkness close to a village called Capellan. He noted some graffiti that seemed to indicate an element of the Resistance within – 'A dit-dit-dit-dah sign, the morse code for victory' – and knocked on the door.

Bob had actually spent some time in Germany as a student before the war, and spoke a little of the language. When the door was opened by a burly young man, who addressed Bob in what he later learned was Flemish, he responded in German. This, plainly, was not the most diplomatic approach. The door was immediately slammed in his face.

He knocked again, and – remarkably – was taken in.

'The family gathered round me in the kitchen – the grand-parents, a lady with a baby, and the young man who had opened the door to me initially. I'd actually knocked on the door of the house of the mayor – the grandfather – and it was him who saved my life as the others thought I was a German infiltrator and wanted to shoot me.' Bob pauses for a moment in his story. 'I'd like to thank Grandad very much indeed for doing that,' he says with a wry smile.

Bob had been doubly lucky – not only had he just happened to knock on the door of a family of some influence but his sav-iour, the mayor, also had connections to the Comet Line. This was to be his route home – he had inadvertently entered a highly efficient network created to spirit escapees and downed airmen out of occupied territory.

'It was called the Comet Line because if they saw an aircraft coming down they would say to their people around, "I have seen a comet."'

The symbol of the line exists to this day, displayed at reunions and memorial services – a bomber falling from the sky with a flaming tail.

Bob was issued with false identity papers. 'I became Robert Simoness, a Belgian seaman who was home on leave from Bor-deaux visiting his old mother who lived in Brussels, in a street called Solzenstraat. My papers said I lived at 19 Solzenstraat, but that house number didn't actually exist – it prevented anyone knocking on the door and asking about me!'

Bob was duly moved to Brussels, and lived for a short period with a stockbroker called Marcel Reinserts and his wife Manee. They kitted him out in civilian clothes, albeit with limited success.

'Marcel was a middle-aged man who was rather portly. He gave me one of his suits, and I'm nineteen years of age, so I could lift out the trousers and look down them! But it was a nice enough suit. And he gave me a pair of shoes as well.'

In Brussels, Bob was also reunited with two members of his own crew – the pilot Bill Randall and an American called Dale Mounts, who had joined them for a single flight on attachment. By a stroke of poor fortune – for all on board of course, but particularly for the hapless Mounts – this happened to be the flight where they were shot down.

'Oh, yes, there's quite an amusing story about the American actually. He didn't have a clue about the kit he was wearing – he'd only joined us for that flight. When he hit the ground, he took out his cigarettes and found out that he only had one match, so he chain-smoked the entire packet. It was only when he checked another pocket that he found the matches we were all issued with – he was that green to the whole thing.'

They stayed only a short time with the Reinserts, as Bob recalls.

'You moved when they told you really, because you knew they were risking everything to help you.' He pauses, overwhelmed by emotion for the first time in his narrative.

His passage to Paris, and then south towards the Pyrenees, was fraught with danger and punctuated with moments when capture seemed inevitable.

'I was on a train, and a German soldier began shouting at me and poking me in the ribs with his machine gun. I just thought that was it, the game was up, but my guide at the time – a chap called Aschiel – just strolled over and said, "He's a silly looking blighter isn't he?" It took the German's attention away from the fact that I still had those huge trousers on. He told me to go away and get on with my own business.'

Aschiel warned Bob to be constantly vigilant, training him to blend in seamlessly.

'If you went to the toilet and didn't leave a coin in the dish for the attendant, they would start shouting at you. The Germans knew this, and would always watch out for these moments. There was the impression after the war – with stories like the Secret Army for example – that the Germans were a bit stupid. That's completely and utterly wrong, they were as crafty as a wagon load of monkeys, they really were.'

Having spent a week in Paris living with a couple called Germaine and Robert Isley, Bob and several fellow escapees were ready to make the run south. By now, they had been gathered in a group of six, and were instructed to follow a young girl to the Gare du Nord railway station, where an agent would pick them up for the journey south.

During the trip to Toulouse, there was one more incident that so nearly ended in catastrophe.

'Dale Mounts had been dozing – the carriage was packed – and looked up to see a woman standing without a seat. He forgot himself completely, and said, "Say ma'am, would you like my seat?" She replied, "Thank you very much," in English, and sat down! We all waited for the whole world to crumble about our ears, but nothing happened. I looked across at our guide, and she hadn't batted an eyelid. They really were very good.'

Bob eventually made his way across the Pyrenees in

mid-October 1942, guided by a passeur he describes as 'a real smuggler – Florentino Guy Cagea, a French Basque. Not a giant of a man, but intensely strong.'

Their group was also accompanied by Dédée de Jongh herself, bringing up the rear of the line. Bob asked her why she did it, why was she taking such terrible risks for strangers?

Recalling her reply, his dry, clipped delivery falters, and his voice trembles.

'She said, "It's there to be done," as simple as that.'

At the time of her arrest on 15 January 1943, de Jongh was making her thirty-third journey over the mountains, having personally accompanied 118 escapees to safety. She was interrogated and tortured before being sent to Mauthausen and then Ravensbrück concentration camps. She survived, though only just – she was described as a 'grey wraith' at Ravensbrück – and after the war went on to work in leper hospitals, which had been her original aim, in Africa. This remarkable woman died in Brussels at the age of ninety, in 2007.

Bob's group crossed the Pyrenees near the coastline, close to Biarritz, and from there were transported to the British Embassy in Madrid. Within a year, the escape route also returned the plane's navigator, Scottie Brazill, to Britain.

'When I was in Madrid,' recalls Bob, 'I asked the ambassador to send my shoes back to the stockbroker in Belgium who had helped me originally, Marcel Reinserts, and they were duly delivered to his house. This meant that he knew I'd made it.'

This simple gesture, the arrival of a nondescript package on a doorstep, would have represented a hugely symbolic moment for the men and women who risked everything to transport the downed airmen to safety. Battered, worn and scuffed, the shoes represented a life saved, a serviceman reunited with his loved ones and an airman back in the fight.

Bob has one last thing to say, one last moment when his words stop being the memories of a distant time, and become a testimony to the people who helped him.

'After the war, they talked about a "Land Fit for Heroes", but in my opinion they were the heroes. They were ordinary people, they did it against the odds, knowing that not only their own lives but their families were at risk. There are people in the world who, without thinking of reward for themselves, do wonderful things, and those people of the Resistance are in that category.'

CHAPTER THREE

Pat O'Leary

Both the Shelbourne and the Comet Lines have rightly been celebrated as successful examples of personal sacrifice, local ingenuity and international co-operation. But there was one other escape line which had such scope, complexity and effectiveness that it has become truly iconic. It was called the Pat O'Leary Line – or the Pat Line for short – and the history of its formation and operation is in itself an extraordinary tale.

The line ended up using a number of routes to move POWs, downed airmen, secret agents and refugees to safety. These ran from Paris via Dijon, Lyon and Avignon to Marseille; from Nevers, Monluçon and Béziers to Perpignan; and Orléans to Toulouse via Limoges, and then over the mountains on the French border to Barcelona. Most users of these routes crossed the Pyrenees, although some made it by sea from small French ports near the Spanish frontier, before sailing on to Gibraltar.

A network of escape routes of this intricacy required meticulous co-ordination and impeccable management. It comes as something of a surprise, then, that the main characters involved in its establishment were a sprinkling of eccentrics and adventurers, although Pat O'Leary himself was a towering figure in the key stages of the line, a man who epitomized Hemingway's summary of heroism – 'Courage is grace under pressure.'

Before O'Leary became involved, the support network and the escape route was set up in the port of Marseille by a cast of characters straight out of a Le Carré novel. They had all washed up in Marseille, marooned by the tides of war, and provided a perfect blend of skills to get the line up and running in the most straightened of circumstances. They did so in a clandestine fashion, but also with a certain raffish style (several of them paid for this approach with their lives). Perhaps the best way to describe them, and to show the initial spirit of the Pat O'Leary Line, is to list their professions. They were – the Writer, the Soldier, the Priest, the Doctor, the Spy, the Banker, the Diplomat and the Femme Fatale. Through their actions, they created an escape network like no other.

The first key character in the story is the seedy, bustling, multi-layered city of Marseille itself – the perfect culture in which to grow a concept of such vision and daring. Marseille has been called the first capital of the Resistance, and not without reason. Until the German annexation of Vichy France, it was the biggest city and the only functioning port in the unoccupied zone. Like so many ports – melting pots of nationalities and conduits for goods and services from around the world – it had always been a hotbed of criminal activity, and had an active and highly efficient black market infrastructure. The docks were open and ships were still coming and going from all over the world. It was easy to blend in among the thousands of refugees of almost every European nationality, fleeing the Germans for all sorts of reasons. It was also completely full, awash with the displaced and desperate, and moving among them those who would make profit from their suffering. Accommodation reached such a premium that hotels were even renting their bathrooms as bedrooms. It was also chaotic and confusing, the ideal environment for plots to be hatched. For one journalist – the American Varian Fry – it was the perfect place to turn words into action, a setting for him to become part of the story of the wider war. He (the Writer) decided to set up the Emergency Rescue Committee, or ERC.

The ERC helped hundreds of Jews, dissident artists and intellectuals get away to safety, smuggling them over the border into Spain or onto ships leaving Marseille. Among them were Hannah Arendt, André Breton, Marcel Duchamp, Marc Chagall, Max Ernst, Lion Feuchtwanger, Claude Lévi-Strauss, Arthur Koestler, Wifredo Lam, Anna Seghers and Heinrich Mann.

In these early days of the escape lines there was – inevitably – a level of confusion and diplomatic uncertainty around the exact status of a refugee or escaper upon arrival in Spain. For one man in particular, this confusion led him to lose his life in the most heartrending of circumstances.

In late summer, 1940, Lisa Fittko, a Jewish member of the German Resistance who also worked for Varian Fry, was guiding the forty-eight-year-old Jewish philosopher and social and cultural commentator Walter Benjamin across the mountains. Benjamin, who had escaped from Berlin, was bringing with him in a suitcase those of his manuscripts he had managed to salvage. A measure of the desperate, exhausted state of most civilians who crossed the mountains is neatly summarized in a story Fittko recounts towards the end of the trek:

On about 23 September we came upon a pool. The water was greenish, slimy, and stank. Benjamin stooped down in order to drink.

'You can't drink that,' I said. 'The water's filthy, and certainly contaminated.'

The water-bottle which I had with me was empty by now,

and Benjamin hadn't complained of thirst at all until that moment.

'Forgive me,' he said. 'But I have no choice. If I don't have a drink now, it's possible I won't be able to hold out until the end.' He bent his head down to the pool.

'Listen to me,' I said. 'Will you just hang on a minute and listen to me? We're nearly there, only one more short stretch and it'll all be behind you. I know you'll make it. But it's out of the question that you drink any of this foul brew. Just think. Be sensible. You're risking typhus.'

'Yes, perhaps. But you have to understand: the worst that can happen is that I die of typhus after I've crossed the border. Then the Gestapo won't be able to arrest me any more, and the manuscript will be safe. So you must forgive me, dear lady.'

And he drank.

The next day, the party which Fittko was leading managed to reach Port Bou, on the coast in Catalonia. But at that time the Spanish government was cancelling transit visas and ordering the police to repatriate refugees to France. Such a measure would have wrecked Benjamin's plans to get away to the USA. But it meant far more than that – it would almost certainly have meant the concentration camps. In despair, he killed himself with an overdose of morphine at the Hotel de Francia on the night of 25 September.

By appalling coincidence, the following day the repatriation order was rescinded, and the other members of his party were allowed free passage after all. They reached Lisbon without diffi-culty on 30 September.

Fry also helped about 300 British soldiers escape. Two service-men who played key roles in building up escape routes at this early stage, and worked with Fry at some points, were Captain Charles Murchie of the Royal Army Service Corps, who had evaded capture after the German invasion, and Sergeant Henry Clayton, who had escaped from a POW camp. Murchie was a fundraiser and administrator; Clayton, married to a French-woman, resident in France, and fluent in French himself, was an interpreter, usefully able to pass himself off as French and so act as an information-gatherer as well. After many initial successes, and under increasingly menacing surveillance, both these men had to leave Marseille in spring 1941.

Meanwhile, word spread of Fry's growing network, which in due course became known simply as 'The Operation'. A safe house was established at the Seamen's Mission at 46 Rue de Forbin, run by a Scottish chaplain (the Priest) called Donald Caskie, who had been a minister of the Scottish Kirk in Paris since 1938. His fearless denunciations of the Nazis prior to the war had obliged him to flee the city to avoid arrest, and he had set himself up nominally as a chaplain on arrival in Marseille. A man of deep principles and abiding courage, he quickly estab-lished himself as a key figure in sheltering refugees and escapees of every denomination.

Also associated with the Seamen's Mission was George Rodo-canachi, a Liverpool-born Greek physician (the Doctor) who had completed his studies in Marseille, settled down to work there, and was now a naturalized Frenchman. Rodocanachi answered the medical needs of the escapers and evaders Caskie was conceal-ing at the mission. Hundreds passed through Caskie's hands, including James Langley, who joined MI9 as one of its senior officers after his repatriation.

Rodocanachi – 'Rodo' as he was known – also undertook the medical examinations of Jews applying to emigrate to the USA, and passed as 'fit to go' as many as humanly possible. Overall, he saw about 2,000 candidates. Another of his official duties was to examine interned Allied soldiers, who (conversely) as often as possible he pronounced unfit, so that they qualified for repatriation. He became increasingly involved with the Resistance, and with what he saw as the humanitarian task of getting escapers and evaders repatriated.

The Soldier, Ian Garrow, arrived in the city in August 1940. A tall man, he was described as looking 'conspicuously Scottish'. As a thirty-two-year-old captain in the Seaforth Highlanders, he had been captured after the battle at Saint-Valery-en-Caux. Along with many others, he walked out of the small town of Belâbre where he and many prisoners were being held, and made his way to Marseille. Here he linked up with Donald Caskie in the safe house at 46 rue de Forbin. Slowly, the key players were moving into place – the Writer, the Priest, the Doctor and the Soldier. They were soon to be joined by the Spy and the Diplomat.

The Spy arrived in the form of British agent Donald Darling, who had been tasked with establishing a Marseille–Barcelona escape route. He had lived in both France and Spain prior to the war and spoke both languages fluently. His role was an important one, as arrival in Spain for an escapee was by no means an assurance of repatriation to Britain. There were many cases of escapees being arrested and even being sent back to France, so there was often a delicate political game to be played once individuals or groups made it across the border. Darling was initially so hamstrung by diplomatic niceties that he was obliged to base himself in Lisbon, moving later to Gibraltar, where he organized the reception end of things. Darling chose the code-name 'Sunday', whereas Airey Neave at MI9 took the name 'Saturday'. 'Monday' was Sir Michael Cresswell, an attaché at the British embassy in Madrid (the Diplomat), who was au fait with the secret operations and who frequently used a diplomatic car to ferry escapers and evaders to safety once they had crossed the border. They almost certainly borrowed their code names from G. K. Chesterton's novel of 1908, *The Man Who Was Thursday*, a dark satire on the undercover life. The philosophy of Chesterton's secret society would have appealed to them:

> So in case you don't know, I'd better tell you that he is carrying out his notion of concealing ourselves by not concealing ourselves . . . He said that if you didn't seem to be hiding nobody hunted you out.

Another key member of the organization was Nancy Wake, codename Hélène, a New Zealander who'd been working in France as a foreign correspondent (the Femme Fatale). She met Garrow by chance in Marseille, later describing him as very tall, good looking, clean-shaven – a man of great charm. Wake herself became one of the most distinguished of the fifty-three female agents deployed in France by SOE, and proved so elusive that the Gestapo gave her a nickname: the White Mouse. They also put a bounty of five million francs on her head.

Her story typifies the remarkable exploits of the many women agents. SOE and MI9 were always aware of the great advantages of using female operatives: 'they made excellent wireless operators, and far less obtrusive couriers than men, and in a resistance organization courier work was essential,' as M. R. D. Foot remarks in his observations on the SOE in France from 1940–44.

Wake operated as a courier, and once explained her technique thus: 'A little powder and a little drink on the way, and I'd pass their posts and wink and say, "Do you want to search me?" God, what a flirtatious little bastard I was!'

She was married to the successful businessman and bon vivant Henri Fiocca and was living in Marseille when Germany invaded. Fiocca part-funded the operation, donating around £6,000, a huge amount at the time. Wake herself sold her jewels and gave the proceeds to the Pat Line.

The core of the organization's ever-increasing membership were French, however. Another member of Garrow's inner circle in Marseille was Louis Nouveau, an elegant, Savile Row-suited, anglophile stockbroker (the Banker). He became involved late in 1940, when he began inviting British officers to his opulent apartment on the Quai de Rive Neuve once a week, for a sort of men's salon. From this, he graduated to providing and organizing funds, giving £5,000 of his money to the operation. As the flow of aircrew evaders grew, he began sheltering them, keeping a secret record of his guests (as he called them) hidden in Volume XLIV of his *Complete Works* of Voltaire. Nouveau's wife, Renée, became an active operative of the Pat Line as well, while Louis also worked as a courier, conveying about fifty people to safety, including Airey Neave.

Garrow swiftly emerged as an excellent organizer and leader, and began to put in place a network of logistics and personnel that operated way beyond Marseille. His only failing as an under-cover agent – as Nancy Wake observed – was that his appearance, mannerisms and speech were unmistakably those of a British officer. In addition, although his French was good, he spoke it with a strong Scottish accent. He'd managed to get away with this in Marseille so far, but despite the vigilant vetting of new recruits as well as of escapers and evaders, who might always conceal an infiltrator in their midst, security for him was always going to be an issue. There was no denying that, even in the melting-pot of Marseille, Garrow stood out like a sore thumb.

Nevertheless, he continued to work successfully, liaising with Donald Darling and MI9, which had taken his organization under their wing, and getting funds via Darling and local sources such as Fiocca and Nouveau. More money came via a French subsidiary of a British company, M. & P. Coates.

Communication in the early days was chancy. Couriers criss-crossed the Pyrenees or managed to sail over to Gibraltar with news and requests. Garrow then awaited coded replies built into BBC broadcasts. Later, life was made easier by the arrival of radios and their operators. But it was always a dangerous game, with the odds stacked against covert operators, and the stakes as high as they could possibly be. Despite these risks, the network continued to grow – Garrow and his companions had achieved a great deal, taking huge personal risks, with limited resources and scant backing from the UK. The line's operatives, as M. R. D. Foot has pointed out, were 'a splendid and daring fellowship of resisters, who would have scorned to steer clear of their personal friends lest seeing them should endanger the circuit.'

But the catalyst that moved the line into another dimension, creating a vast network that would ultimately save thousands of lives, was the arrival on the scene of Patrick O'Leary.

For a name that has such resonance in the annals of escape and evasion, it is ironic that the real O'Leary had absolutely nothing to do with the Freedom Trail that bears his name. He was the son of a Canadian diplomat based in Brussels who had made friends at medical school with a francophone Belgian called Albert-Marie Guérisse.

Guérisse stands beside Andrée de Jongh as one of the greatest of all undercover agents working with the British secret services in the Second World War. He personally ensured the safe return home of many hundreds of servicemen and women between 1941 and 1943. The line that bears his name also saw the passage out of thousands of refugees and displaced people.

Albert-Marie Guérisse, a thirty-year-old doctor in the Belgian army, found himself on the beaches of Dunkirk, where he embarked for Britain on 31 May 1940. After arriving safely at Margate, he set sail a few days later for Brest, where the Belgian army was trying to regroup. In mid-June, as the German army drew near, he made his way to Sete and took a British merchant ship to Gibraltar. From there he got a passage on a French merchant ship which was sailing for England. The ship's commander wanted his vessel to be used by the Royal Navy, and, refitted and renamed HMS *Fidelity*, she became a Q ship, operating out of Gibraltar, working the south-west French Mediterranean coast. This work included landing and collecting agents, and taking off escapers and evaders, by using small skiffs as tenders between the ship and the shore. The ship's second in command was none other than Guérisse. He had been given a commission as Lieutenant Commander in the Royal Navy on 15 September 1940 (backdated to 1 July), six weeks' training by SOE, and a new identity to protect his family if he was caught. SOE suggested he pretended to be French-Canadian as his English was not good – remembering his friend, Guérisse picked O'Leary as a surname and SOE came up with Patrick as the logical match for such an Irish name. For the rest of the war his true identity would remain a secret from those he worked with and from the Germans.

On the night of 26 April 1942 things went wrong, as O'Leary's skiff got into trouble and couldn't regain the mother ship, which was standing three kilometres offshore. Despite their best efforts to remain unseen, the skiff was intercepted by a Vichy French coastguard cutter. O'Leary and his companions were stranded on the beach, arrested, and, after interrogation at Port-Vendres, ultimately taken (via Toulon and Fort Lamalgue) to St-Hippolyte-du-Fort, where there was an internment camp for British servicemen. It was more like a barracks than a camp, with an entrance facing the main street of the town. It was here that O'Leary first heard Ian Garrow's name.

As subsequent events were to prove, O'Leary was an enterprising and determined man, and he immediately began to plan his escape. One almost extempore attempt to get away failed, but it was swiftly followed by another, more carefully planned one. He finally made a successful escape on 3 July with the help of some nuns, who hid him in a trunk containing musty church vestments. They put the Germans off the scent by declaring, with perfect truth, 'in the name of God, there is no Englishman here'. The Mother Superior then led him down to the cellars and through a secret passage to the vineyards beyond the hospice where he'd taken refuge. From here, he made a successful getaway, joining the Garrow escape line armed with a forged ID card in the name of Adolphe Lecomte.

He made his way to Marseille, about 180 kilometres to the south-east, and took refuge with Dr Rodocanachi. There he was introduced to Garrow, who enlisted him as soon as he could, though he had to wait a while for authorization from London. SOE agreed, sending a coded message via the BBC: 'Adolphe doit rester.' Throughout this period, O'Leary continued to use his new nom-de-guerre, Adolphe Lecomte (in fact this was the name he was to use whenever travelling in the north of France). In Marseille, he went under yet another name, Joseph Cartier.

In one sense, his arrival wasn't a moment too soon, for in October 1941 Garrow was arrested by the Vichy police. The organization had actually been under surveillance for some time, and its somewhat loose structure made it vulnerable. It was the first of a series of blows.

The network relied on trust and honour, and as such betrayal by one individual could have a devastating effect. This is precisely what happened in late 1941. Such was the tectonic impact of this that the entire system nearly collapsed, and it was only through the actions of a few exceptionally brave individuals that it somehow prevailed, re-emerging several months later as a route that remained viable and valid.

The man responsible for this betrayal was described as 'the worst traitor of the entire war' by Deputy Commander Reginald Spooner of Scotland Yard. Although his conduct was truly appalling, it is highly improbable that he felt any particular political allegiance, even to the Germans. His track record before and during the war indicates that he thought of nothing but personal gain. Despite his treachery, fuelled by a near-psychotic disregard for anyone but himself, Harold Cole was – in his own way – a remarkable figure. He had a chameleon-like ability to blend in, to cajole, to win over his captors even when the evidence against him was completely overwhelming. He changed sides at least twice during the war (and possibly three times), and there is speculation to this day that he was operating as an agent for the British, for the Germans and even as a double agent. The truth is probably more prosaic – he was operating for himself, with catastrophic consequences for the Pat O'Leary Line.

Cole had been a petty thief and conman in London before the war broke out, and had lied about his military credentials to enlist as a sergeant in the 18th Field Park Company, an engineering unit that was part of the 4th Infantry Division. His true colours came swiftly to the fore, and he absconded with the funds from the sergeants' mess. He was soon recaptured, and was with the unit when they were over-run by the Germans in mid-1940.

It is here that we get a brief glimpse of what Cole might have been, had he used his gift of persuasion, his ability to adopt a disguise, and his nerve – all honed on the streets of London – to more noble effect. Cole escaped from German custody and became instrumental in operating the early escape lines in co-operation with the French Resistance. Under the name of Paul Cole, he guided a number of groups of prisoners to safety, and his bravery and audacity were beyond debate. He was instrumental in escorting the largest group of escapees to date along the line – thirteen servicemen from northern France to Marseille, and from there to safety. He was shaping up to be a model operative, and could have been key figure in the network.

There is the temptation to think of Cole as a rather dapper David Niven-style figure, a dashing spiv with a glint in his eye. The fact was that he seemed to bluff his way through most situations – not an entirely bad thing as a Resistance man of course – although his criminal tendencies never left him. One of the escapers he escorted recalls:

> In my mind (he) did not inspire much confidence . . . His whole appearance was the continentals' idea of a typical Englishman. His French was deplorable and spoken in an accent unmistakably British. He was loud-mouthed, perhaps to cover his nervousness, although while I knew him, he showed no fear.

However, his effectiveness as a guide was never in doubt. Another of his 'parcels' later said: 'I shall never understand how, why or when Cole defected to the enemy, but insofar as it concerned (me) and other evaders, he served us well.'

In 1941, he was re-captured by the Germans, and it was at this point that he may have switched sides (although there is the possibility that it had happened the first time he was in custody, and his original escape was an elaborate ruse in order to inveigle him into the very heart of the Resistance).

In late 1941, the organization began to suspect him of embezzling funds. Donald Darling ran a security check on him, and

O'Leary himself confronted him at Rodocanachi's apartment. O'Leary didn't pull his punches. Under interrogation Cole broke down, and confessed to having done something 'truly awful'. His apparently sincere remorse made O'Leary and his associates hesitate. One of them, Bruce Dowding, was for killing him there and then as a clear danger to their operation, but Cole, who'd been locked in a bathroom while they decided what to do with him, escaped through a window. In a horrific twist of fate, Dowding was one of many subsequently betrayed by Cole, and was duly executed by the Germans.

After Cole's escape, O'Leary and several other agents set off for the north to warn their people in Lille and Paris about him. In this they partially succeeded, but they couldn't get word to everyone. Bizarrely, Cole took part in one last journey transferring a group of escapers south, but he showed his true colours once and for all when, at the end of 1941, he appeared at the home in Abbeville of the twenty-nine-year-old Abbé Pierre Carpentier, a priest who had been active in ferrying Allied servicemen south. Cole was accompanied by three British airmen, which allayed any suspicions in the abbé's mind at first, but two of them turned out to be disguised Germans. The third appears to have been the genuine article, and perhaps an innocent dupe. The abbé was arrested, together with several male and female members of his group, while Bruce Dowding, who'd managed to slip away from this original sting operation having recognized Cole, was arrested the following day.

All those arrested were sent to prisons of one kind or another and most, including Carpentier, were subsequently executed. Before his death, Carpentier managed to smuggle out a deposition against Cole to a fellow resistance worker, Jeannine Vogliamacci, herself an innocent part of Cole's erstwhile network. This deposition helped indict Cole later, though he was never to face a court martial.

Cole ultimately went to ground after the arrests of Carpentier and the others, knowing that O'Leary was out for his blood in Paris. He was later arrested in Lyon by the Vichy police on an espionage charge, and sentenced to death, but he was saved by the German annexation. He then seems to have gone back to work for the German *Sicherheitsdienst* (the intelligence unit of the SS).

By the end of the war, Cole was wanted by both the French and British governments, and was being pursued by MI9. He was captured at Bad Saulgau in June 1945 and imprisoned at the SHAEF military prison in Paris. Remarkably, he escaped once again on 18 November 1945, and a large manhunt was initiated to recapture him.

On 8 January 1946, the French police discovered Cole hiding on the fourth floor of a bar in the Rue de Grenelle in Paris. He was wearing the uniform of a US sergeant at the time, preparing to re-enter society after his next will o' the wisp escape, doubtless to continue wreaking his particular brand of bedlam. But his time, and his luck, had finally run out. He was shot as the police burst into the apartment, and later buried in an unmarked pauper's grave in Paris.

It seems probable that Cole had the kind of self-absorbed, borderline personality disorder which meant that he was entirely egocentric and amoral in outlook, simply doing whatever would both profit him and make for his own survival, regardless of anything else. His disregard for the wider consequences of his actions would doubtless have had implications in peacetime as well as war, but for him to be unleashed into the very heart of the Resistance movement, and the network supporting the escape lines, was truly catastrophic. It's thought that, all in all, Cole was responsible for the betrayal of about 150 members of the Resistance, of whom at least fifty were executed by the Germans. Because of his actions, the very survival of the Pat O'Leary Line was under threat.

The organization was still reeling from the impact of Cole's betrayal when, at the end of April 1942, the suspicious police closed the Seamen's Mission down and arrested Caskie. Lacking enough evidence against him, they allowed the Priest to go to Grenoble, where he had a post as chaplain and continued to secretly help escapees. Meanwhile, Rodocanachi made his own enormous twelve-roomed apartment (which incorporated his surgery) at 21 Rue Roux de Brignoles available as a safe house. The apartment provided a kind of home-from-home, with tea and biscuits and even English books. Nonetheless, its occupants had to be careful, wearing carpet slippers to minimize noise and flushing the lavatories sparingly so as not to alert the neighbours to the fact that the flat had so many 'tenants'.

An overhaul of the operation was carried out in 1942, with new recruits engaged, greater involvement from London and the introduction of a new team of Spanish Pyrenean guides, led by Francisco Ponzan-Vidal, a tough thirty-year-old anarchist/socialist from Huesca who'd fled Franco's Spain and settled in Toulouse, where he'd joined the Resistance. The Marseille end of operations was run by Mario Prassinos. O'Leary, meanwhile, was busy with work in Toulouse and in Gibraltar, where he met James Langley of MI9, who'd flown out specially to liaise. Here he also met Donald Darling, recently arrived from Lisbon. Among other things, there was the situation created by Cole to discuss, and what measures should be taken to block any holes in the operation.

O'Leary was fortunate enough to recruit the indomitable French Resistance fighter Andrée Borrel, codename Denise. At Toulouse, he could rely on Marie-Louise Dissard, aged sixty in 1941, who ran safe houses in the town and arranged escape across the Pyrenees from there for those in her charge. Her apartment, ruled over by her temperamental cat, Mifouf, became the operations centre in Toulouse (the group also used the Hôtel de Paris there). The northern end of the Pat Line was run by Jean de la Olla, who rebuilt the staff there after the wave of arrests following other denunciations by Cole.

Garrow, meanwhile, had been sent to prison at Fort-St-Nicolas, and then to the holding camp at Mauzac on the banks of the Dordogne, after having been tried and sentenced to three-and-a-half years' solitary confinement in May 1942. In an ironic reversal of roles, and indeed a moment that saw power shift within the network itself, Garrow's successful escape would be organized by O'Leary in December, when it became apparent that Garrow was about to be transferred to a concentration camp in Germany. With the help of one of the camp's guards (who was paid an enormous bribe) a uniform was smuggled to Garrow, who walked out of the camp dressed as a German soldier. Garrow was then taken to Toulouse, to a safe house run by Marie-Louise Dissard, and thence across the Pyrenees using one of the established routes. He returned to England in February 1943.

With O'Leary firmly established as the figure running what would become known as the Pat Line, one of the most famous escape routes of the war was now an entirely viable, fully operational entity.

It became swiftly apparent that the line was not simply a route to repatriate escaping soldiers and downed airmen. As the Nazis' sinister policies began to be put into action, huge sectors of the populations of occupied nations started to realize that the invasion of their countries was just the beginning of the horror that was about to be unleashed upon them. The inciting of racial hatred, the systematic deportation of certain ethnic groups and their subsequent murder on an industrial scale made running for freedom more than just a principled choice. It became a means of survival itself.

CHAPTER FOUR

Surviving the Pyrenees

What is most striking for anyone arriving in St-Girons today is its tranquillity. It is the definitive sleepy French settlement – the River Salat rolling through its midst, trout flicking and twisting in the shallows and old men sitting on the banks, gnarled hands resting atop walking sticks as they pass the time of day in idle conversation. The foothills of the Pyrenees present a verdant backdrop, and its narrow alleys and quiet plazas echo to the timeless slow beat of mountain life.

And yet, in the latter stages of the war, St-Girons was a hotspot, a focal point for evaders, refugees and a relentless enemy that loaded the town with agents and troops. Many scenes of high drama were played out here; moments of breathless intensity when the life of an individual could be snuffed out through a second of misplaced trust or a single moment of indiscretion. As I walked across the main bridge of the town, the river thundering over the weir beneath me, a simple glance to the south revealed why.

From this bridge, the wide passage of the river allowed a view through the heart of ancient tenements and steepling ochre townhouses, permitting a clear line of sight to the distant peaks of the Pyrenees. This view represented freedom, the line between incarceration and liberation, between life and death. Cross those mountains and you were in neutral Spain, and from there you could continue your war, whatever that war might be.

Older than the Alps, composed of granite that stoutly resists erosion and weathering, the Pyrenees run for 430 kilometres south-west from the coastline of the Bay of Biscay all the way to the Mediterranean. Such roads and railway routes as do cross these mountains tend to be concentrated at their extremities – the western and eastern ends of the range where it plunges towards to the coast. Crossing the Pyrenees anywhere else means climbing into the clouds, an uncompromising ascent into the rarefied air of mountaineering. This inaccessibility is – of course – the reason why France ends where it does, and Spain begins. Man has been thrown back again and again by these mountains, occupying instead the lower slopes and fertile plains beneath, only venturing onto higher ground in the summer months in a biannual migration of people and livestock known as 'transhumance'. The shepherds who spent part of their year in the mountains, as well as local hunters, accumulated knowledge of the paths across the high mountain passes, mental maps to which no occupying army had access.

Renowned for its local guides, St-Girons had long been a launching point for anyone who wanted to pass through the Pyrenees. In the early days of the war, when southern France was under the rule of the Vichy government, this meant that a steady stream of refugees used the town as a launching point for their run into Spain. Even after the town was occupied by the Germans on 8 November 1942, the passage of escapees continued unabated. This was despite the fact that the Nazis established a twenty-kilometre-wide exclusion zone leading up the mountains, heavily controlled via a series of guard posts and active patrols. As the war took its course, tensions increased within St-Girons itself, with a hugely complex network of local guides being tracked by an equally intricate network of German spies and agents. As a series of betrayals and arrests of the organizers of the various established Freedom Trails took place, the routes through the mountains became more and more demanding, pushing ever higher over remote cols, barren ridges and lofty passes.

Such high passes are rare in the Pyrenees. For its entire, meandering length, the mountain range maintains altitude.

From where I stood on the bridge, the mountains looked otherworldly and magnificent, their peaks solid and dark against the deep blue of the sky. Even in the sweltering heat of the day in St-Girons, I could make out snow on their lofty flanks, a reminder that here is a realm unaffected by the vagaries of lowland weather. The higher reaches of the Pyrenees are a defiantly independent world, generating katabatic winds as freezing air tumbles down steep slopes, creating clouds that erupt overhead with volcanic fury and violent storms that lie in ambush behind ridges and cols.

I walked across the bridge and towards the town square, shaded by high walls, cool and tranquil in the midst of the stifling heat of the afternoon. I was in St-Girons to hear the story of a Jewish refugee who had headed over the mountains in 1944. His son was waiting for me in a pavement cafe in the town, poring over a map. Joav Asscher was a very sprightly sixty-eight-year-old from Holland, who sprang forward to shake my hand as I walked up to him.

'Ah, Monty, how nice to see you. Come, come, sit down.' He pulled a chair towards his table with a rattle of its metal legs across the cobbles and gestured towards a waiter scuttling past balancing a tray full of drinks. 'Please, another coffee.' He turned to speak to me once again, beaming in delight. 'How good of you to come and speak to me.'

Joav was – quite simply – a lovely man, one of those rare characters in life one warms to immediately. He had a thoroughly engaging manner about him which positively bloomed when he talked about how he'd followed in his father's footsteps, retracing his route, the year before.

'Oh, I have such a story to tell you, such a story,' he said. 'For me, it is very emotional even now to talk not only about what my father did, but also my own walk across the mountains. Are you going to try to do it too? Ha! Well, good luck, it is not easy but you will never forget it.'

By now my coffee had arrived, and Joav smoothed out his map and jabbed a finger at where a path intersected a larger road.

'Well, this is where I think my father set out from, a place called Lamaze, but of course I cannot be one hundred per cent sure. He was guided by a passeur called Adriaan, who seemed a colourful character. But then again, I suppose they all were in their own way.'

And so we talked, with Joav my animated and knowledgeable guide, a witness to his father's story.

'You seem very proud,' I said, as he paused for breath, 'is that what spurred you to do it?'

'Oh yes,' he nodded vigorously. 'I am so proud of my father. Without him deciding that he would take his own fate into his hands, I would not be here. I thought of him with every step I took over the mountains.' He paused for a moment, searching for the words. 'He was truly a great man.'

Berrie Asscher's story is typical of those who went over the high mountains in the latter stages of the war, in that he understood the gamble he was taking. No one found the crossing easy, although for local people used to the mountains it was a well-known route to safety (albeit one that was physically demanding even for mountain folk). However, for most people, drawn here from far-away lands and in desperate circumstances, it was a harrowing, near-death experience that came to define them for the rest of their lives. Asscher's crossing is one story among so many, but it represents so much of what was involved in taking the momentous decision to run for Spain by heading over the Pyrenees.

Earlier in the war, Asscher had escaped Holland – assisted by a Dutch businessman called Joop Westerweel – and found himself in the perilous position, as a young Jewish man in Nazi-occupied France, of working on the German defences in Normandy. Although he loathed it, it did allow him a certain freedom of movement, as the Germans issued all of their workers with identity documents. He used these to slip away into the hinterland of France, and from there made his way south towards the Spanish border. He initially wanted only to put distance between himself and Nazis, but on nearing the border learned of the crossing over the mountains. He immediately decided to attempt the route.

He arrived in St-Girons with ten fellow escapees on 10 November 1943, where they met with Adriaan, who immediately took them to a cabin in a remote meadow. Here, Asscher waited for five days, living in complete silence, not permitted to leave the cabin in daylight hours, and talking in whispers to his new companions in the darkness within.

November is a terrible time in the mountains, as the barometer drops precipitously at a moment's notice and localized storms gather in muscular dark vortexes overhead. These weather patterns are entirely unpredictable, even for experienced guides, and many a group found themselves isolated on high ground with a storm breaking upon them with apocalyptic fury, a merciless artillery barrage of thunder and lightning. Temperatures could plummet within moments and, sure enough, when Adriaan returned to the group they emerged from the hut into deep snow and bitter cold.

They set out on the trail, with Adriaan in front breaking track and the group shuffling wearily behind him. As they walked the snow fell ever more heavily, reducing visibility and deadening all sound, their world now reduced to white, swirling, freezing sciroccos inhabited only by the hunched figures of the group. They crested several ridges, ever more exhausted and desperate, and finally arrived at a small hut, where they at last found shelter. Adriaan informed them that if the snow continued to fall, they might have to turn back. And, heartbreakingly, that is exactly what transpired the next morning. Asscher recalls the moment clearly in his memoirs, with the border represented by the summit of Mont Valier clearly in view, a tantalizing mirage, their freedom suspended in the sky above them.

After retreating back down through the mountains, Asscher then had to wait several months, hidden in safe houses – all the while fearing discovery – before being once again informed via the Resistance that a passage across the mountains was possible. Returning to St-Girons in late February 1944, he now found he was part of a group of twenty-three, which included several downed pilots, two French police officers, some older Jewish refugees and two women.

Just before he departed on his second attempt, the group was visited by a truly remarkable – and largely unsung – hero of the resistance movement. Joop Westerweel was a Dutchman who helped an estimated 300 Jews escape from Holland to freedom – this number included Asscher, so he was delighted and surprised to see Westerweel appear in person to wish the group good luck before they attempted the crossing. Westerweel had just helped deliver a number of Jewish children to Spain, and was en route back to Holland. But Westerweel had something more important to say than a simple farewell. Gathering the Jewish escapees together, he told them to bear witness to the world about what was happening to their people. Westerweel – himself a Jew – was impressing on them the importance of their role as global messengers of a story of horror, repression and extermination unrivalled in human history.

Finishing his message, he left to continue his journey home. He was arrested thirteen days later, on 10 March 1944, at the border between Belgium and Holland, and executed at Herzogenbusch concentration camp in August of that year.

Back in the hut, Adriaan handed out provisions to the group prior to their departure. Each escapee was given a piece of bread, some sugar and a small piece of meat. He assured the group that their trip over the mountains would take no more than two days, so these provisions would have to suffice.

On 27 February – a Sunday – Asscher found himself once again heading into the dark maw of the mountains. By a stroke of bad luck, the group was hit once again by a snowstorm, which delayed them considerably in reaching their first refuge – a hut hidden deep in the drifts. Adriaan told the group that the delay meant they were behind schedule and would need more food, so he headed back down the mountain for more supplies, returning a day and a half later.

It is worth considering the details of this situation for a moment. This was a large group of adults – twenty-three people – who had already battled their way through a blizzard and over several high ridges to get to the hut. They had then been left for nearly two days, alone and freezing, and now their guide was bringing them more supplies to continue their journey. But just how much food can one man carry? The most terrifying and exhausting part of their journey lay ahead – the massive, glowering flanks of Mont Valier, nearly three kilometres high and a killer of a mountain in the wrong conditions. Each member of the group was starving and exhausted, and was given – for this monumental feat – another piece of bread, some more sugar lumps and another small piece of meat. Asscher describes part of the journey as they headed towards the mountain, ever steeper and more forbidding: 'We walked like robots, along deep ravines, and knew no more of time or hours.'

After a further day's walking – they had now been in the brutal mountains for three days – they had climbed into an entirely alien world, with blue ice and blasted scree all around. At half past four in the morning, having walked all night, they reached another hut at an altitude of 2,500 metres. This tiny shelter did not have enough room for them all to lie down, so some tried sleeping while leaning against a wall. They were in a truly pitiful state, at the mercy of the elements, physically and psychologically bereft. And that is when Adriaan abruptly announced that, as they were now virtually at the border, he would return home and leave them to complete the last stages on their own.

His words caused immense consternation in the group who felt (not unreasonably) that they were being abandoned to their fate. The motives of passeurs varied enormously – some did it for honour, some out of compassion or patriotic duty, but many did it for money. Adriaan had been paid 8,000 francs for the safe passage of each person within the group – an astronomic sum at the time. In modern terms, that is the equivalent to $40,000, so the complete group would earn him 184,000 francs –$920,000 today. The stakes were – of course – unbelievably high. If he was caught by the Germans, or betrayed by one of his contacts, he would be executed without hesitation, but nonetheless these sums meant that should he survive the war he would be a rich man. One may argue at length about the morality of taking money for assisting the war effort, but other issues of conscience are easier to address. By essentially abandoning the group on the brutal, unforgiving upper slopes of Mont Valier, Adriaan must have known that there was a very good chance they would die. The unwritten code of any mountain guide demands that they keep those under their charge safe. Adriaan betrayed this code, and trudged back through the snow down towards the foothills with the forlorn cries of the group echoing in his ears.

He had told them that the Spanish village of Montgarri was an easy walk once they had passed over the ridge ahead of them. The group gathered themselves together as best they could, and headed upwards once again, this time feeling lost and alone.

It was revealed after the war that Adriaan had abandoned another group in similar circumstances, several of whom had died. In what was perhaps a twist of cruel justice, he was not available to give his account of events, as he was shot by the Germans during another crossing of the Pyrenees in the summer of 1944.

The temperature was now minus fifteen degrees Celsius. On cresting the ridge, the group continued walking all day, still surrounded by snow and ice. One of their number – a French policeman called Maurice – had some experience in the mountains, and had taken charge. Towards the end of the day they reached an impasse, a moment that would decide if they lived or died. Now completely spent, they faced a wall of ice, while to one side was a steep valley. Some instinct, a counter-intuitive sixth sense of survival, meant that Maurice decided to lead them up the ice wall and not into the valley. In retrospect, Asscher believes that the valley would have led them in the wrong direction, and the group would have perished. On such decisions hangs the difference between success and failure, between survival and death, in the uncompromising world of the high Pyrenees.

The group found themselves on an icy plateau as night settled in once more. They were at the end of their tether, completely broken, and Maurice got them to dig a pit in the snow where they huddled together like animals for the rest of the night. His leadership saved their lives, for although the next morning they woke to find that their wet clothing had frozen 'into hard boards', their rudimentary shelter and the warmth of their fellow escapees had kept them sentient and mobile. They were now heading into their sixth day in the mountains.

Somehow, they stumbled on, but now the ground began to fall away beneath their feet, simple momentum leading them downwards. In a blissful change of fortune, they found that they were heading back into the land of people, of grass and forests and life-giving warmth. They descended more than a thousand metres in a few hours, finally entering a wood as the sun began to shine and – for the first time in several days – their clothes began to dry out. Asscher noted simply: 'We understood we were saved. There are no words to express what we felt at that moment.'

They had indeed made it into Spain, along the way writing their own chapter in the many legends of Pyrenees crossings. Their survival had been a testament to their indefatigable spirit, but also to that extraordinary human ability to find some last fading ember of life, some reason to continue, when all else seems entirely lost.

My guide, Paul, met me in the car park at the Col de la Core, a lean figure wearing a large floppy hat, his clothing worn and faded. He smiled shyly as he saw me approach, and introduced himself in a clipped English accent. He exuded quiet competence, and also appeared rather reserved, which was an endearing combination.

'You're a long way from home?' I commented. 'Interesting to

find an Englishman working as a mountain guide here in the Pyrenees.'

'I did this for the first time eight years ago, and I've been hooked ever since,' he replied immediately, his eyes lighting up. 'It's walking a living memorial, really. Footsteps of giants and all that.' He then looked rather sheepish, as though this outburst was in rather poor form and had let the side down.

I decided that I rather liked Paul, and hefted my own rucksack onto my back to fall in behind him as he set out on the path that climbed steadily up the green hill ahead of us.

I was pleased to see that the Pyrenees didn't take long to flex their muscles, with the gradient beneath my feet abruptly increasing, and the trees around me thinning to reveal the grandeur of the challenge ahead. The overall topography of these mountains presents unique challenges to anyone tackling them from the French side. Cut into cross section, the entire range appears as a wedge, with precipitous rock faces to the north-west, and gentle slopes to the south-east on the Spanish side. It is as though nature itself had conspired against anyone leaving occupied Europe during the war, as they would quickly find themselves climbing steep gradients, high beyond the forests and fields and into a moonscape of rock and ice. As an escapee, they would enter this harsh world just as their energy faded and the temperature dropped.

We were climbing up towards a gap in the ridge called the Col de la Crouzette. I could now see it, a shallow parabola against the blue sky, a thousand metres above the car park, and over two thousand metres above sea level. It was a particularly hot day, with the sun warming the rocks at my feet to create a miasma of heat through which we trudged, red-faced and slick with sweat. On one of our water stops by a small lake, a sapphire pool cupped in emerald hills, Paul soaked his hat in the water, placed it on his head, and sat back with a contended sigh as he took in the view.

'They're undeniably beautiful, these mountains,' he said, after a moment's reflective silence. 'But they're killers as well. The average temperature here in the winter – which is when a lot of the crossings took place – is minus two degrees C. Even in spring, they would wait until the snow was cold and crisp enough underfoot to aid walking, which meant setting out in frigid conditions a lot of the time. Storms come up from nowhere – you can be walking blissfully along one side of a ridge, and there can be absolute chaos coming at you unseen from behind another. So many people were lost here you know, this isn't just a tale of heroism, it's one of tragedy, too.'

'The role of the passeur – your role – was a tough one too,' I said in response. 'I can't begin to imagine the pressure of guiding large groups into this environment. Women, children, old men, emaciated, exhausted, desperate people – it must have been horrific for those given the task of getting them over the Pyrenees in one piece.'

'Oh, it was,' said Paul immediately. 'One of the passeurs had to abandon a group of three American airmen who were simply too exhausted to continue, and it was said to have haunted him for the rest of his life. And, of course, they were being hunted too – there were about two thousand known passeurs operating in the Pyrenees, and over a thousand of them were executed or died in concentration camps. They were often well rewarded for taking people across, but they earned their money all right.'

We both sat in contemplative silence for a while, broken only by the cries of two choughs that tumbled and twisted overhead, their calls amplified by the slopes around the lake. Paul glanced at his watch and lifted his gaze to the ridge ahead.

'Come on, Monty,' he said, 'no time to dawdle. It's only a

immensity of the scenery around me, to sleep on the edge of oblivion.

Paul woke me with a cup of coffee the next morning.

'How did you sleep?' he asked cheerfully, as I blearily took in the utterly glorious dawn landscape.

'Ermmm, OK I think.'

'Delighted to hear it,' he responded. 'Because a bear took a sheep a couple of kilometres away last night – I was just chatting to a passing shepherd. I thought I might come down and find just a pair of socks left.'

There are only about thirty brown bears in the Pyrenees, looked after by a force of 150 conservationists (which I think is rather wonderful, an army dedicated to the protection of an animal once so widely vilified). As such, I would have been very unlucky indeed to be dragged out of my tent and noisily consumed – the chances are virtually nil of even seeing one in the immensity of the mountains. Mind you, that's probably precisely what that sheep was thinking as it munched happily away on some grass without a care in the world, idly making its plans for the morning.

The next section of the trail took us – rather depressingly – down a moderately small slope, and then immediately up a rather large one. Throughout the descent of the former I was staring straight at the latter, a vision of rocky, sun-baked toil. It looked formidable, so I decided to stare at my feet for a while and pretend it wasn't there.

In all honesty, I had no idea if I was walking along a heavily utilized segment of the Pat O'Leary line, as the precise route over the mountains changed according to climatic conditions, intelligence on the whereabouts of German patrols and the preferences of the individual passeurs. On entering the higher slopes, the risk of capture by the Germans decreased, and the simple physics of staying alive in the harsh conditions came into play. The colosseum of the high Pyrenees saw many a tragedy unfold, many a drama play out to its inevitable conclusion – yet another figure slumped in defeat to be slowly subsumed in a white shroud. These same upper slopes also witnessed scenes of futile heroism, of sacrifice and selfless valour.

On 23 October 1943, a group consisting of seven French army personnel and seven US airmen attempted the route over the mountains. The former were at least reasonably well rested, and also had the resilience of their infantry training. They were driven by a patriotic fervour, aware that their individual decisions to find a way – any way – to fight, would define them for the rest of their lives.

The other seven were in a truly desperate state. They had been inactive for months, holed up in safe houses, harried from place to place, moved late at night, deprived of sleep and given inadequate food. They were wearing a variety of cast-off clothing, ill-fitting and frayed, and on their feet they had either shoes or French 'ersatz' crampons – essentially football boots with nails hammered through the soles. Two of their number – First Lieutenant Olof Ballinger and Staff Sergeant Francis Owens – had been evading capture for four months, and had travelled over 800 kilometres together since being shot down over Normandy in early July.

Their passeur was called Emile Delpy – himself an interesting figure in that he was working for MI9, not the French Resistance. He set out quickly with the group, keen to put as much distance as possible between them and the threat of German patrols.

In their weakened state, it was not long before the climb took its toll. Ballinger's legs began to cramp up, and he was soon trailing some distance behind the group. They were only in the foothills at Suc, south-east of St-Girons – still well within the reach of the Germans – and to slow the group down at this stage might have been fatal for all. Delpy knew the same and, instructing the main party to rest, walked back to the reclining figure of Ballinger.

'You must wait here,' he ordered brusquely, with no time for sentiment or sympathy. 'I will be back in a week. Try to find a safe place to shelter – the locals here have little time for the Germans.'

The passeur moved swiftly back up the hill and at once continued the ascent. He knew he must push ever onwards, and the group of exhausted escapees must stay with him.

For the next thirty hours the group moved continuously, through an entire night and the day beyond, climbing higher and higher. At the summit, they were hit by a swirling blizzard. One of the American airmen – it is suspected that he had taken several Benzedrine tablets to try to stay awake, over-dosing in the process – pitched forward. Two of his companions carried him for eight hours – a remarkable feat of endurance and selfless heroism in the circumstances – but in their weakened state this simply accelerated their own collapse. The wind twisted in triumph around them, the snow already beginning to claim their motionless forms, entombing them, gathering their bodies into the mountain itself.

Hypothermia cares not about resolve or implacable will – the combination of decreased body fat, the effort of the climb, inadequate clothing and a simple accident of the timing of a storm hitting at the exact moment they had crested the summit ridge created a situation more perilous than any they had faced before. For every one degree that their core temperature dropped below ninety-five Fahrenheit, their metabolic rate fell by 3 to 5 per cent.

(Right to left) Varian Fry briefing André Breton, André Masson and Jacqueline Breton on escaping Vichy France.

Albert-Marie Guérisse (third from the right) on the beach at Dunkirk with a group of fellow Belgian Army officers, waiting to be rescued.

Airmen being smuggled out of France on the Pat O'Leary Line, posing defiantly next to a 'wanted' poster, their uniforms seemingly thrown on over their civvies for the occasion.

One of the ID cards used by the Pat O'Leary Line.

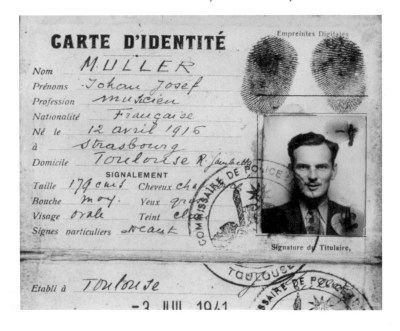

Scottish officer Ian Garrow, an instrumental figure in what came to be known as the Pat O'Leary Line, with Guérisse after the war.

Andrée de Jongh, who founded the Comet Line, receiving her George Medal after the war.

Bob Frost, a British airman who passed through the Comet Line and crossed the Pyrenees alongside Andrée.

Michèle Agniel (née Moet), who worked
as a courier for the Burgundy Line.

Michèle's brother Jean-Marie,
an innocent caught up in events.

Gerard and Genevieve Moet, Michèle's parents, who ran a safe house for
Allied escapees until they were arrested, along with Michèle, in 1944.

A group of airmen in the Moet family's front room.
They were given lessons on looking more French.

The high Pyrenees, taken from the camp on the second night,
showing the harsh terrain crossed by thousands of escapees.

Campo 78, near Sulmona, Italy, an army barracks turned into a POW camp.

Len Harley and his best friend in camp, Albert 'Nick' Nichols.

ABOVE: Pacentro, where Len and Nick found shelter after escaping the camp.

RIGHT: The Spinosa family, who risked their lives to shelter Len and his fellow escapees.

FAR LEFT: Bruno Spinosa.

LEFT: Alberto, the guide who took Len and Nick across Monte Amaro.

Rosina Spinosa today.   Len Harley today.

The plateau of Monte Amaro, where to flag or falter
meant you would probably die.

Capillaries in their skin, dilated by the exertion of the climb, radiated heat away from their bodies, their wet clothing speeding up the process. The very essence of their life force was borne away, degree by degree, on the winds that scour the ridge. As their core temperature dropped further, their mental functions passed from apathetic through to amnesia, and then to total incapacity.

The passeur knew that this moment was critical for all of their survival. If he could just begin the descent, down into the shelter of the southern ridges leading towards Andorra, they could – at last – rest. But if they delayed now, here in the teeth of the storm when the whole group was at its lowest physical ebb, then they would undoubtedly perish.

'Up! Up!' Delpy shouted over the noise of the wind, grabbing the arm of one of the airmen. 'You must move. Allez, allez!'

There was no response. He drew his pistol and levelled it at the three men. Again, no response. Desperate, he fired a single shot close to a slumped head, a percussive crack that left his ears ringing. One of the airmen glanced up at him, attempted to rise, and then slumped forward in defeat.

Delpy turned to look at the remainder of the group, barely discernible through the driving veil of snow, motionless and ghostly on the summit ridge. He tucked his pistol back into his coat and trudged through the knee-deep snow to join them.

Ballinger eventually set out alone, with no mountain equipment or compass, navigating by the moon and the stars, arriving in Spain on 8 November 1943. The three airmen – Second Lieutenant Howard Bailey, Technical Sergeant William Plasket and Staff Sergeant Francis Owens – all perished.

*

By now, Paul and I were trudging through the snowfields ourselves, with the ridge ahead drawing closer, shaded by the immense summit of Mont Valier to our left.

'Over that ridge is the border,' said Paul, waving one of his walking poles dramatically skywards. 'You wait for the view. Even if you're not running for your life, it's enough to take your breath away.'

This seemed to me a largely hypothetical comment, as what little breath I did have remaining was required in its entirety to get me those last few hundred steps. Nonetheless, I took a moment to pause just beneath the ridge, gathering my thoughts before the final moment of ascent. So many desperate people had stood in this self-same spot, salvation only a few metres away. To walk these last few steps with heavy limbs, your heart hammering and breath fogging, meant that you had won – you could cross the border and begin your descent into liberation. With a few strides you had beaten one of the most oppressive and brutally efficient regimes in the history of mankind. You had walked a fine line between life and death, assuming false identities en route, you had relied on nerve, on luck and on the kindness of strangers. And, finally, you had defied the mountains themselves, trudging into the wilderness, breathing thin air, enduring freezing conditions and driving yourself onwards and upwards to freedom.

Having gathered my thoughts, I too walked slowly up and over the summit ridge, the ground falling away beneath me fore and aft as I did so. I turned slowly on the narrow crest that lay beneath my feet, the border itself. Ahead of me lay Spain, and behind me France. For so many who had made this journey before me, it must have felt as if they were looking at life itself. The wind blew up and over the ridge, channelled by the scree slopes below us, to explode over the dragon's back of Valier itself.

It carried the scent of the lowlands, of forests and fields, of rivers and roads.

Paul and I sat on the ridge for a while, talking quietly about the people who had gone before, and those who had perished in their attempts to seek a new life.

'I always think about it, you know,' said Paul quietly, 'and I find everyone who comes along on these treks does as well. It's impossible not to feel something of the poor souls who made this journey all those years ago.'

He paused, looking at the landscape spread before him, mile after mile of glowering peaks.

'I don't really think they need a monument, you know, all those people,' he added unexpectedly. 'I think the only one required is the mountains themselves. There's nothing to match them really. They say everything that's needed to be said about what happened here.'

We sat for a while longer, as the light slowly faded and the late afternoon clouds began to roil and mass on the ridges to the west, before Paul stood and hefted his rucksack onto his shoulders.

'Come on,' he said, 'time to get moving if we're going to beat those clouds. I hear Spain is nice at this time of year.'

And with that we headed down the steep path, slipping and sliding through the scree towards the valleys far beneath.

CHAPTER FIVE

The Price of Freedom

Despite every precaution, changing apartments and moving radio operators around constantly, O'Leary and his team were pitched against increasing German attention, including – devastatingly – the insertion of another informer (and possible associate of Cole) into the operation, an undercover agent named Roger Le Neveu. He had approached Louis Nouveau in Marseille, and volunteered to be associated with the line as a guide. Nouveau was operating alone at the time, acting as a contact point for escapees, and decided to test out Le Neveu with a series of small tasks. These he accomplished satisfactorily, so Nouveau entrusted him with a group of seven airmen to take south. All were delivered successfully, as were a second group shortly afterwards. In February 1943, Nouveau decided to accompany Le Neveu in delivering five more airmen, and Le Neveu seized his opportunity. When they arrived by train in a suburb of Tours, all were arrested. But the real prize was yet to come.

Two weeks later, O'Leary and a companion from the Resistance set up a meeting with the still-unsuspected Le Neveu at the Super Bar cafe in Toulouse. After talking for a while about the general running of the line, O'Leary asked Le Neveu if he had an idea who had been betraying the operation. In a moment of pure theatre, Le Neveu replied, 'Yes,' before giving the signal to the waiting Gestapo that they should move in. O'Leary and his companion were quickly surrounded, and arrested on the spot.

Many more raids followed, as well as arrests including those of Jean de la Olla, who was tortured and saw out the rest of the war in various concentration camps, and Rodocanachi. Rodo died, aged sixty-eight or sixty-nine (the precise date of his death is unclear), in Buchenwald the following year. Nancy Wake fled Marseille, but her husband Henri stayed behind and was arrested in September. He suffered the all-too-common fate of torture and execution at the hands of the Gestapo. They never caught Wake, who worked undercover in one guise or another for the duration of the war. She was ultimately garlanded with honours from Britain, France and the USA, and died in 2011, at the age of ninety-eight. The key Pyrenean guide, Ponzan-Vidal, was also arrested and subsequently executed.

By March 1943, O'Leary's operation was at an end, although Marie-Louise Dissard continued to run the line under her own code name, Françoise, helping 250 escapers and evaders get away. This continued until the Germans got wind of her in January 1944, when she went into hiding successfully until the end of the war. Even during that period, she managed to convey a further 110 servicemen to safety, having moved her centre of operations temporarily to Bergerac. One of these was the American air ace Chuck Yeager (b. 1923) who joined the USAAF in autumn 1942 and quickly graduated from mechanic to fighter pilot. He was shot down on his eighth mission but evaded capture. A silk map sewn into his flight jacket helped him plot a route over the Pyrenees, but he didn't have to make the journey on his own, being picked up by the Resistance. He stayed with the Resistance for a while, helping them construct bombs, though he did not join them in combat. He was very nearly captured crossing the Pyrenees when his companion hung some socks on a bush to dry outside the hut in which they were hiding overnight. The resultant morning ambush from a passing German patrol saw Yeager vault out of a window and drag his wounded comrade – who lost part of his leg – through the snow and over the mountain to freedom. For this action, he was awarded the Bronze Star. He arrived in Spain on 30 March 1944, and then in England in mid-May. On returning to duty, he continued to fight with distinction, and his post-war career as a test-pilot is not only legendary but has also been the subject of a film, *The Right Stuff.*

O'Leary himself was interrogated and tortured, but gave nothing away. His son, Patrick – named one can only imagine after his father's alias – recalled after the war that his father told him he would go out of his way when under torture to provide precisely the wrong information: 'If someone I was recalling was short and fat, I would say they were tall and thin.'

He showed extraordinary mental strength, and when under torture would imagine a scene of total tranquillity to calm himself.

Instead of executing him, and probably in the hope of extracting information in due course, the Germans sent him to Neue-Bremm torture camp in September 1943 and then a series of concentration camps. He arrived in Mauthausen in October 1943 and Natzweiler in June 1944, where he encountered the artist and SOE agent Brian Stonehouse. He sketched a portrait of O'Leary in the camp, which is now in the Imperial War Museum collection.

The two men were in the camp when Andrée Borrel (who had been arrested and imprisoned in June 1943) and three other Resistance fighters, Vera Leigh, Diana Rowden and Olga Olschanesky, were brought there from prison in Karlsruhe on 5 July 1944, and executed at dawn the next day. Other prisoners were confined to barracks as the four young women were escorted to the camp crematorium, given lethal injections of phenol, and 'put straight in the ovens'. For all their protestations of racial superiority and rectitude, the Nazis were always very careful to cover their criminal tracks, as their whole *Nacht und Nebel* programme indicates. As the war neared its end, the Nazis incinerated untold amounts of paperwork relating to the concentration camps. Nevertheless, the Allies still took over thirty tons of it after the close of hostilities.

In September 1944, at Dachau, four other female agents were collected together. Three of them – Yolande Beekman, Eliane Plewman, and Madeleine Damerment – had been brought to the concentration camp from the ordinary prison in Karlsruhe where they'd been held, on account of the officiousness of a prison wardress (the woman also responsible for the transfer of Andrée Borrel and her comrades). The fourth, Noor Inayat Khan, came separately from Pforzheim, where she had been detained in solitary confinement and in chains.

They'd been taken to Dachau by car and train on a sunny day, with no idea where they were going, arriving at midnight. At dawn on 13 September they were brought together in a sandy yard, and knew what was going to happen even before they'd noticed the bloodstains on the sand.

They knelt two and two, each pair holding hands; an SS man approached from behind and shot each of them dead, neatly, through the back of the neck. The average age of the eight women was twenty-nine.

O'Leary, having steadfastly refused to crack under interrogation at Natzweiler, was transferred again, this time to Dachau in September 1944, where he underwent further torture, and where he was finally sentenced to death.

Guérisse's leadership and administrative skills were vividly displayed through his running of the Pat O'Leary Line, but it was during his incarceration that his great humanity truly emerged. It was behind the wire, and under the cosh of constant torture and brutality from his captors, that his legend was forged. His post-war citation from the Royal Navy's Director of Naval Intelligence – Rear Admiral E. G. N. Rushbrooke – to the Belgian Defence Minister reads as follows:

> On his arrest in March 1943, he was subjected to tortures in France, including the bath treatment, refrigeration for hours on end, beatings, etc etc, but never once did he give away any information to the Germans that could be used by them against the Allies or his own organization . . .
>
> During his time at various concentration camps he did his utmost to assist his fellow prisoners in their sufferings, and having considerable medical knowledge, he had himself appointed to render medical aid to other prisoners.

The report went on to note that, after the camp was liberated in April 1945 (just in time to save him from his imminent execution):

> He refused to leave the camp at first, concentrating on saving the lives of as many of his fellow sufferers as he could,* and when at last he was ordered to leave, and might justifiably have been expected to request permission to seek his family in Belgium, he returned instead to France, where he picked up the threads of his organization again to enquire into the well-being of its members.

---

* He had been elected president of a clandestine International Committee of prisoners which took control of the camp on 28 April, after the Red Cross had negotiated a surrender to the US army.

Guérisse became one of the most decorated figures of the entire war. In total, he received thirty-seven awards and medals, from nations including the USA, Poland, Russia, France and the United Kingdom. His British honours included the George Cross, the Distinguished Service Order and appointment as a Knight Commander of the British Empire. He was also ennobled, being given the title of count in Belgium in 1986.

After the end of hostilities, this colossal figure in the history of escape lines went on to fight with Belgian forces in the Korean War, finally retiring from the Belgian Army in 1970 with the rank of Général-Major. There can be no doubt that thousands of men and women, and their many descendants, owe him their lives.

If Guérisse was the driving force behind the line – and an elemental one at that – the mainstay of the operation were the normal men and women of France and Belgium who made remarkable sacrifices to keep it running. Most of them are gone now, having been executed, died in captivity, or simply passed away through old age. But a few remain – the last witnesses to these remarkable times in Europe. They walk among us, each with their memories and their tales to tell, hidden in plain view amid a new generation.

'Coffee, monsieur, or some tea perhaps?' Michèle Agniel looked up at me politely, ever the hostess, welcoming another Englishman in Paris into her home.

'Some coffee would be lovely, thanks, Madame Agniel,' I said. 'It's a great honour to meet you, by the way.'

She smiled and waved a hand dismissively in front of her face, the fingers bent with arthritis, vivid deltas of veins snaking over fine bones beneath skin as fine and pale as gossamer.

'Ah, the honour was all mine. You English gave us all hope, you know.'

This was quite an exchange to have upon first meeting, standing as I was in the hallway of her small apartment. It represented a rather neat summary of what the airmen she sheltered meant to her, as well as a measure of her feelings about the darkest of days in her beloved Paris. Madame Michèle Agniel is a Resistance heroine, a survivor of Ravensbrück concentration camp, and a key figure in the story of survival of at least twenty airmen who made it out of Paris to head south to the Pyrenees. I was conscious that such meetings are rare indeed, and I had a great deal to ask her.

Madame Agniel is now ninety-one years of age, but still has a vibrancy that entirely belies the passage of time. She bustled through to her tiny kitchen, and emerged shortly afterwards with a tray on which were balanced a coffee pot and two blue china cups.

'I know you Englishmen like tea, but it's no good here in Paris,' she said, as I followed her through to the lounge. 'It's the water you know, it is very poor here in the city.'

The front room was immaculate, carefully ordered and pin-neat. Large veranda doors led to a wrought-iron balcony, packed with plants and flowers, with the faint bustle of the morning traffic coming to us on the breeze. Madame Agniel placed the tray on the table in the middle of the room, pointed to an armchair for me, and began pouring coffee for us both. All the while she continued to talk – about the weather, the traffic and how nice it was to welcome a visitor. Her English was excellent, albeit heavily accented, and the words came thick and fast.

'Now,' she said when she finally paused for breath, 'what can I tell you?'

Placing a cup on the table, she settled on the sofa opposite, compact and neat, hands folded on her lap, and looked at me with her head tilted expectantly to one side.

It was a question that threw me somewhat, as I was keenly aware that I was sitting opposite an extraordinary woman, one who had paid a truly terrible price for her valour. As ever in these situations, when one has such a rare opportunity in the face of living history, the mind goes blank. Mine duly obliged, and I looked at her dully for a moment before speaking.

'Ermmm,' I said, 'well, could you tell me what Paris was like at the time?'

Among her many qualities, Madame Agniel had considerable experience of dealing with slightly intimidated, bewildered young foreigners who suddenly find themselves under her care, and she immediately took charge of the conversation.

'Ah, it was terrible,' she said, leaning forward for emphasis, 'to see your home city taken over by another army. It was . . .' she paused, closing her eyes for a second, seeking the right word, 'unimaginable. Yes, unimaginable. To see German soldiers on our streets, to see their flags on our buildings, and all the signs in . . .' again, a moment of contemplation, accompanied by her muttering quietly under her breath, then her eyes sprung open, 'Gothic writing. Yes, Gothic, that's the word. It broke my heart. It broke everyone's heart.'

'But you decided to do something about it, Madame Agniel?' I said.

'Well, no, no, not me really, more my father and mother. They were very good people, very . . .' she paused again for a moment, this time seeking a sentiment, not a word, 'straight. Yes, straight. But I am very proud that they let me, just a young girl at fourteen years of age, become involved. Not many parents would have allowed that to happen.'

It had started in January 1941, with the young Michèle Moet

distributing Resistance leaflets, dangerous work she continued for nearly two years. These simple leaflets soon developed into a newspaper, and she even travelled to Versailles to pick them up in bulk from the printer's where they were produced. At the end of this period she contracted tuberculosis – a potential killer, and a manifestation of the scourge of living in a city under occupation. Her family sent her to stay with a relative in the south of France to recover, but she returned after five months of convalescence in August 1943.

'My parents met me at the Gare du Nord, and they were very excited, they smiled so much that we were back together again. But they also said "We have a surprise for you at home," which I thought was a present!'

On arriving back at the family apartment in Saint-Mandé, an eastern suburb of Paris, the young Michèle was taken aback when her parents opened the front door.

'Ha!' she says, suddenly even more animated. 'There in the corridor was a big American. He said, "Hello Michèle," – he was the first American we had. There were two more very shy young boys in the front room. '

Now the stakes were even higher. In her absence, Michèle's parents had agreed to run a safe house for the Burgundy Line, set up by Frenchman Georges Broussine. Broussine, who was Jewish, had escaped over the Pyrenees (with the help of the Pat O'Leary Line), intending to join the Free French forces. He was recruited by Airey Neave at MI9, trained as a radio operator and parachuted back into France. Michèle immediately began to act as a courier for the line, guiding the airmen arriving at Gare du Nord station to safe houses around the city and then, after they had been prepared for the journey south, leading them back to the station and handing them over to another contact.

'You were only a young girl,' I said, 'were you afraid?'

'I was afraid, yes, but then again I had no choice.' She looked at me with a level gaze. 'To do nothing would have been shameful, and these boys needed our help.'

Just for a moment I thought I heard the ghosts of her parents in that statement, family values passed to their daughter, and as unflinching today as they had been in the years of the war. As was so often the case, resistance was not based so much on fierce patriotism, but more a simple, civilized code that demanded you do the right thing. That frequently meant helping the desperate and lost, which in turn meant defying an occupying army.

'I would wear a blue beret, my school beret, when I met them at the station, and the airmen would know to follow me through the streets. But it was dangerous, particularly with the Americans, who really had no idea at all how to walk like a Frenchman.'

'What do you mean, Madame Agniel?' I asked.

'Up, up,' she said, springing from the sofa. 'I'll show you.'

I placed my cup on the table and stood rather uncertainly (noting as I did so that I seemed to have considerably more difficulty rising to my feet than she did – even in old age Madame Agniel was an effervescent presence).

'Right, now walk for me.'

I duly made the short walk across the apartment, trying very hard to assume a thoroughly Gallic persona as I did so, although I was slightly hindered by the fact that I had no idea at all what that might look like.

'No,' she said, 'no, no, no. Hands out of your pockets! You are too upright, you swagger, you have your head up. No, no, no. You must slouch.'

For the next ten minutes, I was cajoled, scolded and chided by Madame Agneil, walking back and forth along a small section of carpet, until – finally – I shuffled across with my gaze cast to the floor, my shoulders slumped, and my hands hanging by my side.

'There,' she said, 'now you are walking like a Frenchman. Remember everyone was hungry, that no one was openly defying the Germans, and everyone was sad. That is why the Americans always worried us – they were tall, young and full of confidence. They would have their heads up, they would swagger, and they would have their hands in their pockets. They stood out a mile! The British were better, but they still had a lot to learn.' She smiled at the memory. 'They even smoked in a different way to French people. And they chewed gum – no one in Paris had gum! We had to teach them everything, and we had to do it quickly.'

As well as teaching the airmen how to act French, the Resistance also had to clothe them to look like locals, and equip them with the right papers.

'At first it was just a small group of us doing our best, but soon it became a lot more organized. By the time I was arrested, it was very efficient – we could clothe, train and create a new identity for an airman in just two weeks. Then they would follow me back to the station and catch a train to Toulouse.'

The network of the Resistance was now a highly efficient operation, with a series of contacts and co-ordinators handing over downed airmen to the family, who would duly acquire clothing for them and create false papers for their journey south.

'They would have fake papers with them when they were shot down, but those papers were no good,' said Madame Agniel. 'The photographs were all wrong. So I would take them to the Photomaton – you know the Photomaton?'

This was a photo facility in Paris used to create images for identity papers. I had heard of it, and nodded briefly.

'Well, I would turn up with these Americans, and say to the people there that I was in charge of deaf and dumb people as my job, and we needed photos of them. I did many photos this way, and after the war I went back to the shop and said, "Do you remember me?" and the lady says, "Yes, you were the person from the deaf and dumb school." I said, "No, they were all Americans," and the lady was so shocked that my mother had to slap her to stop her fainting!'

At the mention of her mother, Madame Agniel became subdued, virtually for the first time since I had entered the flat. 'I was not all the same, you know, when I went back to the shop,' she spoke slowly, selecting each word. 'I thought the lady would not recognize me. But she did.'

These same false identity papers had been the downfall of the network. They were created by a man called Jean Carbonnet – a significant figure in the running of the line, and one who frequently visited the Moet family in their flat. He had been instrumental in co-ordinating the movements of the airmen, arranging safe houses for them, contacting guides for their train journey south, and sourcing the right papers and clothing to make sure they blended seamlessly into French civilian life. He was visited by a friend who asked him to create some forged papers, a friend who in turn had a Milice acquaintance who was working with the Germans. As an illustration of just how tenuous the safety and security of everyone who worked on the escape lines was, what happened next offers a perfect example of innocent betrayal. A casual conversation with the Milice acquaintance – idle chatter to pass the time of day – resulted in him going to the authorities, who immediately moved in on Carbonnet. He was the very worst person to have been compromised – the very hub of the wheel – and the Germans swiftly traced many of the operatives within the network.

'It was 28 April 1944, and I came back from school, the lycée Héléne Boucher in D'Lissey, to find lots of people in the house.

My mother, my brother, Jean Carbonnet, and two English airmen we had with us at the time. They were surrounded by many Gestapo and French gendarmes.'

The police had turned up in the afternoon, arresting everyone in the apartment. They had then waited for the rest of the family to assemble.

'My father was at work, so my mother – after the police came – had managed to place a piece of white material in the window of our apartment where it overlooked the street. This was a signal that he should not come back into the house. But he did anyway. I think he came back for his family. He knew he would be arrested, but he came back anyway.'

Michèle and her mother were taken to Fresnes prison in Paris, the scene of torture and incarceration in brutal conditions for many who aided the Resistance. Although neither Michèle nor her mother were initially interrogated, their relief was short-lived – after a few days in the jail, the Gestapo came for them.

'We were driven in a special car to the Rue de Saussaies – to the Ministry of the Interior – and taken to a room full of straw. The room smelled of blood, as so many people had been tortured there – it was terrible.'

Michèle was interrogated for two hours, although not tortured, as she managed to convince her questioners at an early stage that she was nothing more than an innocent schoolgirl.

If her mother was tortured, then today as we sit in her small flat, Madame Agniel is not prepared to talk about it. She only speaks – briefly – of others.

'There was a young girl with us in the same cell, and her father was tortured in front of her until he died. She saw her father die before her. As for me, I never saw my father again,' she says simply, glancing up at me as if in challenge, defying her emotions and long-suppressed memories.

Michèle and her mother were returned to Fresnes, and while they were in prison, they heard the news of the D-Day landings on 6 June.

'It was one of the most beautiful days of my life, knowing that soon we would be free.'

Her father had been sent to Buchenwald concentration camp. In early March 1945, a fellow inmate noted that he had not moved from the pallet that served as a bed, and tried to rouse him. By now he was desperately malnourished, and probably very close to death. The inmate had to leave for his work detail, and when he came back, the pallet was empty. He was never seen again.

'It was just weeks before the end, before the camp was liberated, you know?' says Madame Agniel.

Michèle and her mother had been sent to Ravensbrück, and from there to forced labour camps at Torgau and then Königsberg on the Oder (in Poland). The Germans abandoned Königsberg as the Russian army drew near and the prisoners were marched back to Ravensbrück. Michèle's mother was left behind, being too ill to walk, and Michèle hid from the guards. Miraculously, they both saw the end of the war.

'I survived because of my mother,' said Madame Agniel. 'She kept me alive. When we left the camp, when it was liberated, she weighed just twenty-eight kilogrammes.'

By now we had been talking for over an hour, and it was late morning in this little flat off the Rue de la Paix in the Vincennes district of Paris. And yet still she talked, this grandee of war who spoke of things I could only begin to imagine.

But there are certain stories that abruptly bring the reality of war to life, that reach back through time to draw a scene into the present day. Despite the horrors Madame Agniel had experienced, there was one such moment, a tale so touching as to be almost unbearable.

The damage to the network from the arrest of Jean Carbonnet was very real, but could have been so much worse if not for his quick thinking at the moment the arrests took place. Hidden in the Moet apartment was a small book containing all the names and addresses of many Resistance contacts, and the safe houses from which they operated. As he was being bundled out of the apartment, Carbonnet asked to use the toilet, and – remarkably – was allowed to do so. Reaching up into the cistern – where the book was hidden – he retrieved it, and pressed it into Michèle's hand at the very last moment.

'Jean Marie,' he whispered as he did so, his last words to her.

Jean Marie was her young brother – twelve years old – an innocent caught up in events beyond his understanding. Michèle asked if she could be allowed to change his trousers just before being taken away and – again, quite miraculously – was allowed to do so. She hid the book in his pocket, and then returned to her captors.

'As I was in the Gestapo car, I looked and saw my little brother outside the house. He looked completely lost. He had gone to his bedroom to get his favourite teddy bear, the one he slept with as a small child, and was sitting on the pavement holding it tightly as he watched us all being taken away.'

The thought of this scene – a single moment in time and place, a mere stitch in the vast tapestry of the Second World War – affected me profoundly, and I struggled to contain my emotions. A family destroyed at a stroke with a single lost soul remaining, clutching the last trace of his childhood.

Jean Marie was taken in by family friends, who found the book and had the presence of mind to call the phone numbers within it, warning them they had been compromised. When the

Gestapo returned for him, Jean Marie had become ill with colic, and – showing great presence of mind for one so young – used a visit to the toilet to cut up the book and flush it away. The Gestapo took the family that had helped him, leaving him once again on the streets. But liberation was only weeks away, and he survived the war and was eventually reunited with his mother and sister.

'But he never speaks of those times,' said Madame Agniel. 'Even now. It is too hard for him.'

By now it was time to take my leave, and I stood up from the armchair, hands in the small of my back, stretching as I did so. The time had slipped by, and – aside from my brief lesson in undercover life – I had been entirely immobile listening to Madame Agniel speak. Her words had been positively mesmeric, and her conviction undimmed. It seemed to me, listening to this commanding, redoubtable woman, that the German occupiers of Paris were never going to prevail. It really was as simple as that – as long as a defiance and resolve such as hers continued to burn brightly, as long as a small number of people worked together, against what must have seemed overwhelming odds, then hope always remained. I glanced back as I walked away down the Rue de la Paix, and saw her out on the balcony watering her plants, the city of Paris before her.

PART TWO

Crossing Monte Amaro
Sulmona, Italy

'How far that little candle throws his beams!
So shines a good deed in a weary world.'

William Shakespeare, *The Merchant of Venice*

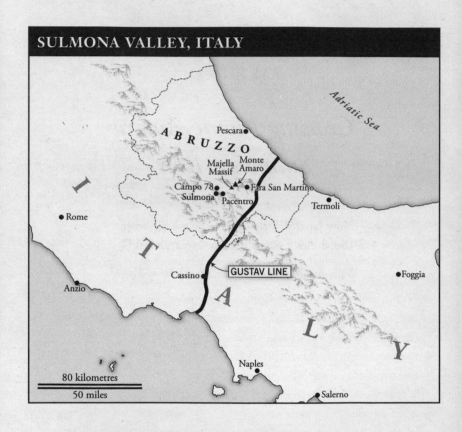

SULMONA VALLEY, ITALY

Adriatic Sea

ABRUZZO

Pescara

Majella Massif

Monte Amaro

Campo 78

Fara San Martino

Sulmona

Pacentro

Termoli

Rome

ITALY

Cassino

GUSTAV LINE

Foggia

Anzio

Naples

80 kilometres

50 miles

Salerno

CHAPTER SIX

Campo 78, Sulmona

As you crest the final rise of the main road into Sulmona, you look down into a fortress. The great buttresses of the mountains rise on all sides of the flat plain, the city in their midst. The valley may be wide, but this is still a citadel, a natural amphitheatre dominated by the glowering peaks to the east, rising nearly three kilometres into the sky. They cast a long shadow over the region – a constant reminder that once you are here, you will struggle to leave.

The drive from Rome airport to Sulmona had taken me two hours, the latter half spent on roads that hugged the mountainsides, gliding along elegant concrete viaducts or vanishing into the heart of the rock via a series of tunnels, only to emerge into the bright spring sunshine to reveal yet another staggering vista or strikingly beautiful mountain village.

The Abruzzo region of central Italy covers an area of nearly eleven thousand square kilometres, yet only has a population of just over a million people. Much of the region is simply too arid, too steep and too rugged for human habitation. The scattering of villages and towns that cling to rock faces or sit on high plateaux are visually stunning – but despite the ingenuity of the local people in occupying every habitable ledge and clifftop, this remains a largely unsettled landscape.

The Sulmona valley abuts the Parco Nazionale della Majella, a region of noted beauty and great natural riches. The serrated ridges of the Majella Mountains cut a meandering path across cobalt skies, with the forests, spurs, cols and peaks home to golden eagles, wolves, bears and chamois. Within this range alone there are over sixty peaks that rise more than 2,000 metres, with the tallest being the majestic Monte Amaro – the craggy spine of its summit ridge topping out at 2,793 metres. Over 2,000 different types of plant flourish in the valleys, plains and steep sides of the mountains, meaning nearly a third of all the plant species in Italy can be found here. Man has always been drawn to this region, inhabited since Palaeolithic times, and it is now a beacon for tourists, who stroll through the narrow alleys of ancient medieval towns and sip wine at terrace cafes, watching the life of the valley laid out like a patchwork beneath their feet.

But for all the beauty of the present, the haunting memories of the past remain. In the Second World War this was a dark place to be sent as an Allied prisoner of war, heavily patrolled by the Germans, and Italian Fascist militia of many different stripes. Escape was thought to be virtually impossible, with the only routes to freedom being valleys alive with the enemy or mountain peaks passable only by experienced alpinists. Once you entered Sulmona valley as a prisoner, common sense dictated that you would have to wait out the war before meekly making your way home.

But I was here to seek out a remarkable story of escape and sustained evasion within this very region. Len Harley spent six months at large under the noses of the Germans, relying on luck, locals and his wits, before making a final desperate charge at the glowering monster of Monte Amaro. He had to exist in the shadows, scuttling from bolt-hole to hiding place, before breaking free to climb into the open skies. And all this from a young man who, prior to the war, rarely ventured beyond the East End of London.

Len's story was, it seemed to me, one worth telling, and I was travelling to the place where his escape began – Campo 78, near Sulmona.

Italy (like Japan) had been Britain's ally in the First World War. In those days, Campo 78, a barracks which had been converted to a prison, held Austrian prisoners. During the Second World War, Italy was until September 1943 part of the Axis, along with Germany and Japan, and the camp – a huge, sprawling affair – housed around 3,000 Allied prisoners This included officers (in a separate section) and other ranks.

Benito Mussolini had, from the moment of his accession to power in 1922, been inclined to form an alliance with Germany, with the aim of squeezing France and making Italy one of Europe's dominant nations. The Italians had a king, Victor Emmanuel III, but he was a constitutional monarch, not an especially strong personality, and in any case was initially disposed to favour Mussolini, whose control of the political scene was complete. As was the case in Germany, the political Right misguidedly facilitated totalitarianism. There was no political opposition to Mussolini's Fascist Party, and the ruling ideology found a natural ally in Nazi Germany.

Italy declared war on Britain and France in June 1940, but by early 1943 the people of Italy, never ardent supporters of Hitler's ideology, were showing signs of disillusionment. Back in 1935, Fascist Italy had engaged in a costly and largely ineffectual colonial takeover of Abyssinia (Ethiopia) – although the Ethiopians still praise the splendid roads the Italians built there. The war had not helped military morale, especially when it turned out that the Abyssinians didn't take kindly to their invaders: Eritrean askaris fighting for the Italians, and later Italian soldiers themselves, were frequently castrated when taken prisoner. Italy had also committed huge amounts of materiel and manpower, especially aircrew, on Franco's side during the Spanish Civil War (1936–39). Mussolini – showing commendable ambition but little grasp of financial reality – later sent Franco a bill for the equivalent of £80 million.

All of this meant that Italy's resources were already depleted before the Second World War even began. By the end of 1942, its military had suffered irreversible setbacks in North Africa and on the Eastern Front. Worse was to come, as the Allies launched Operation Husky – the invasion of Sicily – on 9 July 1943. On the nineteenth of the same month Rome was bombed for the first time – a terrible blow to morale. But there had already been strikes and civil unrest in northern Italy by then, and the German presence in the country was increasingly resented, especially by families whose menfolk were fighting far away on the Eastern Front in what was popularly seen as a futile conflict.

Things weren't going well for Mussolini. By the time he had an emergency meeting with Hitler on the same day that Rome was bombed, his nerves were shattered. On 24 July, he was made to convene a meeting of the Grand Council of Fascism, at which a vote of no confidence in him was carried by a huge majority. He was arrested later the same day, Victor Emmanuel's constitutional powers were reinstated, and Pietro Badoglio (1871–1956), who'd been Chief of the General Staff from 1925 to 1940, was installed as the country's leader. Badoglio proceeded to play a double game. While keeping the Germans onside, he dissolved the Italian Fascist Party and entered into secret talks with the Allies, finalizing an armistice with them on 3 September, which was publicly announced on 8 September.

Italy had – in essence – changed sides. But far from putting an end to uncertainty, this plunged the country deeper into chaos. Its army was left without orders, and the Germans threw division after division into Italy to fill the vacuum and secure as much territory as they could. Badoglio and the King, meanwhile, decamped to the relative safety of Brindisi, which was under Allied control. From there, Badoglio and his new government came to terms with the left-wing partisan movement in order to present a united front against the Germans and the remaining Fascist loyalists. Badoglio's Italian Co-belligerent Army of (at its height) 50,000 men fought alongside the Allies and alongside a disparate force of some 350,000 partisans representing a variety of socialist ideologies, which operated right across the country.

Meanwhile, Mussolini had been confined under close guard at the isolated alpine resort of Campo Imperatore in Abruzzo, at the hotel there of the same name. On 12 September, he was sprung from his imprisonment by a detachment of German paratroopers under the leadership of SS-*Hauptsturmführer* Otto Skorzeny. On 23 September, under German protection, Mussolini became head of the newly formed Italian Social Republic, centred at the town of Salò, north-west of Verona, and notionally covering the area between Italy's northern frontiers and a line across the centre of the country, roughly between Anzio and Pescara. The new republic was no more than a representation – this was territory occupied and controlled by Germany, and none knew better than Mussolini that he was a spent force, propped up by Hitler for propaganda purposes.

This, in its basic form, was the backdrop for any Allied prisoner of war considering escaping – it truly was a journey into the unknown, and escapers from any camp relied heavily on meeting with exceptional support from the local Italian population. It should be remembered that escapers were not going out into an occupied country like France, but into a country which until only recently had been an enemy nation. In September 1943, Italy was riven by political difference and in addition was the scene of a massive Allied–German conflict.

Going on the run in Italy was anything but simple. Every corner turned, and every stranger encountered, held the threat of betrayal, incarceration, or even death. The dreaded and efficient Italian secret police – Arturo Bocchini's *Organizzazione per la Vigilanza e la Repressione dell'Antifascismo* (OVRA) – were Mussolini's equivalent of the Gestapo, and were justifiably feared and loathed in equal measure. You might be denounced by Fascist sympathizers, who themselves may have been coerced on account of a family member held hostage. Italians are by nature curious and open. For an escaping prisoner discretion was obviously at a premium, however many escapers had the nerve-shredding experience of being followed in a village by a knot of small children gleefully and innocently calling out *Inglese! Inglese!* at the tops of their voices. And, as if all this were not enough, the geography of Italy presented real challenges to anyone attempting to head south from the occupied north – with stark mountain ranges creating a near unbroken barrier across the country. But south was unequivocally the direction to travel, as the British and the Americans fought their way north, their lines drawing ever closer. Most escapers struck out alone or in small groups, with only rudimentary maps, and depended entirely on the kindness of locals who risked their lives to help them. As if it were not enough that the thickly forested mountains were home to bears and wolves, some of the territory they had to cross was mined.

Few people escaped successfully from Italy before the fall of Mussolini. As the American Major Philip V. Holder remarked, 'It is not difficult to break out of any prison camp in Italy. It is, however, extremely difficult to get out of Italy itself.'

Yet another variable was introduced after Mussolini's fall, and this was an issue entirely of the Allies' own creation. Up to that point in the war, captured soldiers had been instructed that, wherever possible, it was their duty to attempt to escape. From 8 September 1943, as prison camp guards abandoned not only their posts but their weapons, there was an assumption that the Allied push from the south would be swift. As such, the Allied prisoners, many of whom had spent years incarcerated and were now presented with open gates, were ordered by High Command to 'stay put'.

This order was sent by MI9 in a coded message through radio broadcasts:

> On German surrender or collapse, all P/W all Services including Dominion and Colonial and Indian must stay put & await orders.

The now notorious Stay Put order, as it affected POWs in Italy, was perhaps a result of general confusion related to the situation on the ground. It was probably well-meant, as it seemed logical that POWs should sit tight and await the arrival (thought imminent) of Allied forces. But Allied High Command had not reckoned on the strength of the German countermeasures under the highly experienced command of *Generalfeldmarschall* Albert Kesselring. Kesselring, whose early HQ at Introdacqua was only about ten kilometres south-west of Sulmona, threw a series of defensive lines across Italy as he slowly retreated. The Gustav Line, which stretched across the Apennines between Gaeta and Ortona, slowed the advance of the Allies between December 1943 and June 1944. The last, the Gothic Line, roughly between La Spezia and Ravenna, held until spring 1945.

MI9 had also seemingly not considered the possibility that those beleaguered POWs obeying the order and sitting tight would simply be swept up by the Germans and taken to camps in Germany.

Logically it can be said that thousands of Allied POWs wandering towards the Allied lines in no order at all would not only have put themselves in danger, but hampered the Allied offensive. As such, the Stay Put order did have merit in certain situations, but in others it was disastrous – in many cases (Campo 78 included) the departing Italians were simply replaced by German guards, with a crucial window of opportunity missed as prisoners failed to slip away during the confusion of this transition.

Such a golden opportunity for escape did not stop some senior officers among the POWs carrying out the Stay Put order with missionary zeal. Not only were POWs considering escape in these circumstances threatened with the charge of desertion, but in some cases it created the farcical situation of Allied soldiers literally picking up abandoned Italian rifles, re-locking Italian prison-camp gates and preventing their own men from making a getaway.

We must also throw the state of mind of the POWs into this mix. Many accounts, from memoirs to fact-based fictional works, attest to the debilitating effects of life in the big Italian camps. Because of the complicated political situation from 1943 onwards in Italy, official documentation of the camps is patchy. Thus the 'unofficial' memoirs, some of which are listed in the bibliography, are of huge importance in reconstructing the grim reality of camp life. The posthumously published novels of Dan Billany, *The Trap* and *The Cage*, are examples of such records. Billany was a socialist Yorkshire schoolteacher who served as an officer in the East Yorkshire Regiment. He and three companions disappeared without trace in the Apennines in November 1943, while attempting their own escape soon after Billany's thirtieth birthday. They are believed to have died in the harsh winter conditions.

In the closing pages of *The Trap*, Billany wrote:

How to draw a moral from it all I do not know. But I know this: that I am very, very tired of the talk and the bitterness and the life we lead that is no life: it is a long time since my heart has been at rest. I am tired of the sneers at our 'enemies', and of their respectful hostility or simple callousness to us. There is a time to have done with the responses of the nursery. I do not 'believe' in the war – in this or any other.

Billany's manuscript for *The Trap* had actually been written in thirteen exercise books that he left with the Italian farmer who had hidden him, along with strict instructions that they should be posted to him after he left. They duly arrived in Britain and were delivered to his family.

Some men preferred to stay put. When MI9 agent Jock McKee managed to reach Sulmona in the latter stages of the war, working alone, he found about a thousand POWs still there, in no hurry to get away. They were institutionalized, even unhappy about not being guarded any more, just waiting for someone to take charge of them. Some of them had organized a fairly comfortable life for themselves, trading out of Red Cross parcels (those provided by Scotland and Canada were thought to be the best – one former prisoner remembers 'Canadian parcels with milk and meat and biscuits') with the locals. Some had established relationships with local girls. McKee was able to convince only twenty-three men to come back with him to Allied lines.

Those who remained should not be too harshly judged. They were not professional soldiers, but had been conscripted into a conflict few of them truly understood. They were afraid of exposing themselves to danger again, and in the inevitable swirling of camp gossip, rumour and counter-rumour, the majority believed that the Allied advance would be upon them within weeks. Above all, they had fallen victim to the indescribable lethargy and sapping of will which is the most disabling effect of long incarceration and lack of stimulation. Large numbers of healthy young men have written, for example, of the total atrophy of their sex drive – Eric Newby, who escaped and later returned to marry the Italian-Slovene girl who was one of his helpers, describes this tellingly in *Love and War in the Apennines*. In a time when all the local menfolk had been sent off to war, girls would parade past the camp he was in just to catch a glimpse of the young men inside. Newby writes:

> . . . we were not unduly troubled by the lusts of the flesh – perhaps it was something to do with the diet. As one of my friends said . . . while craning out of one of the windows . . . 'It isn't that one just wants to poke them. I'm not sure if I could do it any more, but it would be heaven just to be with them,' which for him was a pretty profound remark.

Add to this the opinion of another former POW and three-time escaper, who saw the same pattern of behaviour in those around him while never quite succumbing to it:

> People can get used to mosquitoes in Summer, lice, fleas and bedbugs all the year round, the crushing heat in the Summer, the iron cold in the Winter, the clothes that are never-quite-clean, the boredom of the same people, the same food, the same sex, day after day, nowhere to go, nothing to do. What I want to know is, how can they? It was the sheer staleness of life in the camps that got to me. Now that I'm old, I

actually feel less impatient at the way time steals life away than I did when I was young, and a prisoner.

Echoing that sentiment, one Sulmona escaper, Donald I. Jones, recalled the line of the philosopher Ovid, himself from Sulmona and celebrated in the town to this day. Ovid noted that *tempus edax rerum* – 'time devours everything'. It seemed that – nearly two thousand years after Ovid's birth – the words rang true in Campo 78 in 1943.

Something else made life in the camps disagreeable. Eric Newby has pointed out that officer POWs still came largely from middle- and upper-middle-class public school backgrounds, and tended to look down on everyone else, regardless of intelligence or ability. Overall, although some loose sense of camaraderie existed by dint of a shared fate, a large group of men thrown together doesn't guarantee great fellow-feeling or any sense of one-ness, or even personal loyalty. The only thing the POWs had in common, in fact, was the red patch the Italians had had sewn onto their uniforms to distinguish them as prisoners.

It is therefore no surprise that prior to the armistice in September 1943, some POWs were motivated to escape. Of those who evaded recapture, some joined the partisans and others made their way successfully to the Allied lines. Some were never heard of again. And a few – tracked down, if at all, decades later – simply dropped out, weaving themselves into the fabric of Italian country life. This was not an unpleasant or difficult thing to do – the locals were almost all welcoming, helpful and friendly, and men were needed to work the farms.

It should not, however, be forgotten that the local people were risking their lives and those of their families, as well as their animals and property, to give aid. They were not only at risk from Germans. At least one recaptured escaper had been foolish enough to keep a journal in which he'd listed – perhaps as a reference for a future book – the names of all those Italians who had helped him. When he was recaptured, their fate was sealed. Luckily, most escapers had the wit to avoid such indiscretion, but it's been estimated that four Italians died for every Allied POW who made it to Switzerland or the Allied lines in the south. Beyond direct arrests and executions of those caught aiding escaping prisoners, there were also more systematic reprisals, designed to instil fear in the civilian population. The resilience and the fortitude of the Italians should not be underestimated – without their aid, few escapers would have succeeded.

Interestingly, there was never any official recognition of the sacrifices made by Italian civilians in this regard. After the war, several of them did receive financial compensation for their help, but it wasn't generous. Some individual escapers got in touch with their helpers after successfully making their way home, and managed to make their own personal restitution by way of thanks, but very few even bothered to write. One hopes that this is because they simply didn't realize the immense risks that had been taken on their behalf. The alternative, a display of apathy and disinterest now they were home safe, does not bear thinking of.

For Len Harley, his own escape story would become woven deep into the fabric of the life of at least one local family in Sulmona – a family who took the most extraordinary risks on his behalf.

I nearly missed the turning, a small track tucked away next to an olive grove, its verges overgrown and its narrow thoroughfare overshadowed by tall cypress trees. My journey had led me to the outskirts of the picturesque village of Fonte d'Amore, and I slowed down as I approached an overgrown junction. Squinting through a windscreen covered in a fine film of white dust, I just made out a small, hand-painted sign. It leant drunkenly, weathered and careworn, but the words on it were unmistakable:

Camp 78

I quickly indicated and turned up the track, drawing an annoyed, very Italian, toot from the car that had been following me. A little way along the lane, I pulled into a small car park in front of a massive, grey metal gate and stopped the engine.

It was an absolutely beautiful day, warm and still with the gentle hum of insects a soporific backing track. I stepped out of the car into a heady scent of pine and eucalyptus, the road continuing alongside the wall before me, a green tunnel made gloomy and lush by overhanging branches and riotously encroaching hedgerows.

In this tranquil setting, the entrance to the camp was brutal in its raw functionality – a military base originally designed to keep the enemy out, but then redesigned to keep them in. Even after all these years of descending into decay, being slowly reclaimed by the undergrowth, there was no denying what this place was, what purpose it served. As if to reinforce this point, a green watchtower stood above the wall by the gate, its windows cracked, paint peeling, with its gun ports pointing down the track, still carrying out its duty with a baleful eye.

I had arranged to meet a member of the Italian Army at the gate – Camp 78 remains the property of the Italian state – and as I inspected the gates I heard a vehicle draw up behind me. The grey-haired, rather portly man who got out was dressed in an immaculate uniform, and greeted me with a firm handshake before theatrically producing a huge key ring which he jangled in the general direction of the gates, gesturing me to follow. After a couple of false starts, the key turned in the vast lock and he harrumphed in triumph before putting his ample frame to the weight of the handle. The gate groaned on its castors and slowly edged open, gathering momentum to finally crash to a halt. He turned to me, beamed, and stepped aside to wave me into the camp itself.

Abandoned spaces, particularly those that have held large numbers of people, are always slightly eerie, but it seemed to me that Camp 78 had taken this to another level. Although the camp had been utilized for a time after the war, the scene before me was now faintly apocalyptic, with undergrowth intertwined with deserted guard houses, sentry boxes becoming emerald caverns, and green tendrils creeping over every roof and into every doorway. Long grass waved and twitched over once pristine verges and lawns, and rusting barbed wire sagged high above meandering fences. The immediate feeling was of a place that had been entirely forgotten. This was not a tribute, a monument to the men who had been held here, it was a place that was quietly decaying, a forgotten corner of history being subsumed into the terrain around it.

It is a remarkable sensation to walk as one man through a space that once held three thousand. Senses are heightened, with every tussock, cracked flagstone, and empty doorway holding something of those who have gone before. Nowhere was this more apparent than in the row of nine accommodation buildings that sit inconspicuously on the northern perimeter of the camp. As I saw them for the first time, I paused to take them in. They actually looked quite large in the middle distance, a neat row of buildings in fading white paint that made them stand out starkly against the deep green of the undergrowth around them. On the horizon, towering over all, was the rock massif leading ultimately to Monte Amaro, a glowering reminder for every prisoner that their incarceration was not simply a matter of fences and wire. If they wanted to escape, their best chance was over mountains that must have seemed impossibly intimidating to them, craggy and fissured, stark and threatening, and topped with snow for most of the year. Already war had forced them to transform themselves from civilians to soldiers, and now their imprisonment had turned them from soldiers into convicts. If escape was to be a realistic proposition, they had to transform again, from convicts to undercover agents, losing themselves in the valleys and villages of the region, and then make a final transformation into mountaineers. Failure in any one of these roles could result in death. It took a special type of man to successfully make these transitions, requiring qualities possessed by only a select few. For the many, it was a case of doing whatever it took to stay sane in the confines of the camp and the desperate tedium of its routine.

I walked over to the middle accommodation block and lifted the heavy screen door at its entrance. It ascended with a death rattle of ancient metal, a sound that echoed into the dark recesses of the empty space behind it.

I found myself standing in a long, high-ceilinged barrack room. The plaster on the walls was cracked and flaking, but was still unmistakably etched with the markings of the men who had called this home. At intervals along each wall were sketches of old regimental crests, distant memories of the occupants' previous lives. Imprisonment, particularly in times of war, means that innocent men – on both sides – were stripped of their pride, their identity, the very essence of what made them who they were. And so they tried to recreate it, to keep it alive, to remember that in another time, and another place, they had been someone. I was looking at the evidence of that search for meaning when there is none, and for pride when all is lost.

There were some fine old county regiments among the

drawings – the Hampshires, the York and Lancaster Regiment – and there, among the crests and elegant symbols of historic battalions, the words '50th M.E. Commando', particularly poignant for me as an ex-Royal Marine. Below these words were some pictures of impressive fighting knives, two dimensional memories of a time when the men who drew them were warriors but were now reduced to scratching into the plaster to while away a few moments of their long vigil.

I turned on my heel and walked quickly out of the shed, heading out into the sunlight to make my way down the hill to the gate. It is strange how even a brief glimpse of incarceration, the fading signature of the tedium and the solitude of imprisonment, can create an urge to strike for the wide-open spaces of the hills. I had a long walk ahead of me, and yearned to see the open skies and long paths of the Majella Mountains.

As I approached the open gate, it struck me forcibly just what a pivotal moment this must have represented for the men who had decided to make the run for freedom. By stepping over that line between incarceration and liberty – the metal runners on the ground along which the gate travelled were a neat symbol of that final physical commitment – they had made a decision of immense fortitude and resolve. In one step, they left what little certainty existed for them – the routine, their friends, the advice of their senior officers. They also had to shake off the slough of captivity, to lift their eyes to the mountains, and square their shoulders for the challenge ahead.

Would I have done it? I wondered. Would I have been driven enough, motivated by pride and a fire that had never been entirely quenched, to walk through the gate and take on the challenges beyond? As I stood there I realized that I simply had no idea, beyond an inner hope that I would indeed have been one of the men to go, to walk into history with their heads held high. Len Harley – and a small number of his fellow prisoners – made the decision to go. As soon as they stepped across the line they were being hunted, their great adventure underway.

CHAPTER SEVEN

Hackney Boy

From the moment he was born, life was difficult for Leonard Harley. He entered a world that was struggling with economic depression, and his family, who lived in Hackney in London's East End, could not readily find work. Added to this was his personal battle with ill-health – as a child he was so small that he was sent away to an infirmary for malnourished children. Len's early years were defined by struggle, by an absence of excess, and by a dogged determination to survive. The latter quality would stand him in good stead in what would become one of the classic escape and evasion stories of the war.

Len had a number of jobs as a teenager, mostly menial and mostly transient. He worked as a messenger boy and took on basic clerical work. By the time war broke out, he was twenty-one, had never left England (in fact he had barely left London) and yearned for adventure. He joined the Tower Hamlets Rifles – later the 9th Battalion, the Rifle Brigade – and prepared for war. After some moderately eccentric training – the unit was a Territorial Army outfit, and was run by what might be described as enthusiastic amateurs – he was finally called up to the regular army on 1 September 1939.

Len quickly showed himself to be a capable and resilient soldier, rising to the rank of colour sergeant due to his administrative experience. But the chaos of war, demanding the rapid recruitment and training of large numbers of young men, meant that even as a regular soldier there was a degree of turmoil in his day-to-day life.

Seventy-eight years later he chuckles at the memory of his regiment's first march through London to 'reassure the local population':

> Now you can imagine what we looked like. We'd all been up and down the previous night, we'd had nothing to eat, nothing to drink, we were bedraggled. God knows what the local population thought of the British Army at that time.

Sadly, such logistical and administrative shortcomings persisted even when the regiment was sent into the brutality of the battle for Tobruk in the North African conflict. Up to this point Len had seen no action, and one can only begin to imagine the men's sense of anticipation as they disembarked from the requisitioned liner *Duchess of Atholl* in Port Said on New Year's Day, 1941. From there they were swiftly transported to a desert training camp at Qasasin, and after a brief acclimatization and training period, moved several hundred miles to a site called Fort Aguila. Here they dug in, and waited. After the initial Allied successes of Operation Compass, where the Italian 10th Army in North Africa had been defeated, much of the Western Desert Force (WDF) had been redeployed to Greece. This left the remainder – in reality a skeleton force attempting to hold a vast area – vulnerable to attack. Rommel needed no second invitation, and Len's regiment found itself at the vanguard of what was to be a futile and costly rearguard action. Len clearly recalls the first reports reaching his unit that the Germans were advancing towards them:

We moved to a location about 200 miles from Tobruk, and that's where we dug in. We were told that the Germans had got into Tunisia and were in the desert coming down into Libya. And that was the first intimation that Rommel was in the desert.

And so he waited, a newly promoted colour sergeant fighting in an inadequately prepared, undermanned force, peering down a rifle sight waiting for one of the world's best equipped, brilliantly led, highly motivated armies to appear out of the heat haze before him. He did not have to wait for long.

One day, the Germans attacked, and it was a rout. They came with tanks and we only had six Matildas with six-pound shells and some Bren carriers. It was a complete rout. We were given the order to retreat, and did so for the next two days.

After further engagements with the enemy, Len was part of a demoralized and fractured force. On the run, his unit eventually found themselves at the port of Derna. Making a break for the open desert, the convoy was attacked by German tanks. 'They blew the front of the convoy to absolute pieces,' recalls Len. 'My Company Commander and the Company Clerk were killed. So we had to backtrack.'

The remains of the convoy headed onto a plateau in the desert and found a military policeman, who directed them to a vast aggregation of British vehicles.

We thought, Oh good, we're back with the Army again, but we weren't. The Germans had already gone round the back and we were completely encircled. And I'm sure that Military Policeman was a German – I can never prove it, but I'm certain he was.

If it was indeed an elaborate ruse, it had worked to perfection. Len and his unit were now prisoners of war. He recalls the moment of capture to this day: 'It was a horrible thing. You can't describe how you feel when you know it. It's the bottom of you, your life has fallen away.'

What followed was a humiliating – and physically debilitating – period of being shepherded between German and Italian forces, sometimes working as free labour, sometimes sitting in the open desert, surrounded only by barbed wire entanglements, for days on end. Eventually, the POWs were shipped en masse to Naples. And it was here that Len first encountered the miraculous spirit and seemingly endless bonhomie of the Italian civilian population – something that would ultimately save his life, and create memories for him that would linger for the rest of his days:

> We got to Naples, and marched through the streets. And the most amazing thing was that the people watching us march through Naples, they were running in between us, giving us water, apples, anything they could give us to eat. A complete, utter difference to how we were treated in Libya.

Despite this kindness, there was a hellish journey north ahead. It left Harley, who had never been physically strong, emaciated and exhausted. But finally, he arrived at Campo 78 in early 1941 where he was to spend the next two and a half years.

He remembers life in the camp very graphically. The soul-destroying monotony (as a senior NCO he was not allowed to work) was combined with a physically debilitating diet:

> A little bowl of soup which I'd never seen any meat in, so it was just watered rice, you know. That's all we had, one meal a day. And we had this little, little, very hard roll which was

made of rye bread so you could cut it up. But it was a monotonous life – sometimes you'd get a bit downhearted and crawl into the corner of the camp, trying to get over your misery. Everybody would leave you alone. It was a life of nothing.

The one thing which sustained him was the thought that one day he might get out. On 8 September 1943, a football match had been organized between the different nationalities within the camp – with the camp commandant acting as the referee. Such scenes may seem incongruous viewed through the prism of the intervening years, but one must recall that both the prisoners and the guards were caught up in the conflict together – with both yearning for home and the end of war. Len recalls the moment the news of the Italian armistice swept through the camp:

During the match we heard a lot of shouting coming from the village. It was heard by the guards, who then began to shout and jump up and down. THE WAR IS OVER. Everyone began to go wild with excitement, football forgotten. One cannot measure the emotion of that moment, no words can describe our feelings.

The prisoners were ordered to parade, and were addressed by the senior British officer present, who issued the 'stay put' order passed down from High Command. After the initial exultation, it became clear that the Allies were not as close as originally thought, and that the Germans were making a stand. On 11 September the rumble of tanks was heard, and – perceptively as it turned out – the senior British officer called the men together once more, and addressed them: 'Well lads, you're on your own now. It's everyone for himself.'

With those words, Len's war may have theoretically been over, but his battles had only just begun. As part of a large group of prisoners, he broke down a section of the rear wall of the camp, and – with four companions – walked out into a turbulent and unknown landscape.

Accompanying Len were fellow POWs John Cox, Ted Emmerson, Nick Robinson and Albert Nicholls. The latter was Len's best friend within the camp, and was known universally as Nick. The two would share every step of their remarkable evasion and escape over the next few months.

When they started walking, they were faced with three stark choices – none of them particularly appealing. The first was to head into the lush countryside of the valley; but that, they knew, would mean almost certain recapture. Another risky possibility was to try to jump a train to Rome and hook up with the escape route set up by an Irish priest, Monsignor Hugh O'Flaherty, who is so central to the history of escaping that he merits a short digression: During Mussolini's ascendancy, O'Flaherty (1898–1963) had made it his business to visit as many POW camps as he could, trying to locate men who'd been reported missing in action. If he succeeded, he would then use Vatican Radio to relay news of them to their families. By this means, he became a well-known figure among prisoners, and after the Armistice many of those who'd been liberated and managed to avoid recapture by the Germans sought him out in the neutral Vatican City in the hope that he'd help them get home. He initially acted on his own initiative, but soon enlisted the help of such people as the British Envoy Extra-ordinary and Minister Plenipotentiary to the Holy See, Sir D'Arcy Osborne, as well as Osborne's resourceful butler, John May, and a French diplomat called François de Vial. He also recruited Delia Murphy, the wife of the Irish ambassador, and an assorted group of priests, secret agents and Resistance fighters. With their help, he set up an escape network so efficient that he succeeded in protecting and saving over 4,000 fugitives, both escapers and Jews, whom he hid in convents, farms and apartments. This earned him such a reputation among the Germans that the Head of the German Security Service in Rome, SS-*Obersturmbannführer* Herbert Kappler, had a white line painted on the pavement at the west end of St Peter's Square, marking the border between Vatican City and Italy, and declared that if O'Flaherty crossed it he would have him killed instantly. The SS tried several times to assassinate him, but failed.*

Back in the Sulmona Valley, travelling by train without being able to pass oneself off as Italian, and in a country now swarming with Germans on high alert, was not an option Harley and his companions thought their best. There remained choice number three, the one made by most escapers from Sulmona: to cross the Majella massif and make contact with the Allied forces on or near the Adriatic coast.

The group of escapees were now seven in number, as two other prisoners had joined them while they sheltered in the countryside around the camp. At this stage they were rudderless, seeking a route, a plan and a purpose. Doubtless frustrated by their lack of progress as they worked the lower slopes of Monte Morrone adjacent to the camp, John Cox and Nick Robinson decided to make a break for it through the valley itself. Len recalls the moment of the split: 'We were pretty worn out, you know, we were tired, and so we stopped for the night. The next morning two of the group decided to try their best to get further along.

---

* Kappler was arrested in 1948 and sentenced to life imprisonment for war crimes (he was not a pleasant character). O'Flaherty visited him in prison often, and as a result, Kappler converted to Catholicism. Kappler died in 1978, six months after escaping from prison with the help of his second wife, who smuggled him out in a large suitcase: he was dying of cancer and weighed 47 kg at that time.

And away they went and were captured. I found out later that they were sent to Germany.'

The remaining five prisoners were now in a world of complete unknowns. Their one great overarching fear was that they might miss making contact with their own people and find themselves in the wild and trackless wastes of the massif, to vanish forever into the mountains.

There is a special type of heat in these foothills, a merciless flaying sun knifing through the thin air, beating down from above and being reflected by the stones on the ground beneath your feet. It was hard work trekking up and away from the prison camp, following a series of switchback tracks and paths up the flanks of the Majella massif, with the village of Fonte d'Amore shimmering in the haze of the valley below. Although I had set out early, the sun had quickly crept over the peaks of the ranges on the far side of the plain and I was soon trapped in the blistering heat of the mountainside, a tiny figure sizzling on a vast stony skillet, with no respite, no natural water supply, and no shade.

Despite the discomfort, it was a beautiful walk. For the first time, I was getting an eagle's eye view of Sulmona, sitting in the plain in the middle distance beneath me. The mountains beyond, some of their gullies and flanks still in deep blue shadow, lay in tumbling ranks on the horizon, disappearing into the haze of the far distance. As I walked, I heard the quartzite shriek of a golden eagle echo around the ridge far above as it worked the first of the morning thermals. From beneath my feet rose the heady scent of thyme and rosemary, crushed underfoot as I traversed the path.

I was heading for the village of Pacentro, following – as best I could – Len's first foray out of the valley and away from Fonte d'Amore. Although his exact route is not known, simple topography forces any walker to contour around the flanks of the mountain as they head up and out of the valley floor. Although I could not be certain, I was trying to base my route on the simple animal instinct to flee, to move as fast and as covertly as possible.

I was walking along a clearly delineated path, but Len and his companions would not have had any such luxury. They simply knew they had to put distance between themselves and the camp, and – presumably – knew that the villages and settlements at the fringes of the valley might offer sanctuary of sorts. But they were running blind – no guide, no fixed destination, no supplies and no clear plan. Just hope, and the primal urge to move.

Eventually, I came to a wall set into the side of the hill. This was the first sign of human habitation I had seen since departing Fonte d'Amore, and in itself represented something of a feat of architectural endurance. The wall weaved along the side of a steep slope, creating a great step in the hillside, with the flattened ground above it – something of a premium locally I imagined – planted with scattered olive trees.

I followed the wall for a few hundred metres, then brushed aside a low hanging fir branch to abruptly reveal Pacentro beneath me. This is unequivocally a mountain village, framed by the immensity of the ranges behind it. It seemed to me that the only way to view it for the first time is from height, with aching feet and sweating brow. I settled down on a rock, feeling rather pleased with myself, and took in what has been nominated as 'Borghi più belli d'Italia' – one of the most beautiful villages in Italy (and that's up against some pretty stiff competition, as you can imagine).

Pacentro is a tumbling series of interconnecting alleys, ancient stone buildings and ochre roof tops. It follows a ridge called Colle Costello that juts into the heart of the valley, carving an elegant arc through the air, with houses perched on the shoulders of precipitous slopes that plunge towards deep ravines that in turn cut into the heart of the mountains. Although the village suffered terribly in the Second World War, initially used by the Germans as a strategic base, then having much of its population forcibly evicted as the occupying forces left, its sheltered location at the base of Monte Morrone actually saved it from Allied bombing. Thus its ancient architecture is preserved almost completely intact.

The village has been a site of human settlement since at least the tenth century – and probably before – and has developed with increasing complexity over time. I was looking down on a veritable labyrinth of narrow alleyways and passages which created a venous network on the surface of the ridge. But this was a truly three dimensional picture, as beneath it lay cellars, caves, stores and caverns. In short, this was a perfect place to hide escaping prisoners. The village became the site of a complex and deadly game of cat and mouse during the war, with escapees frequently hidden only metres from German soldiers; sometimes beneath their feet, sometimes over their heads. Any local sheltering a prisoner would be taking a huge gamble, relying on their ability to move around Pacentro unseen, as well as on luck and the honour of their neighbours. Sadly, at enormous cost, both could sometimes be found wanting.

By now Len and his companions had been wandering the hills between Camp 78 and Pacentro for several days, surviving on foraged vegetables and water from streams. What had become obvious to them was that they could not do this alone – without local help they would either have to return to the camp or give themselves up to the Germans. Neither was an attractive option. Time wore on, and they were beginning to despair – caught between the relative security of their lofty hiding place overlooking Pacentro and the need to contact a local. As luck would have it, the decision was made for them. They happened across a young goatherd tending his flock on the mountainside. This was the moment of truth. Through hand signs and a few words of Italian they succeeded in telling the boy who they were, and that they were in dire straits. The boy nodded in apparent understanding and went away. Len and his four companions waited for hours, on tenterhooks, until at last a man appeared, strolling up the mountain. His name was Fiore Fabilli.

'An absolutely fabulous character,' recalls Len. '"I speak American," is what he said to us first – very proud of the fact that he'd lived in Pittsburgh before the war. He was lord of the village!'

Fiore took them back to his home in Pacentro, which was then a community of *contadini*, peasant farmers and farmworkers. They were mountain people – fiercely independent, labouring in conditions of great poverty – but their generosity was unrivalled. They had nothing, but gave everything.

Guido Fabilli – Fiore's son who played a key role in the drama that would unfold in the next few months – recalled after the war:

> We [the Fabilli family] had hidden thirty-six prisoners, who were dispersed or moved in twos and threes. The German SS placed notices on the walls of the town stating that if anyone was found attempting to protect the prisoners of war, their entire family would be shot.

Despite such brutality, the people of Pacentro had mobilized in their own, quietly defiant way. Len and his fellow escapees were – for the time being anyway – in the best possible hands.

Of all the tales of selfless sacrifice and quiet heroism among the people of Pacentro, there is perhaps one that stands out more than most. It is a beacon of hope, a vivid illustration that no matter how desperate your own circumstances, there is real nobility in helping others.

Thirteen-year-old Silvio Alboni had discovered three escaped POWs sheltering next to a neighbour's barn, and took it on himself to look after them. Silvio had nothing, often went without shoes, and like most in his community had little or no education. He was so poor, so bedraggled, so abject, that he was known locally as the 'Beggar Boy'.

I had been informed that Silvio was still alive and lived nearby, and would be happy to meet me. I lifted my pack once again onto my back, and made my way unsteadily down the vertiginous scree slopes towards the village, now glowing in the amber light of dusk. It looked every inch the haven for the weary traveller, and – I hoped anyway – hearing Silvio's story would reveal why so many risked so much to help the total strangers who appeared in their midst.

He is an old man now, with hands that tremble and a voice made querulous and faint by time, but when Silvio speaks of his deeds in 1943, his eyes blaze and his chin lifts.

'I did what any decent person would do,' he says, staring straight into my eyes and gripping my arm. 'I was not frightened. If someone has no food, you feed them – it is the Christian thing.'

Silvio had been young and alone when the first prisoners started arriving in Pacentro. He was something of a lost soul himself, scouring the streets and alleyways for food, and living barefoot in rags. His had not been a happy childhood – neglected by his mother, forced to care for his younger sister who had died in his arms, he had known only hardship and hunger. His appearance and behaviour meant he was invisible to most of the townsfolk. Such a cloak of anonymity would serve him well, and save the lives of the three men he encountered one afternoon while foraging for eggs in some bushes.

'They were here,' he said to me, pointing to a nondescript piece of ground in the very heart of the village, surrounded by a low wall. 'They were lying on the ground. They looked so pitiful, so hungry.'

To this day, he remains unaware of the irony of that sentiment, coming as it did from a half-starved beggar boy who had stumbled upon the men while desperately seeking food for himself.

'One of them spoke to me, I didn't understand what he was saying, but I knew he meant me no harm. His name was Jimmy.'

The young Silvio – with that instinctive knowledge of imminent danger inherent in those that live on the edge of society – had gestured for the men to wait where they were, and scuttled off to get the key to the building against which they huddled. Initially the owner refused to hand it over, knowing that to do so meant death if discovered, but Silvio persisted.

'I told her to give it to me, and that if I was found I would say I stole it,' he thumped his chest as he spoke, standing a little taller. 'I had nothing to lose anyway.'

Returning to the men, Silvio let them into an old store and indicated that they should be silent while he went off to look for food. No one notices a beggar boy, so he could move with impunity, the perfect undercover agent going about his covert business. What's more, his skills in finding scraps and raiding food stores meant he could gather what the prisoners needed to stay alive – albeit at huge personal risk. Soon, Silvio was delivering food to them on a nightly basis, using an elaborate pulley arrangement to lift supplies to the hay loft above the store where they were now hiding. He was a starving waif, a child, handing over everything he could gather to three grown men who relied on him completely. Silvio had, at last, found a family.

'Jimmy was a wonderful man,' he said, as we stood outside the same store. 'He used to talk to me, to make jokes, and he even knew a little Italian. He was so kind, so intelligent, and such a good person. He was the first real friend of my life.'

After several weeks of taking care of the men, Silvio noticed a German motorcycle with a sidecar and mounted machine gun checking out the road above the house. On making some enquiries, he discovered that this was to be the new headquarters for the Germans in Pacentro. The game was up.

'I had to get them out. That night I moved them out of the store, guided them to the top of the village, and told them exactly where to go to skirt the mountains. It was dark, it was foggy, and very cold, but it was their best chance.'

'And do you remember the moment of saying goodbye, Silvio?' I asked.

His eyes, which moments before had been afire with the memory of the story, suddenly filled with tears.

'It is a moment I will remember all my life. Jimmy embraced me and thanked me for everything. Then he was gone. I never saw him or heard from him again, but I think of this kind Englishman every day.'

By now he was openly crying, and I reached out a hand to comfort him. He grasped it in his own.

'Did you ever hear from the British Army, Silvio?' I asked. 'From someone who knew Jimmy perhaps?'

'Nothing,' he replied quietly, once again a frail old man, 'I heard nothing. I hoped every day, I waited, but I heard nothing. The mountains are a hard place, very dangerous, so . . . who can say what happened to them all?'

He shrugged again, and settled into silence, small and frail, staring at his feet. I didn't know what to do. I reached out and held his shoulder – bony, fine, impossibly delicate beneath my hand.

'I was a British soldier, Silvio,' I said. 'May I say thank you now? Thank you for what you did. For helping Jimmy and those men. I don't know what happened to them, but I do know that they would never have forgotten you.'

He nodded, and looked up at me.

'You,' he said, 'you must come to my home for lunch. With my family. You say my name exactly like Jimmy did – please come.'

The next day, I drove to the small hamlet of Contrada la Corna at the edge of Sulmona. After the trauma of the war, Silvio, made invincible by hardship and deprivation, built up a business based on collecting wood from the hills of the Majella mountains. He carried it on his back, saved every penny, employed local men, and one day the ragged beggar boy discovered he had become a successful local businessman. He built a grand house with a terrace that overlooked the mountains, and having created a home, he then created a family. Having lunch with us would be twenty-six people, all direct relatives – Silvio was an old man surrounded by love and affection, the lost little boy who had finally found it all.

Lunch was very, very long. And very, very large. I sat at Silvio's right hand – 'You are my honoured guest' – as a series of exquisite dishes were placed before me by smiling family members. Throughout, he told me stories – of the forests, of the men, of Jimmy and of his family. We raised glasses of local spirit, as fiery as molten metal, toasting the mountains that stood immense and forbidding on the horizon. Finally, when it was time for me to say my farewells, I rose with considerable difficulty, hefting my pack onto my shoulder and weaving my way glassily away from the table. I departed amid a chorus of '*Ciaio*'s as the family stood en masse to send me on my way. I decided it would be sensible to leave the car and pick it up the next day, so was standing at the gate wrestling with a recalcitrant strap on my rucksack, blearily trying to remember whether I should go left or right, when I felt a hand on my elbow. It was Silvio.

'Be careful,' he said quietly, 'be careful in the mountains.'

He gestured once again at the meandering ridges of the Majella in the distance, white snow packed into steep gullies.

'It's cold and dangerous, very dangerous. Be careful.'

And with that he released me, sending me on my way, the memory of Jimmy alive in his final farewell.

CHAPTER EIGHT

A Wonderful Woman

As for Harley and his group, Fiore Fabilli had hidden them in the basement of his house, relying on the solidarity of his neighbours for security. They were safe for the moment, and the Fabillis cared for and fed them. After about five days, Harley was ready to be on the move – being in the basement was 'basically like being a prisoner all over again'– but the best course to take was unclear. In the end, the decision was taken out of his hands, for Fiore came to them one morning in great haste and told them that the Germans were in the vicinity. They had to get out. There was a door that opened into the basement from behind the house, and it was through it they made their getaway. Guided by Fiore, they scrambled down a gully until they came to a rocky outcrop, where they stopped at a cave. This was to be their next refuge.

It wasn't ideal. The five men had to be careful to make as little noise as possible, for fear of German patrols, and they had to crawl on their bellies to get inside. But once inside, the cave turned out to be quite spacious, and that night Fiore brought them food and candles. They stayed there, as far as Len remembers, for about a week. But they were not alone in the cave by any means: 'We were running with lice, absolutely running alive. We used to take all our clothes off and sit on the outcrop of rock outside, killing the lice. We were just like monkeys. It was really, really bad.'

At the end of a week they were going stir crazy and had to be on their way. They had heard through local gossip that by now their own lines were a mere fifteen kilometres away, but that was across a mountain range as high as the Alps, and riddled with German troops. They needed a plan and they needed a guide. After speaking to Fiore, he arranged for them to meet a local man called Alberto.

There is a certain spirit that emerges time and again in the stories of such guides, who were, after all, operating under the threat of immediate execution, and relied on their knowledge, fitness and animal instincts developed over many years in the rarefied world of the mountains. As such, Len should not have been too surprised to find that at their first covert rendezvous with Alberto, he was accompanied by a number of other local people, several women, and a great deal of wine. These ingredients were duly combined to create a drunken meeting of some dimensions, which meant that no one could leave the following morning as originally planned. Frustratingly, Len and his companions had to return to their shelter to await further developments.

The foremost of these developments was that the snow in the upper slopes of the mountains was considered too unstable to attempt a crossing. In fact, it would be several months before the conditions would be deemed suitable, and after a few more weeks hiding in the cave and safe houses in Pacentro, Len and the others decided that they couldn't endanger Fiore and his family any longer. Bidding farewell, the group took off into the open coun-tryside, looking for shelter further afield. After a few hours' walking, they came across a barn which seemed like heaven at first – warm and light and full of stacks of straw which would provide them with a comfortable bed. But they soon found that appearances could be deceptive. The place was alive with fleas, which gave them no peace at all. They stuck it out for a few days, but winter was coming on. Heavy snowfall made it impossible to forage for food, the barn was bitterly cold, and if they did venture out they risked leaving telltale footprints in the snow. They decided that they would have to go to the farmhouse to which the barn evidently belonged and throw themselves on the owners' mercy. It was now November 1943, and they knew they had no chance of survival without help.

When they knocked on the door, the farmer, Panfilo Spinosa, answered immediately and told them to be off – there were Germans nearby and the danger was too great. But as they turned to go, his teenage daughter Rosina overrode him and invited them in.

Rosina was to make an indelible impression on Len, with her beauty, defiance, spirit and unquenchable humanity. Seventy-four years later, he still comes alive at her memory:

'An absolutely wonderful woman. So brave – she brought us food even when the Germans were close. It's all because of her that we survived, all because of her.'

There is a theory that Italian women showed less fear of Germans than the men – perhaps because, as Eric Newby remarked, 'soldiers always make an exception for the women of the enemy, for otherwise they would feel themselves completely alone' – though nobody could count on every soldier sharing that sentiment. There are many tales of what appear to be acts of suicidal defiance by Italian women in the face of their oppressors – whether that be the Germans or the Italian Fascists. Rosina Spinosa was very much cut from that cloth, and it was she who persuaded her family to shelter and feed the five escapees. Like Fiore and Silvio, the Spinosas didn't have much, and they were a big family of ten or so members, but what they had, they shared. Ultimately they became proud of looking after the Allied soldiers, as Rosina's nephew, Bruno, remembered when I visited the farm: 'My aunt invited them in because it was so cold outside. We gave them a drink by the fire, let them warm themselves up.'

Bruno looked at me earnestly. Plainly he felt he was not getting his point across.

'Right here,' he said again, pointing at the front door, 'the Germans came in right here, and the whole family had nowhere to run. You understand, nowhere.'

Bruno was eight years old when the Germans came for the escapers, on Christmas Day 1943. Over the weeks preceding the raid, the Spinosas hadn't just fed and sheltered the prisoners, but had also grown close to them. The men had worked in the fields for the family, had played with the children, and one had even attracted the attention of a local girl, who had fallen in love with him. When the decision was made that the prisoners should make their final run, she was devastated, and – in a peculiar act of thwarted love – had gone to the Germans to tell them that the Spinosas were hiding POWs. Her rationale cannot be known – perhaps she thought it would keep them in the country, that she would save their lives before they headed into the brutal environment of the mountains. But whatever her motivation, the timing of the German raid was impeccable.

As a measure of the bond between prisoners and family, the entire Spinosa clan had gathered for a farewell meal – nineteen family members and five escapers in one room.

'My father, he went to the door when he heard knocking,' said Bruno, now a very sprightly and animated eighty-two-year-old. 'He opened it, and saw a German with a rifle. He shouted *'Tedeschi!'* – *'Germans!'* – and then there was pandemonium, total pandemonium.'

The family scattered, as did the prisoners. One POW dived out of a window and was immediately apprehended. He was led straight back into the house, where a few family members – and one other POW – remained sitting at the table, stunned. This was, in fact, quite a clever move by the seated prisoner – whether calculated or not we will never know. He was dressed as an Italian peasant, and many of the Germans spoke no Italian at all. He may well have got away with it, and simply been taken for a family member, but the German guard escorting the captive POW asked him if there were any others in his party.

'No,' he replied, before adding, in the belief that the POW at the table had already been apprehended, 'Just me and him.'

So now the Germans had two prisoners in custody. But they knew there were three more somewhere, and set about finding them.

'The Germans had a Turkish soldier with them,' said Bruno, 'he was a brute. He smashed my older brother here –' he pointed to the back of his neck – 'with a rifle butt.'

Bruno's older brother was marched at gunpoint to each room in the house, at last reaching the master bedroom.

'My brother looked under the bed with the candle he was carrying, and saw a skinny POW – a naval lieutenant – clinging to the underside of the mattress. As the Turk bent down to look, my brother lifted the candle up, so he could see nothing.'

Bruno chuckled at the memory of this small act of defiance, when all had seemed lost.

'Ha! The Turk thought there was no one there. My brother fooled him! Come, let me show you the attic.'

As the Germans turned the house upside down, Bruno's uncle had ushered Len and Albert 'Nick' Nicholls into this very attic. Bruno led me to a door in the corridor outside the bedroom, and pulled aside a rusty catch before gesturing that I should climb the stairs. I moved past him and gingerly climbed the twisting, ancient wooden planks that doubled as a stairwell. Unequivocally, these were the very same steps that Len and Nick had hastened up as the clamour of the search on the floor beneath them grew ever closer. I poked my head up into the claustrophobic darkness, and tried to imagine being crouched there, stricken with fear, staring at the door at the foot of the stairwell, knowing full well that should it open, it was all over. This was the final play, their last throw of the dice. If the shouts and muffled sound of blows beneath their feet came close to the door, and that same door opened, they were caught like rats in a trap.

Showing great presence of mind, even as the jackboots clattered in their approach, Rosina and her Uncle Antonio had pushed a wardrobe in front of the attic door. As the Germans ran onto the landing, shouting and gesticulating, they found Rosina and Antonio waiting for them, offering to show them the remainder of the house.

Miraculously, the ruse worked – the cool heads of the Spinosas and their devotion to the young men under their charge had done the trick. The sounds of the search receded, and when the attic door finally opened it was a friendly face beckoning Len and Nick to come down.

But they descended the steps to a subdued, grieving family.

'They took Rosina's father and my brother,' said Bruno. 'Initially, they wanted my brother Emilio, but my other brother Constantino stepped forward and volunteered, as he had no wife and children. He was a brave man.'

According to Len, the Germans had, in the end, taken three prisoners into custody, so it can be assumed the naval lieutenant was ultimately caught too. But the Germans knew there were still two escapers in hiding. To balance their books, they took two of the Spinosas into captivity. The family had no idea where they would be taken, but knew all too well what their fate would be. In a scene repeated throughout Italy, the simple humanity of an

Italian peasant farming family – the *contadini* – had come at a terrible price.

There was no staying at the farm after that, so Harley and Nicholls were taken to a hut in the woods nearby where they could hide, at least for a time. They were badly shaken, didn't know what to do next, and needed to recuperate. They hardly thought they'd see any of the Spinosas again but the next morning Rosina arrived, bringing with her some pasta for them to eat. Astonished at her bravery, Harley felt moved to ask her why she was taking such a risk in helping them. Her reply was simple: 'I hope that by looking after you, God will reward me by looking after my family.'

Everyone knew the risks; the reprisals were harsh to discourage the locals from helping the Allies, and to break their spirit. But there is an extraordinary postscript to this particular reprisal against the Spinosas.

Panfilo and Constantino were now in German custody. They were given the job of typing up notices in the administration centre of their prison camp, and one day Panfilo noticed that he was typing up a death warrant for a number of prisoners. Reading down the list, he saw that his name, and the name of his son, were included.

In a single moment, driven by desperation, Panfilo ate the notice and moved on to other work. Much has been written about German efficiency and bureaucracy over the years, but in this case it worked very much in the Spinosas' favour. No death notice, no death sentence – Panfilo and Constantino were spared. They survived the war, making their way home and arriving hideously malnourished but alive. No meal Panfilo ever ate was as important as the one over his typewriter that day.

But not everyone shared this remarkable stroke of good fortune. While Len and his fellow POWs were hiding near Pacentro in autumn 1943, elsewhere in the valley a shepherd called Michele del Greco had been arrested. Michele had been entrapped by an SS officer posing as a POW on the run. He'd given the man a meal and told him what direction to go in before another SS man appeared and the two of them took Michele away to prison in Sulmona.

News of his arrest swept through his home village of Anversa, and his family was shunned – the other villagers were fearful of being arrested for even talking to them, as his daughter Raffaella, seventeen years old at the time, remembers. Raffaella and her three siblings all tried desperately to find their father and it took an agonizing four days before they were finally told of his location. Weeks passed, but finally a date for Michele's trial was announced. It was a trial only for protocol's sake, but Raffaella was able to watch some of it through a crack in the courtroom door. She saw her father's initial resolve, and finally his acceptance of his fate. She pressed a parcel of food into his hand as he was bustled out of the courthouse by a German guard, but he gently pushed his daughter's hand away and said, 'I don't need anything any more. Look after mother.'

The sentence was inevitable: death. It was announced in German on a poster pasted up in the village. The date of execution was to be 27 November 1943. Michele's wife, in despair, tried to kill herself by jumping from the balcony of their house, and only failed to do so because Raffaella managed to restrain her. There was a glimmer of hope when the family was given leave to appeal, but this was probably another process for form's sake – the kind of process the Nazis were notorious for. The appeal was, of course, rejected, and Michele was shot by a firing squad on 22 December. He met his end bravely. He could have escaped, but didn't do so for fear of further reprisals on his village.

Michele had successfully helped fifty escapers before he was caught. In prison, he told his priest, 'They accuse me of collaborating with the enemy. I have not collaborated with anyone. I only put into practice what I was taught in church as a child: Give food to the hungry.' His tombstone reads:

Michele del Greco.
An Example of the Italian Spirit to All.
Fallen under Enemy Fire.

Amid what Rino Panza described as 'the inhuman whirlwind of war' in Italy, there are certain stories that hold a particular power, resonating through the ages. Michele del Greco's arrest and execution is one such tale – a simple, honest, decent man trying to do what is right, and paying a terrible price. Indeed, his story seemed to me to encapsulate the price paid by ordinary Italians for the decisions of others, for political and military machinations that were carried out far away yet had a tectonic impact on their lives.

As the father of two small children, I had been profoundly moved by Michele's story, and during my last day in Fonte d'Amore I particularly wanted to visit the site of his imprisonment and execution to pay my respects. It is tempting to dismiss such thoughts as overly sentimental, self-indulgent acts that attempt to pay homage to just another victim of a war from another age. But I felt – indeed, I feel – that to walk in the same courtyard, to stand in the same spot where the fatal rifle shots rang out, and to touch the same ancient stonework, means something, even if the sentiment is an entirely personal one.

The site of the prison is the Abbazia Santo Spirito al Morrone, an exquisite building in the centre of the village that was once a monastery. A clock tower stands proudly above the large main entrance, overlooking a courtyard that was originally created as a place of contemplation. The sun was still low in the sky as I walked into the courtyard, my footsteps echoing from the four walls, the shadows long and the air perfectly still. It is – by design – a cool, quiet sanctum at the heart of the village that surrounds it.

Having stood for a moment in the very centre of the yard, slowly circling to take in the barred windows that surrounded me – monastic cells repurposed by the Germans for more sinister needs in the war – I carried on to a shaded door in the far corner. Here a long, airy corridor led to a sunken garden, green and silent. As I appeared, two crows were startled into flight, their clattering wings and raucous calls amplified by the crumbling stone keep around them.

It was here that the sentence had been carried out, three gunshots resonating like thunderclaps in this confined space. Retracing my steps, I found the plaque to Michele in the middle of the corridor. It reads:

Michele del Greco
Martyr of the Second World War, an example of
rare moral integrity and Christian spirit. Shot by Nazis in
this abbey on 22nd December 1943, for having assisted
English, French, Russian and American prisoners.

I walked back through to the main courtyard and sat on the elegant curve of the main steps beneath the clock tower. While researching Michele, I had found a short document written by his daughter – Raffaella – over fifty years after her father's death. In the rush of preparing for my trip to Italy, I had not had a chance to read it – now seemed as good a time and place as any.

Her words, even though written five decades later, resonated with such fury, such impotent rage, and such longing, that they sprang from the page. This was more than a simple eulogy from a daughter to a father, it was cry of anguish, a howl of baffled loss that held as much power today as it would have done the day Michele was shot.

The sentence was carried out without the family's knowledge – they were told by a neighbour – and he was buried in a pauper's grave. After a harsh winter, the family eventually found the grave and exhumed the body – still perfectly preserved in the cold earth. Raffaella's mother had lifted the coarse blanket he had been wrapped in and seen the bullet hole over his heart:

> She put her hand on the hole as if to transmit her warmth and receive the courage to go on. It was her last farewell to the man she had loved, to her companion in life that she now had to face alone.

As a final postscript to her story, Raffaella recounts the last words her father wrote to his family, scrawled in pencil on a page of an exercise book in the darkness of his cell. They received the letter after his death sentence had been carried out. In it, he directly addresses his wife:

> Carminnucia, I am comforted by the fact that I saw you last time and you brought me all four children, just so I could kiss them and I place a kiss on this sheet of paper. I kiss my wife together with our children, dear children.

I folded the paper and sat alone for a while. Glancing upwards, I could see the first rays of the sun appearing round the fluted edges of the clock face, touching the cobbles beneath with soft light. After a few moments, I tucked the letter into my pocket, rose to my feet, and walked back out through the exquisite stone archway of the Abbazia Santo Spirito al Morrone.

CHAPTER NINE

The Run for Monte Amaro

Six months into their escape, Harley and Nicholls were still being cared for by the Spinosas – at great peril to the family. Most of that time had been spent simply familiarizing themselves with the territory around them. Now, with the winter nearly over, they decided that they had to attempt the mountains. They knew they couldn't keep the Spinosa family at risk any longer – they had already done more for them than anyone could reasonably expect. It was time to strike for home.

Over the next few weeks, they would try three times to head over the mountains, and three times would be thrown back. During one of their attempts – with no moon and very low visibility – they climbed into the foothills of Amaro and then found themselves descending a steep shale bank. Making a great deal of noise – with clattering stones and tumbling rocks at their feet – they finally found themselves at the base of a wide gulley. Allowing their eyes to adjust to the gloom, they saw they were surrounded by strange, lumpen shapes in the darkness.

They were standing in the middle of a German tank park.

Hastily scrambling back up the shale bank, they returned to their place of refuge. They now knew beyond doubt that they would need a guide, and once again – through what was now an established network of local contacts – managed to get in touch with Alberto.

They rendezvoused with Alberto at a small hut outside Sulmona, at the very base of Monte Amaro. This was to be their final run at the mountain, an all or nothing attempt at freedom. They had used every local contact, had survived countless close shaves and ridden their luck as far as it could carry them – it was time to make one last bid for freedom.

Among the group who met them was Fabio Fabilli, the man who had originally shielded them in Pacentro, who had come to bid them farewell. He had with him two other escapees – one of whom was a British major. Subsequent events would reveal that there was more to him than met the eye, indeed there is speculation that he was working undercover for British intelligence or Special Forces. Also accompanying Fabio was one of his sons – Guido – who would act as a guide and porter in the mountains. Years later Guido recalls the exact moment they decided to make for the summit:

> It was 27 February 1944 – an extremely cold day with continuous snow, over a metre high. It was, fortunately, completely iced over and was exactly the right opportunity. The watchword was 'one for all, and all for one.'

Fiore had brought meat – Harley doesn't remember if it was lamb or goat, but he hadn't eaten meat for years, and the stew they made in the big cauldron in the hut was nothing short of ambrosia for him. That same evening the snow hardened, the sky was clear, and Alberto decided that it was time to get a move on. The group set out at 1800 hours.

Len and Nick were desperately ill-equipped for the climb, with threadbare clothes and poor footwear. One of their companions was a smartly dressed Italian civilian who was – incongruously – carrying a suitcase. He soon fell behind and began to shout and rant bitterly about the experience. Len and Nick dropped back and tried to encourage him, and then – eventually – to threaten that he would be shot unless he kept the volume of his complaints down. They had to hurry upwards to rejoin the main party, and Len recalls that he did not see the man again. Len notes in his post war account, 'I never knew if he made it.' Such was the brutal reality of their situation – to flag or to falter was, in all probability, to die.

The first deep snows on the slopes of Amaro took a terrible toll on their strength, demanding that they push on through soft drifts, contouring the steeper sections to traverse ever upwards. Their movement generated heat but expended great energy, and so they trod a fine line between survival and exhaustion.

They kept going all night, zig-zagging up the mountain paths, keeping a fearful lookout for another hazard (albeit one that in reality bore them very little real threat) – bears and wolves. At dawn – twelve hours after setting out – they had reached the summit, but no sooner had they done so than someone called out urgently, '*Tedeschi!*' Guido recalls the scene:

> An English major at the end of the line saw the pinpoints of two dark uniforms. He shouted in English and Italian, 'Hurry, two ski patrols are pursuing us and they have machine guns.' They were in close range and we thought we were all going to be shot. The English major was equipped with a radio and transmitted to his command for help. He stayed back. The response was immediate and soon two attack planes had killed the German skiers and the planes accompanied us until we made the final crossing.

Plainly the major had not only the right equipment, but immediate contact with higher command, reinforcing the view that he was more than just a regular escapee. But their troubles were far from over. Having defied the enemy, they now had more elemental problems to deal with. They had barely reached the summit when a blizzard hit them, accompanied by a wind of brutal intensity. They were completely exhausted, totally exposed, and at the end of their tether. Their survival depended on their ability to keep moving down towards the shelter of the eastern slopes of Amaro, and towards their ultimate destination of the advancing Allied army.

My guides met me on a flat stretch of road between the villages of Cansano and Campo di Giove. They presented two very contrasting figures – one was a whip-thin young man, dressed in cutting-edge equipment, unmissable in lime-green Gore-Tex and a luminous yellow headband plastered with sponsors' logos. He flashed me a broad smile, with bright eyes and perfect white teeth set against the deep mahogany of his mountain tan, before springing forward with an outstretched hand.

'Ah, Monty, it is my pleasure to meet you. I am Marco.'

He spoke in English with a heavy Italian accent, and looked every inch the alpine guide, the sort of chap who would bound up precipitous slopes all day then do something clever with a belay and a tiny hissing stove before retiring into a sleeping bag for the night to write epic poetry about the wind.

'And this is Nico. He is local to here, so he has great knowledge of the region.'

This was – of course – one of my main rationales for doing the trek. To truly follow the footsteps of Len and Nick, I needed an Alberto. And here he was, a man as craggy as the craggiest crag. He looked as if he had been roughly hewn from granite and then left outside to gently erode for a century or two. His face was deeply lined, his bald pate shaved clean, and a wisp of a grey beard sprung from his lower lip like a tiny stalagmite. When he smiled, he revealed a row of peg-like teeth, dark with nicotine, and his palm was so rough his handshake elicited an audible rasp as he pulled his hand back. His clothing was more basic than Marco's, his rucksack simple. His legs bowed gently like banded steel, and I immediately felt very safe and slightly intimidated in his presence, which is an odd combination but I'm sure reflected the feelings of Len and Nick when they first met Alberto (even if he was fairly drunk at the time).

After exchanging the briefest of pleasantries, we set off at a clip, leaving the road quickly behind us. It was early in the morning and the mountains were shrouded in low cloud, which was probably not a bad thing as the highest point on my immediate horizon was a row of thirty-foot-tall pine trees, as opposed to the glowering peak of Monte Amaro in the distance, hidden behind the mist. All I knew was that beyond the trees lay a long trek, most of it – in fact, all of it – uphill. I would be constantly moving in two dimensions – distance and height. Every step took me closer to the summit and lifted me into air that grew ever thinner.

The lower reaches of the trek took us through beech forests, with Nico and Marco moving fast and easily ahead. I silently prayed that we wouldn't end up with an 'old bull vs young bull' race between them, as in that case there would only be one casualty (and it wouldn't be either of them). As it was, I settled into my own pace, thighs burning, pulse racing and breath sawing, as Nico and Marco pushed on ahead.

After an hour of hard trekking we stopped at a small water fountain – a simple tap and hose emerging from the side of the hill.

'The Fountain of the Bears,' said Nico unexpectedly in rather good English, gesturing for me to fill up my water bottles.

Having done so, I settled down to drink and asked Nico where he was from.

'Here,' he said, with an expansive wave of the hand. 'My home is in the mountains. I work for the Parco Nazionale della Majella.'

It sounded delightfully lyrical when he said it, the opening line of a song about the hills and their inhabitants. I grinned at him and raised my water bottle.

'*Salute* to that!'

He laughed, nodded vigorously, then leapt to his feet.

'We go,' he said simply.

By now we were reaching the lower edge of the alpine vegetation, and the upper edge of my stamina. I paused by the fountain for one last, long drink, then moved off once again.

The mist had begun to clear, revealing a series of interlocking valleys, spurs and ridges in our wake. Even these foothills looked wild and impenetrable, and not without reason. There are in fact eight packs of wolves that roam the park, preying on natural food such as chamois, deer and stragglers from hiking groups. The latter meal was – admittedly – only in my own fevered imagination, but it struck me forcibly just how alien this landscape must have been for any escaping prisoner not used to mountains and forests. Their dependence on their guides really was total.

After another good few hours of trekking – upwards, ever upwards – we had passed through dense forests of Apennine pine and at last emerged into the tundra of the upper slopes. Although I allowed myself the briefest moment of self-congratulatory triumph on doing so, it also gave me the first glimpse of the upper reaches of Monte Amaro proper. The clouds parted as if by a celestial hand, swept aside theatrically to show the quailing mortal on the slopes what lay ahead.

I was hiking with two knowledgeable, professional guides, using state of the art equipment (my GPS watch informed me that my activity for the day so far had been 'moderate', which made me feel like Frisbee-ing it into the void). It is only when you see the mountain up close, when it hangs over you, squaring those great dark shoulders and icy peaks, that you fully appreciate what the escapers went through. This was mountaineering, pure and simple, but carried out by men who had no training, no equipment, little food, and no knowledge. What they did possess was a burning desire, a desperation to escape, to hear a familiar language, to return home. But even with that as the most potent of fuel, their feats were Herculean – and it is only when you walk those same weary steps that you truly appreciate this.

Another hour and we were into the snowline. By now the slopes around me were devoid of trees, but nonetheless still had small explosions of colour, a firework display of alpine blooms against the dark grey of shattered rocks and tumbling scree. There were wild crocuses, orchids and pansies – a defiant sprinkling of yellow, purple and red, and a celebration of life itself where there should be none.

There are a number of Freedom Trails through these mountains, and at our next stop I asked Nico if we were following a particular route.

'The trail is here, there –' he gestured at a distant saddle between two peaks – 'there, there and there!'

As he gesticulated in all directions I looked back at him, puzzled.

'They took the prisoners over wherever they thought was best,' he explained. 'They knew about the snow conditions, where the patrols were, they knew everything. Do same route, again and again, you get caught. They were clever.'

By now, for this latter-day Englishman anyway, another factor had begun to creep into the equation. It was cold, that special cold one only experiences at altitude, when your body aches, your defences are at their lowest, and a light sheen of sweat raised in the climb spirits away any warmth that remains.

Many, many escapes took place in winter, at night. The rationale was simple – at night the chances of being seen were slight, and the extreme cold meant that the snow hardened, making it more stable and easier to walk over. But there was a catch, a potentially lethal one. Such conditions were quickly fatal if a strong wind sprung up, if a blizzard ambushed a group at altitude, or if anyone stopped for any length of time in the open. The guides had to drive the exhausted prisoners on, cajoling and threatening, as to falter would be to die. Many prisoners – among them possibly Silvio's dear friend Jimmy – perished en route, particularly those who chose to run for the mountains without a guide. Exact numbers are not known, but the total number of prisoners who escaped throughout Italy after the September 1943 armistice is in the region of 11,500, and of those a great number simply vanished. It is not unreasonable to assume that many of these died in the mountains.

I trudged up to where Nico and Marco were now waiting for me, both sheltering behind a large rock at the foot of a ramp of deep snow. This in turn led to the ridge that was the main spine of the mountain. As I walked I could feel my breath labouring and my heart hammering – we were now at over 2,300 metres above sea level and each step had become more of an effort. The wind, which so far had been harnessed by valleys and vegetation, was now unfettered by obstacles and whirled and shrieked gleefully over smooth scree slopes. Snow whipped from the ridge above, spiralling and twisting and creating white vapour trails and vortexes in the deep blue sky.

'Hey, Monty,' said Marco, when I finally arrived. 'You used crampons before? No? Well, now is a pretty good time to learn.'

The slopes leading to the summit ridge are – if not quite precipitous – certainly very steep indeed. Slip on the snow and you face an exhilarating period of acceleration, all pin-wheeling arms and scrabbling feet, before your abrupt and messy arrival on the rocks below. We were all keen to avoid this, so – with Marco's careful tutelage – I strapped on the crampons, stepped onto the snow, and began my ascent. They were wonderful – four-wheel drive for feet – and the slope quickly fell away behind me. Twenty minutes of deliriously rapid progress later, I hauled myself over the sharp ridge that led to the summit, still some way off in the distance, to have my back slapped and hand pumped by a delighted Marco and Nico.

There was still a way to go but we had broken the back of the climb, and after a further hour wending our way along the ridge, an otherworldly path snaking its way through the heavens, we arrived at the summit. Below us, nestled at the head of the valley beyond the ridge, the one that led off the eastern flanks of the mountain, lay our *rifugio* – an old stone building where we would be spending the night.

As I stood briefly on the summit – not a place to linger, as even on this spring day it was scoured by icy winds – the true nature of Len and Nick's climb became fully apparent. As I had set out from the valley floor far below, I had been magnificently well-equipped, well rested and well fed. Several hours later, standing on the summit, I could feel the investment of energy it had taken to get this far, with tired limbs and a deep weariness setting in. I could also feel that wind, cutting and uncompromising – to stop here in a debilitated state would have fatal consequences. As I turned to trudge down to the *rifugio*, still half an hour's walk away, I marvelled at the escapers' resilience and inner drive. They were men on the run, driven by fear and chased by the enemy. They were also pursuing the chimera of freedom, the powerful incentive that on the other side of the physical barrier of the mountain lay liberation. But theirs was nonetheless an immense physiological effort, a do or die attempt to get home, and deserves to be lauded and celebrated.

I still had to cover a considerable distance the next day, as between me and the small town of Fara San Martino – final destination for both Len and me – lay fourteen kilometres of snowfield, scree, forest and stony track dropping precipitously over 2,000 metres in altitude. I would walk this route having had the benefit of a night's rest in the *rifugio* (now only a few hundred metres away, a blessed relief) but Len and Nick had done it in one push. This was their moon shot – there would only be success or failure, with no compromise, no middle ground.

The next day I hobbled to the end of the trek, a point marked by a steep rock canyon that narrowed overhead, eventually closing to an atmospheric passage that I could touch on either side with my hands outstretched.

'This is called the Throat. The end,' said Nico simply.

When Len, Nick and the remainder of the group had reached the summit, even though they were urged ever onwards by their guides and were still within the maelstrom of the blizzard, in a quintessentially British moment they decided to toast their achievement. Before setting out they'd been given a bottle of cognac by Fabio and now, at their moment of maximum peril sitting on top of Monte Amaro, Nick suggested they broach it. Harley had never tasted cognac before, and as they toasted each other, he thought he had never felt better in his life – the warmth of the spirit coursing through his system bringing the realization that they could, they would, make it home. Such was his enthusiasm for this new found drink that the initial sips soon turned into something slightly more elemental: 'We quickly downed the whole bottle!' recalls Len.

The large quantities of alcohol had an immediate effect on their exhausted bodies, and led to Nick suggesting a rather novel means of extracting themselves from the summit: 'Nick suddenly decides, "I know the quickest way to get down – on your backside." So he got on his backside and we both slid down the mountain. Quite a bit down.'

This unconventional – and potentially lethal – method is known in mountaineering terms as 'glissading', and is only practised by experts in carefully judged situations. Nonetheless, for the two (mildly inebriated) escapees, it proved marvellously effective, and they were soon in the lee of the summit. With the rest of the group and their guides, they made their way down the two kilometres' vertical descent towards the valley floor. As the slopes levelled out, they still had several kilometres of twisting path to negotiate. By this stage, Len and Nick were incoherent with fatigue, shambling and tripping, their onward movement enabled by gravity and the final remnants of that stubborn endurance that had seen them surmount so many obstacles over the previous seven months.

I tried to imagine their feelings as they walked through the canyon, their final steps to freedom. Although they had heard that Fara San Martino was in Allied hands, they did not know for sure (and in fact, a mere three weeks beforehand it had been held by the Germans). As they emerged from the confines of the rock walls on either side of them, they could have found themselves at gunpoint, their dream shattered and their guides led away for execution. They were completely exhausted and knew their fate would be decided in the next few agonizing minutes.

When at last they arrived at the village it seemed deserted, an eerily silent place, forbidding and barren. By this time they were at the end of their tether, and Harley felt that whatever happened next, he'd go along with it, he was so exhausted. They made their way along the road which led through the village and away from Monte Amaro itself, when suddenly a group of armed men appeared from behind an outcrop of rocks. Harley and Nicholls had no idea who these outlandish-looking fighters were and put up their hands, praying that they were partisans, not Germans or the remnants of a Fascist militia.

The two groups continued to size each other up, a moment that seemed to last a lifetime. All the while the fate of Len and Nick hung in the balance – they were at the end of a monumental journey, they had defied the odds again and again, living on their wits, overcoming tremendous physical and mental obstacles, and yet it could all come to nothing in a heartbeat. And then, from behind the same rock, a Sikh officer of the Indian Division of the Eighth Army appeared.

Emotionally and physically spent, Harley collapsed into the arms of the partisans. The journey was over and the escape complete. He'd made it against all the odds.

I was a skinny little thing, you know. I was always ill until I was about twelve years of age, always in and out of hospitals and that. And I think basically my inner willpower kind of kept me going, and that has stood me in good stead all the rest of my life.

Len Harley finally arrived home on 18 March 1944, the Hackney boy who had experienced more in a few short years than most men do in a lifetime. The conflict had left its mark, as war does on all involved, but the deepest impression for him had been left by the kindness of the ordinary Italian people he met, who had saved his life again and again. And above and beyond them all was Rosina Spinosa, who – even as she grieved for the perceived loss of her father and her brother taken by the Germans only the day before, had still brought the men food, and had shown them compassion and humanity.

Very shortly after his return to England – indeed on his first period of leave – Len married his fiancée, Win. Nick was his best man. After he was demobbed, and once he had settled into a new life as a civilian, he wrote to the Spinosas to tell them his news. They replied, and they have kept his letter to this day, as he has theirs.

Len wrote:

We arrived back in England on March 18th last year and I went home that same day. My family had just been informed that I was well and safe. Imagine their surprise when I knocked on the door? They looked amazed to see me. Then there was a lot of handshaking and kissing and many tears. Only a few hours earlier they still believed I was dead. They had no news about me for eight months. I have often spoken of you all with my wife and my family. They too asked me to write and thank you for everything you did for me. I will never be able to thank you enough for all your help. It was magnificent. I know that so as to help me and my friends you suffered a great deal.

I will never forget that.

And Rosina's Uncle Antonio replied on the Spinosas' behalf:

Dear Mr Leonard Harley and family,
I was delighted to receive your long letter a few days ago. We were all so happy to learn that you had successfully made it back to England and that your family was lucky enough

to see you were alive. For us the best news was your wedding and together with my family we wish you all the best for a happy future. I now hope that you and your wife have made all your dreams come true. We are all in good health for the moment and Constantino is back with us. The Germans are on the run and we are now free and waiting for the world to be at peace.

In your letter you often thanked us for everything we did for you, but I do not think that is necessary because it was our duty and also I believe that any father would have done the same if ever in the same position.

We are happy that you always remember us.

As I turned into the drive I noted that the house looked neat and tidy, with manicured lawns and carefully tended flowerbeds. Sitting on the outskirts of Sulmona, it was more part of the mountains than the town, surrounded by swaying fields of poppies and quiet, dusty lanes that weaved and dipped over the foothills around it.

Seeing several other vehicles were already parked outside the house, I realized I was nervous. So much rested on the next few hours, years of uncertainty could at last be ended, debts cleared and honour finally satisfied. But it relied on fickle technology, and I was aware of just how much could go wrong, of just how high expectations were and how deflating reality might be.

Waiting for me in the house were the Spinosas – gathered once again for a special occasion, as they had been on that terrible day in 1944. And also, waiting in England, on his sofa with his daughter, sat Len Harley.

I knocked on the door and was greeted warmly by the host, Raffaelle Spinosa, a dapper man in his mid-fifties. His wife and their two children stood behind him, each shaking my hand in turn and ushering me in. And there, sitting at the dining table, was Bruno. He sprang up when he saw me, an invincible man of the mountains, hard as teak, eighty-two years old and still with a piratical glint in his eye.

But there was really only one person I wanted to meet. I walked over to the settee, where a little old lady, dressed up in her Sunday best, was waiting. She glanced up as I approached, her features still strong, her mouth set, and her gaze steady. I gently took her hand.

'Senora Rosina, it's my great pleasure to meet you.'

Beside her was her daughter, Venny, who whispered a translation in her ear before listening to the reply.

'She says she is happy to meet you too.'

Len had returned twice to Sulmona to find the family, the most recent visit being in 2009, and yet he had failed on both occasions. The Spinosas had moved to America after the war, although they ultimately returned after several years overseas, and during his visits Len could not find anyone who knew where they were. This deeply honourable man had never known, in the seventy-three years since he had left the care of the Spinosa household, whether his eternal gratitude was truly understood or acknowledged. And now, within moments, he would at last be able to look into Rosina's eyes and tell her for himself.

In front of Rosina sat a laptop computer on a coffee table. Bruno took a seat beside her on the sofa, the family gathered round, and without further ado I touched the key to commence the call.

The harsh electronic ringtone lasted only a few seconds, and then Len's face appeared on the screen. I had no idea what the reaction would be, whether time had softened his feelings, whether age had taken its toll, and whether the conversation would be short and stilted.

I saw Len, ninety-eight years old and still a survivor, immediately lean forward towards the screen. There was a flicker of recognition, a moment of confused and tumbling emotions, and then his face crumpled as the tears flowed.

'Oh, Rosina, how wonderful,' he said, in a trembling voice. 'How lovely to see you. I'm lost for words, lost for words.'

And then the voice trailed off, and the tears came again. Beside him his daughter Chris was also crying, and put her hand on her father's shoulder.

Rosina had also leant forward with a smile of recognition and delight, and quickly spoke to Venny beside her.

Through her own tears, Venny said, 'Len, she is very happy to see you.'

And then Len began to talk. Seventy-three years of not knowing, seventy-three years of carrying a debt of gratitude almost too weighty to bear, and seventy-three years of pent-up emotion, all came tumbling out in a delighted stream of consciousness.

'You are wonderful people, wonderful people. Thank you for what you did, thank you, thank you.'

Beside Rosina, Bruno beamed in delight, and leant over to mutter something to Venny, who let out a great shout of laughter. She turned to me.

'Bruno said he always knew Len was in love with Rosina, he just didn't realize how much.'

And so they talked, nodded, and smiled at one another, carrying on a conversation interrupted by over seven decades of separation. A lifetime to catch up on, and a treasure trove of shared memories to explore.

PART THREE

Gordon Lett and Operation Galia, Rossano Valley, Italy

'Unhappy the land that needs a hero.'

Bertolt Brecht – *The Life of Galileo*

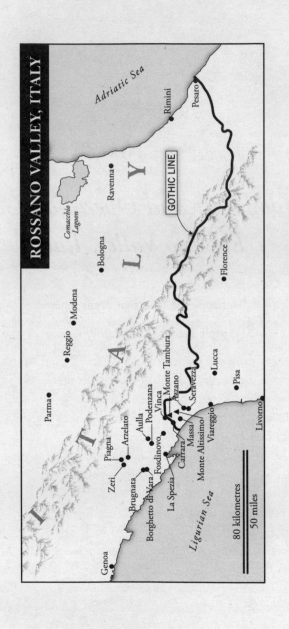

ROSSANO VALLEY, ITALY

CHAPTER TEN

The Partisans

By all accounts, Tom Redhead was a large, powerful man, four-teen stone in weight, with big, very strong hands. Paradoxically, everyone who knew him commented on how quiet and gentle he was. Such a benign disposition did not, it seems, extend to those who attempted to incarcerate him. By guile, by strength, by nerve and through sheer dogged determination, Tom escaped again and again. And – just for good measure – again.

Tom came from Hull, and worked as a carpenter before the war. He was in his early twenties at the outbreak of hostilities, and joined the Military Police. He must have presented quite a spectacle in the famous red cap, quietening any bar-room brawl or recalcitrant soldier just by entering the room. In June 1942, he was captured in the North African desert by German troops, and sent to Camp PG82 just outside Florence. Here he remained until the surrender in September 1943 (an unusually long period of incarceration for Tom, a lapse he certainly made up for later). After the Italian surrender and armistice, he took the decision to go on the run, and with three other prisoners he reached the nearby mountains and the settlement of Deccio, a tiny cluster of houses perched improbably on the pinnacle of a mountain. They took shelter in a barn there, ultimately befriending the family who owned it. This family – the Pieruccinis – took extraordinary risks to protect the prisoners, with the group spending seven months in the village under their care. The three daughters in the family (Beatrice, aged fifteen, Argene, seventeen, and Dora, thirty-two) were fearless and feisty. When a German patrol tried to take the family's only cow, they stared them down, pitchforks in hand, and the soldiers – possibly quite sensibly – decided to seek meat elsewhere.

For considerable periods in 1944, the Pieruccinis' large house was positioned almost equidistant between the advancing Allied lines and the entrenched German forces. Only half an hour separated the two armies. Being caught in the crossfire was a regular hazard, as was the sudden appearance of German patrols scouting for encroaching enemy, seeking supplies, looking for hidden prisoners, or hunting out collaborators.

'Oh, we were crazy,' says Argene today. 'At one point, we had two German soldiers sleeping in the kitchen downstairs, while upstairs at the same time we had seven prisoners of war sleeping in the main bedroom! Our grandfather told the Germans that there was someone very sick upstairs and they shouldn't go up, so they didn't!'

I was with Tom Redhead's son, John, having taken him to Deccio to meet Argene and Beatrice (Dora had passed away a few years ago). Both in their nineties, they were as vibrant as they had been as teenagers.

John abruptly reached out and grasped Beatrice's hand.

'Thank you, thank you for what you did for my dad,' he said.

She smiled broadly, while a delighted Argene shouted, 'Hah, yes! We were crazy back then. Crazy!'

As the ladies ushered us into the house we passed one of the windows, and I noticed the metal grate covering it was pock-marked and dented.

'A bomb,' said Argene, seeing the direction of my gaze. 'They weren't aiming at us, but they used to drop their bombs on the hillside by mistake sometimes. This went off when Dora was baking bread – she had just moved into the next room. She would have died otherwise, no question.'

In the centre of the kitchen table was a large earthenware bowl, and within it a series of small items. Beatrice leant forward and picked out a grey fob watch.

'My dad's watch,' said a delighted John. 'He said that he'd left it here. Can I hold it?'

Beatrice beamed in delight, and placed it on John's out-stretched palm.

'I can't believe that I'm holding this watch,' John murmured. 'Dad talked about it, but I'm amazed that the ladies have kept it for so long.'

He turned it slowly in his hand, a simple watch stamped with a serial number on the side. It was one of hundreds of thousands of watches issued to Allied troops, and yet it was one of a kind, precious beyond measure to the Pieruccini sisters. They had kept it close for seven decades.

'Tom was special,' said Argene. 'We were fond of the other prisoners of course, but Tom was like family to us. Every time he came into the house he would pick a flower from the garden outside and hand it to our mother. We all loved him.'

'Where were the men of the household?' I asked.

'All off fighting in the war,' said Argene. 'We just hoped that if something happened to them, then they would be looked after by strangers the same way we looked after the boys who came to us for help. It was nothing special – just the Christian thing to do. Our duty.'

Despite the protection of the family, the prisoners were finally captured again – happily at some distance from the house, so they didn't compromise the family in the process – and Tom was taken to Florence. Here he was imprisoned in the intimidating Fortezza da Basso. As the guard locked him in his cell, he told Tom that the fortress was ancient, impregnable and that escape was impossible.

Within three days, Tom was on the run again.

Using a bent piece of steel, he and four other prisoners had chipped away the bars from the windows – covering the noise of the work with loud singing – and then drew lots to see who would climb out to face an uncertain fate. Tom's name came up first.

Under cover of darkness, he clambered out of the window and crept through a large central courtyard unobserved, in the process slipping past several guards. He was joined an hour later at the base of the high wall surrounding the fortress by his four companions. They had brought a blanket with them, which was cut into strips and fashioned into a rope, which they duly used to scale the wall. They then negotiated the streets of Florence – heavily patrolled, crawling with the enemy – and headed once again into the mountains. And that is where Tom and a South African prisoner called Johnny met up with the local partisan brigade. Already Tom's adventures read like something out of a sensationalist novel, but with this development, a new chapter of remarkable exploits was about to begin.

In Italy, the fall of Mussolini had encouraged many anti-Fascists to come out of hiding and declare themselves. In the north, *Il Duce*'s return to power within a matter of months forced them to go underground again, or face arrest. Many were caught and executed, but from July 1943 the Italian Resistance had already begun to take shape. It had fertile soil to grow in – in cities and countryside alike, fierce depredations had turned the majority of the population against the regime. In the countryside in particular, the change from traditional indifference to political rule to active resentment of the dictatorship was provoked by the confiscation of food and animals – both working stock and those bred for meat.

This behaviour had another effect: it strengthened the Communist movement in Italy. Thus, yet another dynamic was set up – this one within the Resistance, whose various groups included some which supported the Badoglio government and the King, as well as liberals; socialists; Christian and social democrats. There were also some who promoted Communism as Italy's post-war political engine as well as those, more or less apolitical, whose principal aim was liberation first – politics would come afterwards. Many just fought because they were fed up with seeing their cows and mules taken away, and it mustn't be forgotten that the degree of poverty among mountain *contadini* was such that the loss of one pig could mean ruin. (The grinding poverty of the south described by Carlo Levi in *Christ Stopped at Eboli* could equally well be applied to the rural north.)

These groups fluctuated between uneasy co-operation and (sometimes violent) rivalry. Add those Italians remaining loyal to Mussolini, and the hardcore Fascist paramilitaries of the *Brigata Nera*, and you got what amounted to local civil wars within regional civil wars within a world war. A further complication was that Italy was a new country, scarcely a generation old. The last twenty-one years of that short history had been dominated by Mussolini. By 1943, no one under thirty could remember any other regime than his. His removal from power – even after being reinstated as a puppet dictator by Hitler – meant that a vacuum was created which numerous factions and ideologies moved hastily to fill.

In an attempt to organize, control and give some cohesion to the various resistance groups, a Committee of National Liberation was formed in September 1943, immediately following Italy's formal secession from the Axis. The CLN (in Italian *Comitato di Liberazione Nazionale*) was apolitical, and represented all shades of the non-Fascist political spectrum, united in the aim of the liberation of Italy. The CLN established agencies in cities still under German occupation and these agencies tried to co-ordinate the efforts of partisans within certain designated broad areas or divisions, as well as working with Allied liaison officers embedded within the partisan groups.

In addition to the conflicting political views within the Resistance, there was also a world of difference between the industrial north and the agricultural south, between the city-dweller and the countryman. Accents and dialects were so disparate that a Neapolitan would have as much difficulty in understanding an Apennine farmworker, and vice-versa, as an outsider would. And the outsiders, in this case the Germans on the one hand and the Allies on the other, both had their reasons to mistrust the Italians. In German eyes, the Italians had let them down, even betrayed them. Their apparent ineptitude as fighters had earned them unwarranted contempt in some Allied opinion. Either way, the complexity of the Italian situation entirely escaped most foreigners.

Tom Redhead was one of many escaped POWs who joined the partisans, a decision that was fraught with danger. Why he made this decision is not known – as is so often the case it was not something he discussed even with close family after the war, a measure of the age perhaps, when the right thing to do was keep your emotional cards close to your chest. He may have been coerced into fighting – many escaped prisoners were, as they were considered of great value to the partisans as well-trained servicemen. Or he may have willingly joined the fray. What we do know is that Tom was a formidable individual, and the partisans would have welcomed such a redoubtable fighting figure into their ranks. And so it proved – although initially suspicious of any escaped prisoner due to their fear of German agents, the partisans soon realized that they had someone rather singular in their midst, and before long Tom was taking part in hit and run raids alongside them. For two months, Tom lived with the partisans, until their location – a hut on a Tuscan mountainside – was compromised, and Tom was captured along with several of the battalion and a number of other POWs who had joined them in the fight.

The group – numbering eleven in total – were immediately put up against a wall and, without trial or ceremony of any sort, a firing squad was assembled in front of them. At the very last second, one of their captors came running, waving his arms and shouting. They had realized that they had valuable English POWs among the group, and the order was that they should be spared. Tom and the other prisoners were removed from the line up, and duly witnessed their companions being executed. When one considers the emotional implications of this moment, the shattering impact of watching your brothers in arms being murdered before your very eyes while you are spared, then perhaps his reticence in discussing this phase of his war becomes more understandable. He had fought alongside these men for two months, lived with them in the same rough shelters, broken bread with them, and relied on them wholly in the thick of the fight. They would have undoubtedly talked of life after the war, of their own loved ones, of good times to come, and formed the uniquely strong bonds that are forged in the heat of battle. The survivor's guilt he carried must have been immense, rendering him silent about this event for the rest of his life.

Finding himself once again in a cell, he immediately began to plot their escape. This time the stakes were as high as they could possibly be – the group had been tried by the Germans, and duly sentenced to death. Their brush with death at the hands of the firing squad had, it seemed, just postponed the inevitable.

They were held in the camp for several days awaiting execution, and whenever there were air raids, they were all moved to a small dungeon. Identifying this as a moment when they might make their move, they fashioned coshes out of an old pair of trousers and some sand they had smuggled into their cell (presumably in their pockets while exercising in the prison yard). Sure enough, the sirens wailed later that day, they were hastily moved, and Tom – ever to the fore – led the assault on the guards. Having incapacitated them, he then charged into the office of the camp, knocked out the German personnel there, and stole the keys to all the cells. He released all the other prisoners, except for three Americans who refused to leave (doubtless alarmed by the sight of a large, furious man wielding a trouser leg as a deadly weapon).

The group of escapees managed to make contact with a UK operative in the local area called Major Magee, and found themselves spirited away to the Allied lines.

For his considerable heroism throughout this period of repeated escape and sustained evasion, Tom was awarded the Military Medal. After the war he returned to Hull, and spent the remainder of his life largely unsung, working as a joiner – perfect employment for a large man with powerful hands, a gentle disposition, and memories of many years of creative destruction of any obstacle that stood in his way.

While Tom was fighting with the partisans, the overly-confident Allied invasion from the south had stalled in the face of determined German resistance. The Gustav Line held up the advance until June 1944, and when that was finally breached the Germans fell back on the seemingly impregnable Gothic Line. This ran from a point just south of La Spezia on the west coast, all the way across northern Italy to the Adriatic coastline between Pesaro and Ravenna. The Allied progress wasn't helped by the fact that, following D-Day on 6 June 1944, the Germans hit back on the Western front with everything they had. For a moment, during the Battle of the Bulge at the end of the year, things seemed touch-and-go. In fact, the Germans were out of money and out of resources, and Hitler's vaunted secret weapons – the V1 flying bomb and the V2 rocket – were too little, too late. But, on the ground, no one knew this for sure.

German forces in Italy were under the control of Albert Kesselring – 'Uncle Albert', as the British forces dubbed him – who was a Luftwaffe field marshal, and as such Hitler gave him freer rein in his strategies than he would have given an army officer. The Luftwaffe was effectively a new military arm, and Hitler had been able to stock its officer class with men sympathetic to him. Consequently, he trusted it more. Hitler had described himself in 1943 as 'the greatest war-lord in history' – but the reality was that without the Führer's interference, Kesselring found he could operate much more effectively. By June 1944, Kesselring, increasingly frustrated by partisan activity, ordered that the fight against them be conducted with the 'utmost severity' and promised to protect any commanders who exceeded their 'usual restraint'. He went further in July, issuing a series of orders declaring that there would be reprisals against any civilians helping the partisans – from burning down an entire village if the German army was fired at from that location, to shooting anyone offering the partisans food, shelter or intelligence.

In spite of this, there was one great constant, one consistent badge of honour that the Italian people wear – justifiably – to this day. As the Gothic Line held, the Italian *contadini* took on a new role – they were now not only helpers and guides for escapers and evaders, but aiders and abettors of specialized Allied strike forces operating behind the lines. The co-ordination of these operations became easier as the American OSS and the British SOE (which operated in Italy under the title No. 1 Special Force) were able to set up command centres in Rome (liberated in June 1944) and Florence (September 1944). Allied missions were set up behind German lines, with Allied officers (either escapers or dropped in by parachute) working with the local Resistance. Some escapers worked with the locals on their own initiative until formal contact could be set up with the Allies. In any event, contact between them and Florence (increasingly the centre of operations as the Allies drove north) was established by dropped-in radio transmitters or by use of couriers – intrepid men, often only sixteen or seventeen years old, who knew their local countryside intimately – who weaved their way to and fro across the front line.

The young men of the partisan forces were not trained soldiers, of course, and they fought with rudimentary weapons until they could either 'liberate' more sophisticated arms from their oppressors (the expression used for anything thus acquired was: 'I found it under a tree') or get them via Allied air drops. There was no military discipline at first, and partisans had to make up their own minds about what was morally and ethically the right thing to do. Some of the more hard-line Resistance groups had no compunction in killing any of the enemy taken prisoner, whether Fascist Italian or German. Such actions didn't help when reprisals came, and whole villages were razed, their occupants slaughtered in massacres of unrelenting horror and brutality. For their part, Resistance and organized Allied military attacks on the Germans had to be weighed against the possibility of provoking such reprisals against entirely innocent civilian settlements. It was a moral dilemma beyond measure – engage with the enemy for the higher cause, but in doing so be aware that horrendous acts would be meted out when your operation was complete. The Italian Fascists, more feared and loathed than even the SS, had a chilling name for such reprisals – a *rastrellomento*, a raking.

Such attacks against the Germans were nevertheless vital, since they had the important psychological effect of preying on any remaining sense of security the enemy might have had, as well as tying up large numbers of enemy soldiers who might have been deployed to greater effect elsewhere. As the chaotic political and military scene in northern Italy flexed and pulsed on a nearly daily basis, the Gothic Line was becoming increasingly important as a point of focus, a physical barrier where the destiny of two opposing armies, and the future of an entire nation, would be decided.

The Apennine mountains, over which the Gothic Line stretched, were home to a large number of village farming communities, largely isolated from the rest of the world. Despite the constant threat of reprisals, the locals unstintingly helped evaders, and the escape routes across the mountains set up for POWs were smoothly run by local guides. The area was a stronghold of the Resistance, with one of its crucial roles being the diversion of defensive forces from the Gothic Line.

One area of vital strategic importance was the section of the Apennine Mountains that overlooked the port of La Spezia. This was the westernmost point of the Gothic Line, and potentially an area of vulnerability that the advancing Allies might exploit – the mountains there presented less of an immense natural barrier, allowing large weapons to be moved by rail and road. The ports of Genoa, La Spezia, Viareggio and Livorno were essential for transporting supplies to the Germans, but the Americans were putting pressure on the region as they made good progress up the coast. Against this backdrop, some of the most heroic actions of the war took place, often small in scale, but devastating in effect.

I travelled to the Rossano Valley, approximately thirty kilometres north-west of La Spezia, to research the story of a few key individuals operating in this area to weaken the Gothic Line. In doing so, they altered the momentum of an entire theatre of war. They could not have achieved their objectives – nor could the soldiers involved have made their escape – without the collaboration of the local partisans and wider populace. Every class of society had its reasons for hating the Fascist regime, but aid was not given just because of that: it was given in a spirit of simple humanity and decency – a stark contrast to the barbaric behaviour meted out by the occupiers and their Fascist sympathizers. War, as ever, brought out the very best and the very worst in people, many of whom had previously lived side by side in relative harmony. And yet even the cruellest reprisal failed to weaken their resolve: if anything – and perhaps this shouldn't be surprising – it was strengthened, and stood defiant in the face of escalating horrors.

Giovanni Tognarelli is a stout figure in his early nineties, giving the impression even today of immense solidity and strength. He met me outside his flour mill in Piagna, a small village set in the foothills of the mountains. His features were burnt to a deep brown by nearly a century of working under the Italian sun, and his eyes sparkled in delight as we met. His handshake was firm, and his smile radiant.

Giovanni was – indeed, he is – very much a survivor. Unbowed by the horrors he witnessed during the war, there is something elemental about him. During my travels through Italy, I was to meet many such people – those who defied the enemy, and lived long lives after the war. I wondered briefly if the two factors might be connected in some way – an indefatigable spirit and an ability to adapt to any circumstance (and indeed prevail against it) might be used to defy the onset of age as much as the ravages of an occupying army.

My reverie was interrupted by Giovanni, who led me down a short hill to the mill. It sits at a sharp bend in the road, perched on the edge of a green slope that falls away gently into the valley floor. This is far from the harsh landscape of the uplands, and it is easy to see the impact of generations of local farmers in the elegantly shaped terraces and shaded groves of olive and chestnut trees. The latter were particularly significant in the war, as Giovanni was quick to point out.

'The Germans came and burnt all the wheat fields,' he said. 'They killed the animals, too. They burnt the villages of Chiesa, Liguria and Castoglia. In Zeri, they rounded people up and shot them as if they were wild boar. Local people were frightened, they had nothing left to eat, so they came to us. Come, I'll show you.'

He led me through a pair of ancient double doors, cracked and weathered by the freezing nights and blistering noons of the mountains. It was a short journey in terms of distance, but seemed to span centuries – mills such as this have worked these valleys for many hundreds of years. During the war, they came into their own, changing from local artisan industry into oasis of survival and beacons of hope for so many of the surrounding population. The mills fed many local families, and indeed the partisans in the hills as well as the prisoners being hidden in nearby buildings. I suspected that this room had changed very little since the war – and indeed in the decades before that – with its three immense stone grindstones sitting in the gloom, and large wooden chutes overhead to deliver the chestnuts into a hole in the middle of each. The entire space – the beams, the floor, the windows and the grinding mechanism itself – was coated in a layer of fine white powder. It even hung in the air, twisting in the dim light, spinning and tumbling in the wake of our passing.

'We fed everyone from here,' said Giovanni proudly, touching one of the stones with a hand as weathered as the rock beneath it. 'We turned no one away. The partisans were accustomed to food made from normal flour, not from chestnuts, but they ate it anyway! We made bread, chickpea polenta – everything required to feed the people who depended on us.'

'Weren't you afraid of being caught?' I asked.

'Yes, we were afraid, but my father was a brave man. He had been known as being anti-Fascist before the war, so everyone knew he would do the right thing. But it wasn't just him, everyone helped, the entire valley.'

He led me back outside and waved me to a seat set against the wall of the mill. With a brief exhalation of breath he sat beside me, and indicated a building in the middle distance, obscured almost entirely by trees.

'We were sheltering a group of prisoners in that barn,' he said, 'when one of them – an Australian – broke his ankle, so we moved him to my grandparents' house. The *carabinieri* launched a random search, and that was the first place they looked! I thought it was all over, but one of them was actually a local informant for my family, and he was the one who looked into the room where the Australian was lying in bed. He simply told the warrant officer in charge that he hadn't seen anyone, but that was a close shave. Both of my grandparents were in their eighties, but they would have been shot without question.'

After a brief moment of contemplative silence, he gestured for me to stand and we moved over to edge of the road, where it overlooked the valley – a deep-green, verdant dale beneath us. From our lofty viewpoint, we could see for several miles, and as

Giovanni talked, he indicated the hiding places, the tucked-away barns and sheds that dotted the landscape before us. In doing so, he painted a picture of a local population mobilized for one purpose alone – to defy the occupiers by assisting the Allies in any way they could.

'Oh yes, everyone was helping,' he said. 'You had to be very careful of course, as there were informers, but this valley – our valley – would do anything for an escaping prisoner or a soldier working behind the lines.'

He described local boys being used as couriers, himself included, and how Italian soldiers left behind after the armistice of September 1943 were taken in by local families and used as messengers and secret observers. He described covert moves of large groups of prisoners, and of friends in the police force and district administration informing local people of every decision taken by the occupiers. It occurred to me as he talked that the Germans were never going to win, never going to overcome this valley and the people within it. The network was simply too strong, too complex, too refined, and too entrenched.

What is truly remarkable is that Giovanni's valley was not by any means an isolated case – entire communities and regions created networks of safe houses and couriers, and developed their own covert signals and intelligence networks. There are those that may question Italy's role in the war, but what is beyond doubt is the heroic response of the majority of its civilian population, typified by the indestructible figure beside me, gesturing animatedly at the idyllic valley that had defied an army.

CHAPTER ELEVEN

Gordon Lett's International Battalion

It looked entirely nondescript to me, a rather tatty section of wall no more than 200 metres long. It abuts a busy road in northern Tuscany, close to the town of Borgo a Mozzano, running along the side of a dusty car park next to a sports field. But it is a symbol, a defiant echo from the past. This short section of cement and brick is the last piece of the Gothic Line that still stands, the fading signature of a structure that once stretched from coast to coast and was one of the most intimidating defensive lines in Europe. The plan was to stop the Allied advance in its tracks by fortifying the only points where vehicles and heavy weapons could pass – the narrow valley floors, the gorges, the tracks, and the roads. Any movement through the confines of these areas would soon run into the near impregnable barrier of the man-made defences; to mass against the wall and the wire was to be pounded mercilessly by well-established gun emplacements set high in the hills.

I turned off the road and parked the car, climbing out into the still heat of an Italian afternoon. The hot air hung heavy and listless around me, trapped in the confines of the valley, a blanket of oppressive heat with no avenue of escape. To my left as I walked towards the wall was a precipitous rock face rising sharply from the railway line, and to my right a river, beyond which the mountains stretched away to a lofty horizon.

As I got closer, I saw that the wall was much higher than I had realized. Immense at the base, sloping to a ridge of concrete on top still set with rusting eyelets for barbed wire, it towered several feet over my head. I placed one hand on it, pushing against it, some instinct making me want to test its mettle. The wall was only one part of a multi-layered defence system which, in some places, lay fifteen kilometres deep, with every hollow, twist, crag and gulley another stronghold, another killing ground. It had taken 15,000 people, many of them working under conditions of virtual slave labour, several years to construct. Along its bristling length were over 2,300 heavily fortified machine-gun nests, 479 mortar and anti-tank positions, miles of anti-tank ditches, layer upon layer of minefields, and of course the mountains themselves – an eighty-kilometre-long natural barrier, with peaks over 2000 metres in height.

Take out the brutal context of its construction, and this last section of wall before me was strangely admirable in its stolid persistence. Even in this land of soaring peaks and steepling slopes, the line was biblical in its scale, its immensity challenging the terrain through which it snaked. The Gothic Line was a scar on the landscape, an echo of a time when an occupying army used all of its ingenuity to divide the Italian nation. This final section of wall is a last concrete weal, a reminder of a period in Italian history that can never truly be erased.

I knew that the patch of earth where I stood would have been covered by gun emplacements, but none were immediately apparent. By scouring the steep hillside above the railway line I eventually made out a cave entrance, tucked away, heavily disguised, but unmistakable in its intent. This would have been the site of ambush, the point from which murderous fire would have been unleashed.

I left the car park and made the distinctly dicey crossing of the road, running the gauntlet of speeding cars and irate cyclists. On the other side, I made my way under the elegant arc of a railway bridge, and followed a short leafy lane to a barred gate. This was set low in the rock wall, and was a fearsome affair of thick steel and interlocking bars. A cool breeze wafted out of the deep shaft beyond it – plainly this was more than a simple cavern. It was the beginning of a tunnel that burrowed into the heart of the mountain, emerging higher up on the rock face to gather the breeze.

I lifted the gate to one side and stooped to make my way through the entrance. Neat concrete steps took me down into a series of switchbacks and sharp turns designed to be easy to defend, and almost impossible to attack. Each turn represented a strong point where you could make a brief stand then fall back, as your enemy tried to advance, stooped and low, turning into ambush after ambush as they inched along the confines of the stone passage before them.

The tunnel soon opened out into a large chamber, giving me a chance to straighten up, clutching the small of my back as I did so. These larger areas were used as living spaces and for storage. The men occupying this labyrinth knew that they would fight the enemy to the death within the mountain.

A longer, much wider staircase led upwards from the chamber, and I saw the first glimpse of daylight ahead. Climbing towards it, out of the claustrophobic gloom beneath, I emerged into a gun emplacement. This was a monument to functional design, with a perfectly level floor for the gun itself, and a neat side chamber for the storage of ammunition. A perfectly squared entrance looked out over the valley, and it was a considerable relief to walk out onto the gunnery platform itself, into the fresh air and sunshine.

Since the war, a crude barrier of breeze blocks had been built in front of the emplacement – presumably to stop people straying onto the railway line and road below. I looked back at the entrance and realized that the rock face above it was actually carefully disguised concrete, ridged and pitted by hand to make it blend into the cliff. This was a structure where nothing was left to chance, and it seemed to me that the surprise for the enemy in the valley floor beneath would have been absolute.

I climbed onto a small ledge that gave me a vantage point overlooking the wall, and there – laid out beneath me – was the killing zone. The ground leading up to this section of the wall would have been cleared, meticulously paced, measured, and marked. The gun crew would have been drilled to perfection. And then they simply would have waited, the trap baited, the enemy siphoned and channelled by distant valleys towards this patch of bare earth, death hung high in the hills overlooking it.

Although much vaunted as a truly impregnable barrier, a vast killing zone that would either force the Allies to withdraw or create the necessity for negotiations, no defensive line of any length in military history has ever been totally impervious to enemy assault. The Gothic Line was in fact breached on several occasions, with one such action being the Battle of Rimini in September 1944, but such was the nature of the defences that the Germans could withdraw in an orderly manner before counter-attacking to devastating effect.

Although in control of these lesser incursions into his defences, Kesselring was keenly aware of the crippling effect that the breaching of the entire barrier would have on the German campaign in Europe as a whole. The damage would be as much psychological as military. He was so keenly aware of this, in fact, that he renamed it the Green Line, perceptively noting that should something fail that was so closely associated with Germanic culture – signalling the fall of Gothic identity itself – then the impact on morale at home would be catastrophic.

From an Allied perspective, it had become apparent that something beyond an all-out assault was needed. What was required was a daring military operation that would create confusion behind the entrenched positions of the enemy. This would lead to the diversion of enemy assets and troops, and thus weaken the barrier for further direct assaults from the south.

For this plan, the planets aligned in late 1944, through the work of one remarkable man – Gordon Lett – and the arrival of six Dakota transport planes flying low over the Rossano Valley. From them leapt a troop of SAS, descending into the chaotic world beneath, and into a mission that would cement their place in military history.

Major Gordon Lett (1910–1989) was born in Papua New Guinea and raised in Australia and India. He had an enormous love for mountains – prior to the war he led two Himalayan expeditions and was a Fellow of the Royal Geographical Society. He was also a professional soldier with the East Surrey Regiment who was taken prisoner close to Tobruk in North Africa. Still a relatively young man – he was in his early thirties – Lett had been a POW at Campo PG 21 Chieti, a particularly tough camp in the Abruzzo region, but was subsequently transferred to Campo PG 29 Viano in the Reggio Emilia district of Emilia-Romagna, some sixty kilometres west of Bologna.

At Chieti, he'd made the acquaintance of Bob Walker Brown (1919–2009), an officer in the 2nd Battalion, Highland Light Infantry who had been captured in North Africa in June 1942.

They were to meet again, in truly extraordinary circumstances, later in the war. Walker Brown escaped from Chieti, re-joining Allied ranks in early October 1943. He was lucky to do so. When Chieti was abandoned by its guards following the armistice, its Senior British Officer (SBO), Colonel Marshall, enforced the Stay Put order. Faced with a near mutiny as a result, Marshall threatened any POW who attempted escape with a court martial, and appointed his own set of guards to enforce the order. The result was that when German paratroopers arrived, they found about 1,300 men waiting for them, more or less passively. Showing precisely the sort of qualities of judgement and audacity that would serve him well in future operations, Walker Brown and a few fellow POWs on the camp's Escape Committee had hidden in a tunnel and broke out of Chieti that night. The other men in the camp – POWs simply obeying an order from a misguided senior officer – were duly sent to camps in Poland and Germany.

At Viano, it was a different story. The Italian camp commandant there, an aristocratic older officer of the pre-Mussolini era who also happened to be an Anglophile, communicated news of the armistice to his prisoners, told them that all telephone links with Rome had been cut, and permitted their SBO to advise them to take to the hills. Gordon Lett did so, in the company of Sergeant Bob Blackmore and Rifleman Mick Miscallef. Lett was not the kind of officer who would choose to associate exclusively with other officers, instead preferring to pick his companions on merit. The initial plan was to make for the Italian coast and await the arrival of the Allies – then believed imminent. But fate had decreed that Lett would play more than a bit-part role in the region through which he travelled, and indeed in the wider conflict that unfolded around it. He was an individual of singular quality, one who found himself in a situation perfectly matched to his abilities and background. On 30 September 1943, after a three-week march, he arrived in the Rossano Valley in the rugged Apuan Apennines, the mountains which look down on La Spezia and the coast, about twenty-five kilometres to the south as the crow flies. Lett was to stay there for eighteen months.

What confronted him were conditions as bad, or worse, than any he'd ever seen, either in India or Africa. Added to a life which was already hard and poverty-stricken were curfews, aggressive sweeps by the enemy to round up dissenters, heavy taxes and the appropriation of animals and food from a population already struggling to make ends meet. These measures had long since made the locals impervious to the dire threats and clumsy anti-Allied propaganda issued by the Germans and the Fascist authorities, if they'd ever paid any attention to them in the first place. Despite the oppression and the unpleasant attentions of OVRA, Mussolini's secret police, the locals remained stalwart in their support of any escapers whom they could help; even though, it has to be said, some escapers were heedless of the sacrifices and risks taken on their behalf. Not so Lett, who could already speak Italian and developed a great sympathy for the locals, who in turn immediately took him and his companions under their wing.

Lett's arrival in the region could not have been more impeccably timed. The legal government in Brindisi had no power here in the north, where the Fascist Republic of Salò held sway under the Germans, and the *contadini* found themselves leaderless and confused. In the interests of self-preservation, they fought back instinctively by helping the Allies, who at least treated them like human beings, and to whom they looked for liberation. Their actions were not so much aggressive as passively obstructive – hiding livestock and food stores from their oppressors and leading German search parties astray in the mountains. But they had to be careful. In these tiny communities everybody knew one another; yet no one knew for sure who could be trusted outside family circles or who might be a Fascist informer. The enemy had placed a bounty of 5,000 lire plus two months' supply of food and tobacco on the head of any escaper – a princely reward – whereas anyone caught abetting an escaper faced summary execution.

Operating in the area were a toxic combination of the *carabinieri* (not all of whom could be trusted), *Brigata Nera*, the Waffen-SS and German-army alpine troops. It was a deadly environment, entirely unforgiving of mistakes, but nonetheless one that was crying out for a leader to rally resistance.

One thing the villagers did have going for them was that for most Fascist Italians and for the Germans, the territory was forbidding, unfamiliar, and deeply hostile. Far from being able to fraternize with the locals, as Allied soldiers could in southern Italy, the Germans shut themselves up in their barracks at night and never went out alone. They knew they were hated, and they knew they were losing. As time passed, more and more soldiers conscripted into Mussolini's Republican Army also deserted, and morale among those who remained sank.

Lett's original intention had been to re-join the Allies at Genoa or Leghorn, where they were expected to invade. As time passed a coastal invasion was looking increasingly unlikely, but he still wanted to escape back to his own forces and was in the process of trying to determine the best way of doing this when, towards the end of October, he was approached by an Italian from the CLN office in Genoa with a view to his co-ordinating Resistance in the Rossano area. Lett had already been involved in a number of close calls whilst on the run, and had been helped greatly by local families. His natural authority and military experience meant that he had also become a focal point for any locals wanting to resist the Fascists, and as such he embraced the chance to create a more coherent force. He immediately set about forming an International Battalion, composed of Italians and many other nationalities caught up in the war. The first recruits were Britons and Poles, but later this core was joined by Danes, Dutchmen, Frenchmen, Russians and Yugoslavs. Some were escaped POWs, although many more were fugitive sailors from ships seized by the Germans in the port of Genoa, who had contacted the CLN there and were duly sent to join Lett's rapidly expanding force.

In time, the region in which the battalion operated became a sort of unofficial republic, with Lett – whom the locals called 'Luigi' – as president. It even developed a rudimentary medical and legal infrastructure. This helped the locals, who were seeking any form of authority and governance, and it is to Lett's eternal credit that he managed to establish order and a sense of structure so quickly – which also created stability for the battalion's power-base.

It wasn't only the nationalities which were disparate. In his book, *Rossano: An Adventure of the Italian Resistance*, Lett recalled that the battalion's complement included 'a barrister, two doctors, a lawyer, an ex-Consul-General . . . several fishermen . . . an Arab merchant seaman from Eritrea, a couple of artists, a musician, shopkeepers and cafe-owners, some of whom owned cafes or shops in London and Scotland, a butcher, a theological student, a dentist . . .' The list goes on, and also takes in the Italian members of the force – *carabinieri*, railway workers and of course the peasant farmers of the villages of the Rossano Valley: Chiesa di Rossano, Buzzo, Castello, Zeri, Calice, Torpiana and more. These recruits were drawn from locations scattered over the mountains between the garrison town of Pontremoli, incidentally the local headquarters of German and Fascist Italian troops, and the coast. Unequivocally, the *contadini* were the backbone of the operation, and at Chiesa and Zeri the inhabitants of the villages paid a terrible price for their compatriots' decision to join the fight. Many other small towns and villages shared a similar fate.

The battalion was ready for action by the end of October, and though only armed at first with a handful of old-fashioned rifles and some 'red devil' Italian army hand-grenades, its presence in the valley gave a huge boost to the morale of the civilian population in and around Rossano. These locals were, as a rule, grindingly poor, and though oppressed by the occupier and Fascist Italians alike, never lost their sense of humour, their generosity or their solidarity. The battalion, however, always had to use their discretion when taking the locals into their confidence. News travelled fast in the mountains and there was always the risk that it would reach the wrong ears.

War Office orders were that no liberated POWs should remain in Italy unless they were on special duty, but when news of Lett's force reached London, SOE and MI9 ratified the battalion's existence, and with good reason. By May 1944, the force had grown to 130 men (though this number fluctuated with the fortunes of war). Thanks to Lett's inspirational leadership and his ability to recruit perceptively at a local level, as well as seek local supplies, it was by now a well-armed guerrilla force, billeted among the houses of several villages, ready to assemble for actions against the enemy. They had no uniform, but they did have a badge: a combination Union Jack and Italian flag, which was sewn on the right shoulder of a member's tunic, shirt or jacket. The great majority of partisans also sported beards, of which they were very proud.

Hidden among the dense chestnut forests of the mountains, the fruit of whose trees provided the staple food of the region, their tactic was to make a foray, strike hard, and get out quickly, disappearing into the woods before the enemy had time to give chase. Attacks were not always carried out with military precision. The owner of a local hostelry, who was generally tipsy on his own wine, on at least one occasion went into battle roaring drunk, only able to navigate by holding onto the tail of his mule, which at the time had more sense than he did. The battle over, and sobered up, his memory was of having been to a terrific *fiesta*.

The CLN, as and when it could, provided equipment and funds. Some of the money came from the big banks in Genoa, which one might cynically say knew which way the wind was blowing by now. And so, by May 1944, the battalion had made several successful attacks on patrols moving in and out of Pontremoli, and on 15 June launched a successful raid on the Fascist garrison guarding the Teglia Dam, which provided electricity for the entire Magra Valley.

In addition to combat duty, MI9's 'A' Force assigned the battalion the duty of acting as a centre for escapers who had made their way into the mountains, providing local guides to take them to safety by various routes. 'A' Force was actually the department assigned to deception operations, but this blurring of responsibility between forces and groups seems to have been a characteristic of MI9 throughout the war. An escape line, known as Ratberry Three, was established and ran from September to December 1944. One partisan brigade – the Val di Vara, led by Dani Bucchioni – took over 300 escapers across the mountains to freedom along this route. Lett's ragtag battalion of lost souls and brave locals had transformed itself into a fighting force of some capability and a rapidly growing reputation, both among the beleaguered Italian population and – alarmingly – the Germans.

Lett was given a codename by the British – Blundell Violet – and the status of the battalion as a military mission was confirmed. Two Italian radio operators were dispatched to join him, and the mission was formally charged with the care of escapers, information gathering, support of local independent partisan groups and liaison between these and the Allies, in the event of an Allied military attack force being sent into the territory to perform specialized actions against the enemy. This eventuality was to arise soon enough.

Fast progress was being made by Lett, but it wasn't always smooth. Unable to pursue and track down the partisan and battalion forces, the enemy reacted by organizing a series of raids. Troops of *Brigata Nera* and Waffen-SS would descend in force on villages suspected of harbouring guerrilla fighters and 'punish' them. The idea was to beat the locals into submission, but the extreme cruelty, ferocity and violence of such raids only crystallized the locals' hatred and hardened their determination to be rid of their oppressors. Remaining steadfast in the face of what was done to them required adamantine spirit. At the beginning of August 1944, the village of Chiesa di Rossano, where Lett's HQ had been up until then, was attacked and badly damaged. The HQ, at the Palazzo degli Schiavi, was destroyed.

But this was just the start of a period of violence that escalated rapidly to acts of medieval ferocity. August saw two raids that came to define for ever Fascist brutality in the Apennine region – the memory of which will linger for generations to come.

On 12 August, Waffen-SS units arrived at the village of Sant'Anna di Stazzema in the province of Lucca, about forty-five kilometres south-east of La Spezia, in order to exact retribution for various acts of resistance and sabotage in the region and as part of a 'cleansing' operation aimed at local partisans. Under the command of SS-*Hauptsturmführer* Anton Galler, the Germans rounded up and killed over 500 people, including 107 children. They were either machine-gunned in groups or herded into cellars and killed there with hand-grenades. The village was then burnt to the ground, and all the livestock belonging to it was slaughtered.

The entire operation took three hours. The average age of the SS men involved was twenty-two. In 2005 ten former SS men, then in their eighties, were convicted *in absentia* at a military court in La Spezia, and sentenced to life – but were never extradited from Germany, and never went to prison. In 2012, the German judiciary dropped its investigation of the atrocity, though eight of the seventeen known perpetrators were still alive at the time. The decision caused outrage in Italy. The Sant'Anna massacre is among the worst recorded of the entire war.

On 24 August, a similar force, this time including the *Brigata Nera*, arrived in no fewer than ninety lorries at the village of Vinca, not far from Carrara, and proceeded to round up the villagers and shoot them. Vinca was a known staging post on the escape routes south over the Razore and Altissimo mountains. This massacre extended over three days, and the *Brigata Nera* men were harsher even than the Germans. It seemed that the ferocity of such reprisals – even when carried out by Italians, on Italians – simply knew no bounds. This village, ancient and venerable, occupied by proud dynasties with long traditions, was never to be the same again.

It was overcast as I approached Vinca, the sky hanging grey and heavy over the rocky cauldron created by the mountains that surround the village. On one of the last hairpins I pulled over and took in the scene – one of staggering beauty and grandeur. It is easy to see why a human settlement sprung up here, the last foothold at the head of the valley before precipitous rock slopes begin, a place to gather your thoughts and your energy before entering a vertical world. Over time, simple shelters grew up, then houses and streets, and the inhabitants began to farm the lower slopes and nearby valleys, growing chestnut and olive trees and grazing sheep. Marble quarries were hewn out of the base of the cliffs. What had been a staging post, a base camp, became a village. This was never a prosperous place, more a community of subsistence farmers and labourers as well as a haven offering welcome respite for the traveller, but nonetheless the village became a bustling little community.

The scattering of houses before me were a collection of ancient walls and red roofs, features characteristic of many villages in the region and the perfect complement to the green of the forests on the lower mountain slopes, as well as the dark grey of the marble hills that overshadowed the entire scene. It looked entirely tranquil, timeless and serene.

I re-started the engine and drove into the village itself, parking in the deserted main thoroughfare. Like so many modern rural settlements in Italy, Vinca teeters on the edge of oblivion. Once home to 400 people, only ninety-five residents remain – most of them elderly. There are an estimated 6,000 deserted villages and hamlets in Italy as a whole, with a further 15,000 in danger of becoming derelict as the inhabitants abandon the old ways to move into the cities. The modern Vinca is typical of this exodus, and the main street was eerily quiet as I walked through it, with the only sign of human habitation an old lady who opened the shutters of a high window to hang out her washing. I waved as I passed, but she did not acknowledge me.

I turned off the paved main road and into an ancient warren of tiny alleys, low arches and shady passes. Old steps weaved crazy angles beneath my feet, taking me to the heart of the village itself, the epicentre of a truly barbarous crime scene.

I had arranged to meet one of the survivors of the massacre, an old man called Andrea. He had asked that we meet on the terrace of his house at the edge of Vinca, a small cottage overlooking a bend in the road as it climbed into the foothills. As I arrived I saw that his family had turned out for the occasion, which made life considerably easier, as his daughter could translate for us both.

Andrea stood as I walked through the gate and smiled at me through a thin grey moustache. Although stooped and bent with time, he still moved with confidence and strength, something I had noticed as a characteristic of the older generation in the mountains of Italy, where every walk is a workout, and family are never more than a street away.

'*Buongiorno*, Andrea,' I said. 'How are you?'

'I am old,' he replied, 'but I am happy.'

He cackled in delight at the reply, and waved me without ceremony back through the gate.

'Come,' he said, 'I want to take you to a special place.'

We walked along the path cut into the side of the hill, a contour line made real. Either side of us were allotments and enclosures – using the folds and fissures in this landscape to eke out a living from the land is as much a feature of Vinca today as it ever was.

We quickly passed through the village, traversing a neat line through its centre, and ended up at a kink in the path where it intersected a small stream – a tranquil glade with an old stone enclosure carved into the hill next to it. Large pine trees overhead meant that we were hidden from the glare of the sun, and with the water alongside it created a natural place to stop, to rest, and to talk.

Andrea led me into the stone enclosure and turned to face me. Behind him was a fresco cut out of marble, a stylized version of a mother holding up a child. As he spoke the cool of the shade assumed a chill, and the dim light a darkness.

'It was here,' he said suddenly, eyes blazing, 'that they rounded up women, children and infants, and from up there –' he indicated a rocky ledge overlooking where we stood – 'that they machine-gunned them.'

As he spoke he edged closer to me, so the final words were uttered close to my face. The anger and the sorrow emanated from him, every word emphasized, the memory vividly alive. I didn't know what to say.

'And you know,' he continued, 'they say it was the *Brigata Nera*, but actually it was more than that. The commander of the battalion was married to a Vinca woman.'

'Unbelievable,' I muttered. 'Did they ever find him after the war?'

'I have not finished,' he said fiercely, aware of the importance of his words and the triviality of mine. 'She left him, and he visited the village a month before the massacre. He spoke to the mayor, and said "I will see you in four weeks". When he came back, he found his father-in-law and shot him himself.'

At this he paused, overcome with emotion, before visibly gathering himself to once again lift his head and look me in the eye.

'These men. They shot a two-day-old baby by throwing it in the air as the mother watched. They cut the stomach of a pregnant woman, eight months passed, and tore her child out. They shot an eighty-five-year-old. They tied the old men to wagon wheels and shot them in the legs so their own weight strangled them. They played music as they did this, and had a party when the massacre was done. They were. . .' he paused again, for once not looking at me directly but staring into the ground at his feet '. . . they were mad, they were like mad animals.'

As he talked, I realized that he was not simply telling me the story, he was making me a witness. Andrea knew full well he was inspiring another person to tell the world of Vinca, to spread the tale over time and space, to keep it alive when he was gone.

'I lost sixteen relatives that day,' he said, more quietly. 'I was away with the sheep in another valley, I heard the shooting and

I hid for three days. When I came home it was over. Three days of slaughter. We had to burn the bodies, as they had started to decompose.'

The energy went out of him at that moment. He rolled his hand at me, and pointed at his watch, looking absurdly large on his bony wrist.

'My animals, I must feed my animals.'

I began to thank him, but he simply smiled at me and reached out to pat me gently on my arm, his work done.

'*Ciao*, Monty, *ciao*.'

He walked out of the enclosure, turning back along the ancient path that hugged the hills of Vinca to continue his timeless daily ritual.

There is a memorial for those killed in the massacre at the northern end of the village, dominating the cemetery and overlooking the valley. It faces in the direction from where the Fascists came, a sentinel at the head of the pass. It is a simple memorial, a large white marble wall with the names and ages of all 174 people killed etched upon it – 144 of whom were women and children. The names are grouped not in families, but in categories of age. Four of the dead were under the age of one and a further eleven were under the age of ten. The monument shows that this was no act of fury, no random backlash, but systematic slaughter by men possessed.

The story of Vinca is truly beyond reason and imagination for someone such as me, raised in the tranquil surrounds of the Western world after the Second World War – ours has indeed been a gilded generation. Soon the last eyewitnesses of the horrors here will be gone; indeed the stubborn longevity of survivors such as Andrea is in itself an act of defiance against the very worst acts of their oppressors. But with their inevitable passing there is a danger that the atrocity of Vinca will itself slip quietly into history, becoming just another sepia-tinted episode of a distant and different time.

But if the rattle of the machine guns here – aimed at defence-less and innocent women, children and babies – is to have any meaning, or any value to mankind, then the story of Vinca must continue to be told without flinching. A new generation – pushed further towards extreme political ideology by the mass movement of people and straitened economic times in Europe – needs to understand just how short the journey is from rhetoric to convic-tion of beliefs, to 'them' and 'us', and so to mass murder.

Although the International Battalion under Gordon Lett had been so successful that its actions had given rise to a rumour among the enemy that a large force of Allied paratroops had been dropped into the region, in reality it faced problems on the ground. Rivalries – usually political – between the brigades made them less efficient, and efficiency was paramount at a time when drops of arms, medical and other supplies by the RAF and the USAAF were becoming more frequent. A drop could be a hit-and-miss operation, sometimes failing because those on the ground hadn't the means to signal to the pilots, or because to light a signal fire at the time of the drop would draw the attention of the enemy. Rivalry between groups could mean fighting over dropped supplies, or stealing from one another. Political rivalries were a fluctuating but constant thorn in the side of those whose aim was to unify the Resistance. Supplies were vital: none of the freedom fighters, whether Italian or foreign, had anything like the right kind of kit for the conditions in the mountains, especially in winter. The locals were hardened to the punishing cold, but not to the extent of fighting battles in it. Boots were among the most valued pieces of equipment 'liberated' from the enemy. As for transport, they used mules, nicknaming them 'Rossano jeeps'.

To facilitate co-ordination between the brigades, the CLN bureau in La Spezia dispatched Colonel Mario Fontana (1897–1948) to the area. Fontana and Lett worked together to achieve the far-from-easy goal of uniting the disparate groups around them, at which point the area was designated the Fourth partisan Zone. Unity became more important, as repeated attacks on enemy targets resulted in a German counter-offensive.

The hideous raids of August did nothing to quench the spirit either of the locals or the Resistance. As the summer of 1944 gave way to autumn, the number of deserters from Mussolini's 'little Republic' army increased to the extent that they couldn't be handled by the International Battalion, or the partisans in general. Although it was tempting to welcome them into the ranks of the partisans, the latter were in no mood to accept last-minute converts. This attitude was hardened by news from La Spezia of the treatment meted out to prisoners taken in the *rastrellamenti* by the ironically named *Maggiore* Mario Carità of the *Brigata Nera*. Carità was an expert in extreme torture who had set a bounty of 50,000 lire on Gordon Lett's head. Lett responded by offering a bounty of double that for Carità's. In the end, it was Carità who lost the game: surprised in bed with his mistress by US troops at Castelrotto on 19 May 1945, he was shot dead in the ensuing gun battle. He was forty-four years old.

The biggest problem of late 1944 remained the fractured political nature of the various partisan groups, whose individual funding was now controlled by the political parties grouping under the legitimate Badoglio government in the liberated south. This led to an unequal and often ill-advised distribution of funds, which it was beyond the power of Colonel Fontana or Gordon

Lett to control. As a foreigner, Lett, of course, could have no say in this debate over funding. Their situation was going downhill.

So far, the International Battalion and the increasingly involved local partisan brigades had been so successful that they had also achieved an important psychological aim – severely rattling the enemy. But they did not want to lose the advantage – a highly trained force was required to drive home any gains, to stir the hornets' nest, and to draw in yet more enemy to a region that was becoming a key battleground in the fight for Italy as a whole. It was now undeniable that to push home any strategic gains made by the International Battalion, they needed outside help.

It was vital that the western end of the Green Line should not be strengthened by the enemy – far from it, the plan was actually to weaken it as far as possible. To this end, major disruptions of German convoys and supply lines using that part of the Via Aurelia (the modern SS1 road), which linked Livorno with Genoa, were necessary. Specialist forces would be needed.

Thus, it came as a huge relief when, shortly before Christmas, news of a dramatic and anxiously awaited kind arrived. The War Office was sending in the SAS.

CHAPTER TWELVE

The SAS and Operation Galia

Operation Galia was the second and most successful of three SAS actions carried out in the Rossano region between late 1944 and the end of the war. The mission was essentially to disrupt any planned German counter-attack on the port city of Livorno, which was defended only by the US Army's African-American 92nd Infantry Division, and to tie up German manpower while the Allies rallied. By pulling German forces away from the Green Line, it was also hoped that this diversion would create a window of opportunity for a larger scale Allied assault.

Gordon Lett first heard about Galia – though such an operation had been long hoped for and half expected – from a message received on a radio borrowed from a nearby American mission, during an encounter with its members on 22 December 1944. Lett had for some time been asking London for a military mission in the region, with a request for three to four hundred troops to exploit the gains he had already made with his own force. So the news of support was most welcome. The receipt of the message was even more significant since Lett's own radio had broken down and he'd been out of contact with Allied command for some time. Unbeknownst to him, this absence of communication had raised suspicions among the intelligence community back in London that he may have been compromised, although of course this was not passed on in any transmissions.

The signal informed Lett that a unit of thirty-three men from 2nd Regiment SAS, were to be dropped into his area five days later, on 27 December. An immediate response was required to let command know that he'd be ready to receive them. Almost in tears with relief, Lett replied: '. . . ready to receive twenty seventh repeat twenty seventh stop signal letter H for Harry repeat H for Harry and British and Italian flags on field already indicated stop regards'.

It is worth noting here that Lett had been operating alone for many months, behind enemy lines, creating a fighting force from a disparate group of men using weapons he had acquired through initiative and carefully cultivated local sources, all the while trying to persuade the Allies that his organization was legitimate, and his need for support absolutely critical. He had also been walking a fine line with the local politics of the various armed gangs, partisan groups and key figures in the valley. Added to this, of course, was the constant threat of betrayal, and the fact that he was actively engaged in taking the fight to the Germans. Lett had somehow managed to pull this off, a feat of great diplomacy, of magnificent leadership, and of highly complex management. But with this must have come immense mental stress. Lett should be lauded as a remarkable figure in this period, this region, and this conflict, and his reaction on hearing that he was finally to receive tangible outside support is entirely understandable. The relief must have been immense.

As it happened, 27 December marked the first anniversary of the first *rastrellamento* in the valley, and Lett knew that the arrival of the SAS on that day would massively boost local morale and possibly galvanize the various partisan groups into some kind of collaboration, however temporary.

The force Allied Command was sending was only a tenth of the size Lett had requested earlier – but it was based on sound military thinking. It was extremely well trained, well equipped, and ideal for conducting guerrilla operations. Lett hoped it would have an immediate effect on his own force, and the population they relied on – and indeed who relied on them – so heavily.

Formed in July 1941 by a twenty-four-year-old visionary called David Stirling for operations in the desert of North Africa, the soldiers of the SAS had quickly established themselves as experts in sabotage, hit-and-run raids and long-distance patrolling. Their recruitment strategy and training methods were initially somewhat Corinthian – many of their assets had to be 'acquired' from whatever local sources were available, an early characteristic that came to define them as eternally resourceful, determined and flexible troops. After some initial setbacks – on their first major raid they lost a third of their force, and inflicted no damage upon the enemy – they soon developed a standard protocol for training and operations that served as a highly effective template for operations much further afield. By 1944, they were superbly trained, extremely fit and battle hardened. Lett could not have hoped for a better force to operate with him in the valleys and ridges of Rossano.

On the morning of 27 December, Lett and his men set about preparing the DZ (drop zone) – a field above the now-ruined village of Chiesa. The local women had made large national flags out of coloured parachute silks sewn together, and these were sited at one end of the field. In its centre, other pieces were laid out to make a large letter H. They waited nervously all day. At last, late in the afternoon, they heard the longed-for sound of aeroplane engines, and six Dakotas flew into view. Operation Galia had arrived.

The first drop was of supplies, and attached to one bundle

was a packet containing letters from home. Among them was one from Lett's fiancée in London – the first news he'd had from her in over a year. At the second pass, a sole parachutist dropped from the side door of one of the planes. His name was Captain Chris Leng of the SOE, and although he does not feature a great deal in the accounts of what was to come for Operation Galia, this simple act of great bravery is worthy of note.

Because of the break in radio transmissions due to the loss of the wireless set, London had concluded that Lett might be operating at gunpoint in order to lure the SAS into a trap. As such, it was decided to initially drop just one man into the DZ, and if he was not taken prisoner or killed, then the rest would deploy. Captain Leng was that man, and his feelings as he hung beneath his parachute, entirely committed to an uncertain fate, can only be imagined. He landed safely and was undoing his parachute harness as Lett approached him. The two men greeted each other warmly. The relief must have been huge on both sides, with Leng laughingly comparing their meeting to that of Stanley and Livingstone. Then he fired a green flare from his Very pistol and the main drop, from about three hundred metres, began.

The commander of the SAS recalled the deployment in an interview after the war:

> Up went the green light, and we dropped into the worst possible dropping zone. It was the steep side of a terraced vineyard, and we had a number of minor jumping injuries on landing. I personally landed just on the edge of a drop, and as my canopy collapsed I came down about ten feet or so and was very badly shaken.

Although the landing was dramatic in the extreme, the welcome on the ground could not have been warmer. The Italians greeted them effusively, as Parachutist Stanley Hann recalled later:

> Old ladies dressed in black kissed me on both cheeks. Half-starved kids with bright, shiny eyes skipped and danced at my feet. Several bearded, swarthy, fierce-looking partisans appeared. Some, rather disconcertingly, wore German uniforms or tunics with ammunition bandoliers criss-crossing their chests. The partisans insisted on embracing me – garlic-breath kisses on both cheeks, bear hugs and hefty pats on the back.

One of the stick commanders (a group of ten parachutists was termed a stick) was Edward Gibbon, known to all as 'Tinker'. He recalls the drop quite clearly, noting in a post-war interview that as they made their final low run into the valley, 'I remember looking up and seeing the tops of the mountains above us.' He also dryly observed that he in particular had quite an 'exciting' landing.

His Bergen – containing all his equipment and suspended from his leg on a rope, as standard – landed in a tree and became tangled. Unfortunately, Gibbon's parachute landed in another tree, and between the two was a ravine. He ended up strung in mid-air between the two, 'like a fly'.

Glancing down, he was alarmed to see that below him was a crowd of men in German uniforms: 'I cut the rope from my kitbag with a knife and swung down with a crash, against the tree, and then found they were partisans. But it was an exciting few moments.'

Although the drop itself went as well as could be expected – this was, after all, a hazardous deployment into a mountainous region – there were hitches. Tom Shaughnessy commanded another stick, and the pilot of his Dakota pressed the green button to trigger the jump a few seconds too late, meaning that he landed on the other side of the mountain. This minor error – one can entirely understand how the pilot may have been somewhat preoccupied at the time – meant that it took Shaughnessy three days to get back to the main group, which Gibbon notes 'didn't please him greatly'.

But, crucially, all the SAS troops had deployed successfully, a process greatly assisted by the preparations of Lett and his partisan brigade on the ground, and the fact that (most unusually for an SAS operation) the drop took place in broad daylight.

There is some evidence that the drop was actually meant to be seen – a clear message sent to the Germans that a large force had landed behind their lines, and was preparing to do battle. Although the essence of the mission was to disrupt and destroy enemy supply lines and convoys, an undoubted secondary aim was to draw forces away from fortified positions on the Green Line. What better way to do so than to deploy a large number of parachutes – over 300 in total, although of course only thirty-three had men beneath them – in broad daylight. This was the most extensive single drop organized by the SOE up to that point in the war, and must have presented a sight of tremendous military pomp, clear intent, and daunting spectacle.

It is important to put this decision into context. This small group of men were dropping into enemy-held territory, and did so in broad daylight to draw as many of the occupying forces and local Fascists onto their location as possible. It was a move of staggering audacity, trusting their training, instincts and skills to survive the inevitable intensity of the German reaction.

There was a surprise in store for the waiting Lett: as he made himself known to the commander of the SAS he recognized him as Captain Bob Walker Brown, his friend from the Chieti POW camp.

'You didn't expect to see me, I bet,' said Walker Brown as he greeted Lett.

It was a remarkable moment – in this extraordinary theatre of war, with defeat or victory hanging in the balance, two of its key players had been reunited.

In addition to the soldiers, the drop included many supplies of all kinds – two Nicholls radio sets, plus weapons, food, medical kit, clothing and blankets. These were more than welcome for the people on the ground, as it was midwinter and their stores were running low. However, the new equipment didn't include proper alpine kit for the SAS unit: they had pullovers, but they didn't have appropriate underwear or waterproofs. Additionally, the men hadn't been issued with white overalls – essential camouflage in the snow-covered terrain. When they later requested these, they were sent a consignment of white vests. They also lacked either skis or snowshoes.

On the other hand, they had Lett's International Battalion and several trusted partisan groups affiliated with it to support them, to guide them through the countryside and to identify the most attractive targets. Radio contact with Allied Command was sometimes patchy, but these were men trained to operate independently, and the knowledge of dependable friends on the ground had already boosted their confidence.

They'd expected to go into action immediately, but so warm was their welcome – villagers competed for the honour of having them billeted as guests – that the first sorties weren't made until the following day. Despite the minor delay, Walker Brown was not a man to waste time, and he needed to strike before the enemy could properly prepare for him. Having successfully negotiated their difficult and hazardous deployment into the Rossano Valley, the SAS were about to go to work. Operation Galia was under way.

*

The main targets would be road and rail links essential to the German supply lines, but it was also important psychologically to undermine enemy confidence, so bold strikes at key military bases were also on the agenda. To effect this, the unit had brought a three-inch mortar with them, the first time such a weapon had been deployed in an action of this kind. This would prove to be a devastatingly effective weapon, and whereas previously the weight of the mortar itself and indeed the shells had been seen as prohibitive for long-range patrolling in the field, the gamble was to pay off.

The unit was divided into five sections, each of about five men, the rest forming a central command HQ. The sorties began on Thursday 28 December. Attacks were planned on the Borgo Val di Taro road to Parma, and on the routes between La Spezia and Genoa. By Friday 29th, Walker Brown was already liaising with Colonel Mario Fontana, the commander of the Fourth Partisan Zone, to plan future joint attacks with the partisans. All seemed to be set fair; but almost immediately the expedition struck a rock.

Led by the unfortunate Tom Shaughnessy, Number 5 Stick had been sent south to raid the Aulla–Reggio Emilia road, but they hadn't got far before they were surprised and captured. It was the night of 29–30 December, and their captors were a force of *Brigata Nera*, to whom the SAS men had been betrayed by an informer. It was as well that they were in uniform, and that they had been captured by Italians, not Waffen-SS, for Hitler had issued his notorious 'Commando Order' requiring the summary killing of any enemy Special Forces troops operating behind the lines. Instead, they were taken to La Spezia, where they became prisoners of war.

Their local guide, Chella Leonardo, was not so fortunate. He, too, was wearing British battledress, for Lett insisted on this when his men went into action in the hope that it might afford them some protection. However, Chella also wore the insignia of the International Battalion on his right shoulder. This was recognized by the Fascists, who beat him half to death and then finished the job with a bullet. Throughout the beating, and even in the moments before his execution, Leonardo did not betray a single confidence relating to the SAS mission, something for which he is remembered in his home town to this day.

On the same day, Saturday 30th, the SAS scored its first hit, taking out a small German convoy on the La Spezia–Genoa road. Walker Brown, in the face of the early setback of losing Number 5 stick, was determined to follow the first success through with a much more significant action. On New Year's Day, he launched an attack on the enemy garrison town of Borghetto di Vara, about twenty kilometres south-west of Rossano on the west bank of the Vara. Using intelligence gleaned from the partisans, and making this a joint attack with them, the SAS successfully targeted a number of garrison buildings using the mortar, while cutting off lines of retreat with Bren guns. Despite the fact that the secret of the attack had been leaked to the Germans, it was a success, driving the enemy from the town completely for twenty-four hours, and having an even more important undermining psychological effect. The SAS had announced their arrival on the scene in some style.

The following days saw unremitting attacks on convoys along a variety of routes, with bridges mined and blown, and the ambushing of a staff car which resulted in the deaths of a high-ranking Italian Fascist and three German officers. Most of these attacks were carried out by men who were suffering such extremes of cold that often their fingers could only just operate their weapons. There were severe setbacks too – after a Dakota crashed during the initial drop, the supply zone was changed. It proved

Tom Redhead, who escaped from three different Italian POW camps and fought alongside the partisans.

Tom's son John with Argene and Beatrice Pierucci, formidable sisters who sheltered Tom and other prisoners.

The men of Operation Galia at Brindisi airfield, 26 December 1944, prior to parachuting into the Rossano Valley. Bob Walker Brown is on the far right.

One of the SAS sticks
on Operation Galia, with
a Vickers machine gun.

One of the local couriers
who helped the SAS.

Three of the SAS troops
operating in snow. They
lacked any proper alpine kit.

On top of Monte Altissimo.

The Marble Mountains, where Operation Galia exfiltrated after
forty days in theatre, exhausted, harried by the Germans and ill-equipped
for the perilous winter conditions.

The *Brigata Nera*, more feared and reviled than even the SS.

Hitler in Maribor, Slovenia, where he demanded:
'Make these lands German again.'

The vast customs shed at Stalag XVIII-D near Maribor,
where Russian POWs were kept in inhuman conditions.

Some POWs playing rugby at Stalag XVIII-D.
Western Allied POWs were protected by the Geneva Convention.

Ralph Churches,
photographed in 1940.

Les Laws, Ralph's confidant
who helped plan their escape.

Ralph in the camp, where his popularity and ability to
speak German saw him elected as Camp Leader.

The site of the escape, by the railway line at Ozbalt.

With Ralph's son Neil at Ozbalt station.

At this farmhouse, near Topolšica, the POWs were ambushed by Germans.

The Crow's Flight, led by partisans, with Ralph in his trademark slouch hat.

A male and female partisan – the women were allotted no different treatment and fought alongside the men.

Ralph and his wife Ronte in December 1944, a few days after his return to Australia.

hard to reach – five hours' march – and by the time the SAS had made the difficult journey to the new dropping zone, they might find their stores already gone, pillaged by rival partisan groups. On one occasion, the SAS men were obliged to return fire from Communist partisans whom they surprised in the act of pilfering, though they aimed high. Despite this, Allied Command refused to change the drop zone back to the original site.

They might have had troubles with partisan groups over whom they had no control, but the SAS were enjoying an excellent relationship with those who came under the auspices of Gordon Lett. One particular figure of note was their guide in the village of Sero, which became for a time the headquarters of their operations against the Via Aurelia and other strategic enemy positions, including the towns of Brugnata and Borghetto di Vara. Local man Luigi 'Pippo' Sibaldi spoke English with a strong American accent, having lived in the States before the war. He was an extraordinary character – a crack shot, and very fit indeed. He became a natural ally to the SAS, and indeed saved a number of SAS men who were trapped within Sero when the Germans unexpectedly entered the village. He did it in some style, climbing a church tower and engaging the enemy with a Bren gun to create a diversion for the SAS to slip away. Such was his status with the men of Operation Galia that he became an honorary member of the SAS (glorying under the alias of 'Frank White'), assisted them greatly in their exfiltration from the region at the end of the operation, and was even parachuted back into the mountains to work with the SAS on a subsequent operation. When he died in 1967, Bob Walker Brown wrote a moving obituary to him in the SAS regimental magazine.

Operation Galia continued to operate with success into the middle of January, thanks to the training and expertise of the SAS and the help of outstanding individuals on the ground. As well as the use of specific guides such as Luigi, they also enjoyed the continuing support of the rest of the local population, and one partisan group became, effectively, a permanent adjunct of the SAS team. Chestnut bread and chestnut polenta – together with a plentiful supply of the local wine – made a welcome change from the usual bully beef. (The SAS were not the only ones to get sick and tired of bully beef. During the war it became a staple, and Fray Bentos of Uruguay exported 16 million tins of it in 1943 alone.)

Reprisals were not far away, however, and one took place on 12 January at Brugnato, just across the river from Borghetto. Brugnato had been the jumping-off point for a second attack on a convoy at the garrison town by the SAS the previous day. The *Brigata Nera* ransacked and set fire to houses in the town, shooting into the fleeing crowd as they did so.

The SAS response was immediate and ferocious, attacking Borghetto again later that very day. A fierce battle ensued, during which the SAS were helped by the chance arrival of a USAAF Thunderbolt fighter-bomber, which dropped a bomb on Borghetto. The bomb failed to go off, but the SAS also attacked the road out of Brugnato with three bombs of their own, forcing those carrying out the raid in the town to withdraw back to safety over the bridge linking the two towns. The battle continued until the SAS, down to its reserves of ammunition, decided to call it a day. At that point, four more Thunderbolts, doubtless alerted by the first, arrived on the scene, bombed the bridge and strafed the road. This use of air assault to back up ground operations – albeit unplanned – proved to be a vivid demonstration of co-operative warfare for the partisans, while the enemy concluded that their attackers had closely co-ordinated air support. The SAS were not only creating waves locally – by now, large numbers of enemy troops from further afield were being deployed to their area of operations to deal with what was thought to be a large and well-equipped force.

But, as the operation progressed, the SAS men began to suffer depredations of their own. Many of these were not due to the enemy, but ill-health. Altitude sickness had been a problem before acclimatization, and now some of the men were suffering variously from pneumonia, dysentery, mountain flu, infected wounds and frostbite. His numbers depleted by illness, and knowing that his stay in the mountains could only be for a limited time, Walker Brown decided to step up his operation still further with a series of major attacks on roads near to the principal enemy town of the inland region, Pontremoli, about twelve kilometres north-east of Rossano on the River Magra. The plan was brilliant, innovative, and cost-effective. It was also faithful to the SAS principle – developed in the North African campaign – that a small number of highly trained men, engaged in lightning strikes, could effect as much damage as a whole regiment.

Three separate attacks on convoys and enemy positions were planned to take place simultaneously over the night of 19–20 January. Though these attacks were partially successful, the Germans had deployed troops in the region and launched a major *rastrellamento* on the 20th. During the several days which followed, the SAS and members of the International Battalion – deployed with the SAS because of their crucial local knowledge – engaged in a tense cat-and-mouse game with the Germans, who were intent on extirpating this dangerous enemy in their midst once and for all. Astonishingly, the Germans didn't think of destroying the church tower at Arzelato, which provided the SAS and the International Battalion with unrivalled views over the terrain surrounding Pontremoli and the town itself, enabling them to plan countermeasures effectively. But the SAS and International Battalion had to perform at an extraordinary physical level to remain ahead of the

Germans, all of which took its toll. At one point during the hunt, as Walker Brown reported later, 'fifty-nine hours' marching without rest or rations over hills deep in snow gave the party sufficient mobility to shake off the German troops deployed in pursuit.'

At last, after seven days, running out of supplies and having little to show for their efforts, the Germans brought the huge *rastrellamento* to an end. In the meantime, thousands of German troops and vital assets had been tied up at a crucial time in the war when both were in increasingly short supply, and could have been deployed to much greater effect on the Green Line.

However, the successes of the SAS and the partisans through this and their other actions were not without cost. Apart from Shaughnessy's stick early on, not one SAS soldier had been captured, killed or wounded, but the partisans working with them, who had frequently saved them by skilful guiding and extreme vigilance, had lost many of their number, including numerous key members. Some of these losses were in the most brutal circumstances, and the slaughter of innocent old people, women and children in the villages had continued.

The combination of battlefield losses and fear of local reprisals saw the gradual depletion of support for both the SAS operations and the International Battalion itself, something both organizations felt keenly. By the end of the month, it was time to recoup and regroup. During January, the SAS had achieved its objectives, but now the men were tiring, and it was getting close to time to pull out. There had been a period of difficulty in communication with Allied Command, who, hearing nothing, began to think that Operation Galia had been exterminated. A supply drop had been promised of more arms, whisky, rum, twenty-five pounds of tobacco and 50,000 cigarettes. Consumption of cigarettes was very high (at least two of the SAS men smoked forty a day) so this last would have been more than welcome, had the drop taken place. A relief party was also to be sent up to Rossano to gather information and to help the SAS withdraw through the enemy lines and re-join the Allied forces – if the SAS had survived. This party was a small one; just two SAS soldiers and a radio operator.

But at last, on Tuesday 30 January, radio communication with base was re-established, and a drop requested at the original zone, since the second was by now occupied by the Germans. On 2 February supplies, together with Jock Milne, an SAS captain seconded from the Royal Army Medical Corps, were parachuted in. Milne jumped from the very low height of just over 100 metres, but made a safe landing on soft snow. His kitbag burst, however, and the SAS men were obliged to gather syringes, tubes of ointment and other medical equipment which had been scattered across the field.

The SAS mission now had fresh supplies, and a doctor to tend the sick – the International Battalion's own doctor had been unable to continue as the aftermath of the big *rastrellamento* required his services locally. Far from starting to pull out, Walker Brown determined on a last set of sorties. On 7 February one SAS stick attacked the road linking Aulla and La Spezia, destroying eight lorries, while another hit the Via Aurelia again. And there was one final sortie at Borghetto which was aided, again by luck, by a group of patrolling Spitfires, which noticed the attack and joined in.

These actions sent a message to the Germans that their surge against the SAS and the partisans had done nothing to dent their prowess. Since ultimate defeat now loomed in the minds of even the most optimistic supporters of Hitler and Mussolini, most ordinary German and Italian Social Republic soldiers wanted nothing more than to throw in the towel. Increasing chaos and uncertainty reigned along what was left of the defensive line – these parting shots from the SAS had indeed battered the morale of the enemy. After more than forty days of near relentless fighting, of raids, of constantly moving from one location to another while only a single tactical bound ahead of the enemy, the military objectives of Operation Galia had been accomplished.

Although Bob Walker Brown had initially considered staying longer in the Rossano Valley, quite apart from the exhaustion and illness of his men, he sensed that at last the locals' hospitality might be wearing thin. He didn't want to outstay his welcome, or expose them to further danger and depredation. The end was near, although that didn't stop the Germans from randomly burning down swathes of chestnut trees to sabotage the local food supply, and continuing their constant assaults on villagers. Walker Brown himself witnessed the machine-gunning of sixteen youths all aged under twenty by the German *Feldgendarmerie* (field police) and six elderly people strung up from lamp posts by meathooks. Despite the indefatigable spirit and consistent decency of the *contadini*, he decided that for the good of all it was time to go, and a fighting withdrawal was how they intended to do it.

The SAS never retreat, they exfiltrate, and ideally they do so under their own terms. But they were a long way from home, and faced moving at speed over an unfamiliar landscape crawling with the enemy. In this regard, Operation Galia had been almost too successful – a captured German informed Walker Brown that the occupying forces were looking for 'at least 400 enemy paratroopers', and were using two brigades to do so. Walker Brown modestly admits that he allowed himself a brief moment of pride before turning to the business in hand – how to get his men out of theatre safely. A successful exfiltration by this group of exhausted men, harried and hunted at every step, would be a feat of endurance to match the military endeavours of the previous forty days of intense operations.

Ever the astute tactician, Walker Brown split his unit into two: he would lead the first out on the night of 10 February. The second, under the command of Lieutenant James Riccomini, would depart twenty-four hours later.

CHAPTER THIRTEEN

The March Over Monte Altissimo

In a small roadside cafe in Rossano, I spread the map out on the table in front of me, the route taken by Walker Brown and the SAS men shown as a convoluted line from Rossano in the north-west all the way to their final destination of Seravezza further south, only a stone's throw away from the coast.

Even this two-dimensional representation of their planned route appeared intimidating. Their path was plotted with the help of a map taken from a German officer killed in a recent partisan operation, which marked every enemy frontline position, but speed was of the essence as they knew those positions would change. The aim was to squeeze through a narrow corridor separating two German regiments. They would be threading the eye of the needle in doing so, passing directly through German lines – and indeed through the Green Line itself on the ridge of Monte Altissimo, directly overlooking the port of La Spezia, with the enemy there on high alert to their presence.

The exfiltration would have to pass close to several major settlements, including significant pinch points at Podenzana and Aulla. At the latter, they would have to negotiate the Magra River, with the inherent hazards of any water crossing – extreme cold, noise and the fact that they would be out in the open as they

waded across. From there they would head due south to Fosdi-
novo, before jinking east to Vinca and then into the ridges and
precipitous slopes of their final hurdle, the mighty Marble Mountains. They would have to climb Monte Tambura, with a peak of
1,426 metres, and after that – their last barrier before the Allied
lines – Monte Altissimo, a great slab of granite with a summit of
1,589 metres. From there they hoped to link up with the Allies
at either Azzano or Seravezza.

It is important to put this route into context. This was one of
the worst winters on record. They were desperately ill-equipped
for such an arduous trek through mountainous terrain, exhausted
after over forty days in theatre, and were being harried and pursued at every turn. To reach safety they would have to make
excellent time, make the most of their local contacts, make use of
the terrain to hide their passage, and make history in accomplish-
ing one of the most arduous exfiltrations in the annals of their
regiment.

On 10 February 1945, Walker Brown's group made their way
south-east towards Aulla on the River Magra. They had originally
planned to engage the enemy en route, but decided against this
as they were keenly aware that the second SAS team would be
following in their wake. Although they might be able to make
good their escape after a raid, the second group would then
encounter a mobilized and alert enemy.

In one of those darkly comic moments inherent in war, the
following day one of their number accidentally lost his trousers
down a well, having taken them off and slung them over his
shoulder in order to keep them dry while crossing the stream.
This was a welcome bit of light relief for his comrades, which got
even better when they had the good fortune to capture a German

Hauptmann, caught with *his* trousers down in the company of a local girl. The SAS trooper was understandably keen to purloin the trousers for his own use, but Walker Brown was steadfast – no man under his command would operate behind enemy lines wearing enemy uniform. Moreover, the prisoner was always placed at the front of the group when approaching uncertain situations ahead in the hope that, in the event of trouble, the German (with a gun in his back) would co-operate and talk them out of it. As Walker Brown pointed out, their prisoner wouldn't have been able to make a very convincing argument to a suspicious patrol in only his underpants.

Despite these lighter moments, their situation was becoming desperate. Although they enjoyed continuing and unstinting support from local communities along the way, every member of their party was kept on full alert. Their nerves were stretched to the limit as they pushed their exhausted bodies onward.

Rather incongruously for such a high-stakes exfiltration, the scenery was staggeringly beautiful, becoming more so as they approached the edge of the Carrara mountain range – famous for its marble quarries and the source of the material which Michelangelo and Donatello used to create their masterpieces. These quarries had also provided treasured building stone for the Romans and their predecessors. But beautiful as it was, it was also harsh and treacherous terrain, with heavy going over broken rock in the depths of winter.

It was now 13 February, seven weeks since the post-Christmas drop into the Rossano Valley. At last they reached the mountains themselves, and prepared to make the ascent and crossing. Their route now took them past Vinca, the scene of the horrific massacre which had taken place only six months before. When they passed through the area, the SAS men found the few people they met subdued, still in deep shock from the horrors they had witnessed.

It was time to make some serious decisions about the amount of equipment they carried. Walker Brown noted:

The party marched to Vinca – a long and tiring march across very rough country. Bren guns had to be left with the partisans as, owing to the physical condition of the men, it was not possible to carry much on the last stage of the march.

They still had a good twenty kilometres of tough terrain ahead before they would reach Monte Altissimo. The following day they set out south across the massif of Monte Tambura, passing Forno, another village which had suffered a massacre the previous June. There they were joined by a group of USAAF aircrew evaders, and also dumped the last of their heavy packs and continued onward with just rifles, ammunition, and the bare essentials of kit and supplies. It was now a run for freedom that faced an entirely binary end point. Either they would succeed in the next few days, or they would dramatically fail – they simply did not have the equipment or supplies to sustain their exfiltration for longer.

The road ahead, along the flank of Monte Altissimo, was mistrusted by their guides, since there had been rumours that not only had it recently been mined, but that it had also come under enemy mortar fire. Monte Altissimo itself was their final and most formidable physical obstacle, its summit over a kilometre and a half above sea level. On its other side lay the Allies. As they moved ever higher into the snowline, their pace slowed, and they became more and more exposed. Walker Brown notes that their dark battledress, 'made us about as inconspicuous as cherries on a wedding-cake' against the side of the mountain.

The guides were persuaded to carry on across the tough terrain. Walker Brown noted:

The march over Monte Altissimo was exceedingly difficult and tiring. It was pitch black and not possible to use the ordinary mountain track, as it was mined. Therefore about 2000 feet (c. 610 m) or more had to be climbed at an average slope of one in four. The pass at the top of Monte Altissimo was reached at about 23h00.

They had already had to endure enemy mortar fire on the track, and there was one direct encounter with an enemy patrol of four men, who passed by them at a distance of about a hundred metres. The SAS got ready to do battle, but the Germans, though they had seen them, chose not to engage and made their way off down a valley. Perhaps they were just too cold and too exhausted to put up a fight. By now, the SAS would have sympathized with that.

The worst experience they had was when one of their number – some say it was the captured German captain – sprang an enemy tripwire and set off a phosphorus flare. They waited tensely in the darkness – surely they were about to be ambushed, their great adventure brought savagely to a conclusion so close to its completion. But nothing happened, and breathlessly they continued through the stark ridges and thin air that surrounded them.

The Marble Mountains look just as impressive from close range as they do from a distance. The peaks are so sharp, the ridges so serrated, that they appear almost as a child's nightmare vision of a mountain – stark, forbidding and hostile. In the drive up to the car park, I had passed several marble quarries, great chunks taken from the sides of the cliffs that revealed the white rock beneath, looking for all the world like fresh scar tissue on the weathered grey slopes of the ancient mountains.

I had arranged to meet a local mountain guide to show me the route the SAS had taken. Cristiano Virgilio had grown up in these mountains, and he had readily agreed to guide me on this final stage of my journey. Our preparatory phone call had been longer than I had expected, as Cristiano had encyclopaedic knowledge of the location of the routes, and shared with me the enemy positions, the weak points and the sites of the paths over the ridges.

When he pulled up in the car park alongside me, his appearance was – pleasingly – precisely how I had imagined it would be. He was lean and tanned, with a classic Roman nose and a swarthy complexion. His hands looked incongruously large – the tools of his trade, tough-skinned and covered in a network of tiny scars. His outfit was entirely luminous – fluorescent-yellow trousers, a bright orange T-shirt and a green bandana that positively glowed in the morning light.

'*Buongiorno*, Cris,' I said. 'We're not going to lose you in a hurry, are we?'

He smiled shyly, and indicated the ridge high above us with a wave of a sinewy arm.

'Up there, it is better to be seen,' he said simply.

He was a softly spoken, rather gentle man, and as we prepared our kit for the day ahead he talked a little of his background and why his connection to these mountains, and these trails, was so very close. In many ways, Cristiano was the embodiment of the travails and intense social complexity that faced this region in the years during (and indeed following) the war.

'My wife's family,' he said, as we began to walk, 'they were Fascists, you know? It is more complex than we think, and sometimes people just picked the wrong side. After the war, many of her family were killed. There were killings here for many years that were simply vendettas – nothing to do with the war, just settling scores. All you had to do was say someone was a Fascist and you could do it. They were terrible times.'

Cristiano had the disconcerting habit of walking ahead of me with his hands clasped neatly behind his back, strolling along as the path took us higher and higher in a series of steep switchbacks. He looked as if he was out on a Sunday saunter, and seemed very contented indeed. This was in marked contrast to me, using my hands to push on my pistoning thighs as I leant into the gradient of the hill.

We worked our way steadily upwards, walking through shaded beech woods with occasional deep grooves in the forest floor where wild boar had foraged for food. We were following an ancient path, used by marble quarrymen since Roman times.

'That quarry in the middle distance there,' said Cris, when we stopped for a brief rest at a natural viewing point, 'that is called Michelangelo's Quarry. He was famous for roping down the rock faces himself to pick the precise slabs he wanted. The people here have always known these mountains well, and helped many, many people over them.'

We resumed walking, and the beech woods started to give way to patches of tough grass and bare rock. I could see the ridge line directly ahead – the end of the vertiginous section of the climb, but the beginning of the long and dangerous traverse leading to the summit of Monte Altissimo.

We crested the ridge line together, to be greeted by a view so entirely stupendous it stopped me in my tracks. Cristiano had known precisely what was coming, and smiled broadly as I at first exclaimed loudly, then laughed out loud at the sheer immensity of it.

Below us lay the coastal plain, with the city of Massa spread out at its heart, an untidy collection of old suburbs and new developments. The blue of the sky high above gave way to the deep sapphire of the Mediterranean beneath, with the coastline weaving its way into the distant haze. To our immediate right the ranks of high mountain peaks glowered – beyond them lay Vinca, and the route the SAS had followed to the point where we now stood. To the left, the ridgeline continued its ascent to the summit of Altissimo.

This view, entirely splendid as it was, would have been lost on Walker Brown and his exhausted SAS men. For a start, as they crested this rise they would have been looking at enemy-held territory – this point in their journey basically looked west, and the Allies were to the east – as such the SAS men still faced a long and very dangerous walk along a narrow path on a high ridge, with drops on either side, before they could descend. The second reason was that they tackled Altissimo in the dead of night, to avoid detection by enemy patrols.

During that most brutal of winters the patrol crested the ridge through snow two to three metres deep. They also marched every step in hob-nailed boots. These were magnificent for the parade ground, and reasonable for long marches over flat terrain, but were about as unsuitable for mountaineering as it's possible to be. The hob nails were extremely slippery on rocks and ice, with the metal conducting the freezing cold of the ground straight into the feet of the men. They were also noisy on rocks, the equivalent of creeping up on someone while wearing tap shoes. Finally, they threw out sparks as they hit the rock underfoot. These men of iron needed boots that were anything but.

The Germans didn't just lay mines on the routes they suspected were being used by partisans and escapees, they also mined the fringes of the paths to discourage any use of the natural breaks that led into valleys down to the west. They were also patrolling the area intensively. As we walked along the ridge line, we passed a circular depression in the rock, with what appeared to be a broken-down old wall around it.

'Bunkers,' said Cristiano, when he saw the direction of my gaze. 'This whole area was fortified by the Italian Fascists so they could cover all the approaches to the mountains.'

The SAS men were now tip-toeing through the most hazardous section of the entire exfiltration. Simple geography conspired against them to create a limited range of route options, all of which were unquestionably being monitored by the enemy.

'Now,' said Cristiano, 'we climb.'

It is, in fact, perfectly possible to walk to the summit of Altissimo without having to climb a rock face, but I had asked Cristiano if we could inch our way along some of the more precipitous faces that dropped far into the valley floor beneath. The rationale was that if the SAS men had not been able to follow the path, then neither should I. This had seemed a simply magnificent idea at ground level – quite frankly I felt faintly heroic even having the conversation – but seemed eminently less logical now there was a yawning gap beside me, an echoing void through which I could clearly visualize myself falling at a meteoric rate.

But I need not have worried. Cristiano was the epitome of professionalism, and soon had me tethered behind him on a short rope as he made sure-footed progress ahead of me, the rock face dropping away beneath us.

'This,' he said, waggling the rope at me as we paused on a ledge, 'is not designed to hold you if you fall, as it is only tied to me and not the rock face. It is designed to stop you falling altogether. If I feel you beginning to topple, I simply tighten like this –' he hauled vigorously on the rope – 'and you will be pulled towards the rock face.'

'And what about if you fall, Cristiano?' I asked.

'Oh, in that case we would both die. No question at all. Now, we continue, yes?'

We edged along the face for a further hundred metres or so,

me with a somewhat preoccupied facial expression, before I suggested to Cristiano that I felt we had now 'explored enough of the "off-route" section for historical integrity to be maintained, and could we get back up on the path again please . . .'

Having walked along the ridge for a few more minutes, we finally stopped at the head of a steep gulley that led to a road in the valley floor. Halfway along the valley lay Azzuno, the small village that was the furthest northern point of the Allied front line in this region, the tip of the spear.

'I'm sure it was here,' said Cristiano, as we both looked down the slope. 'This was where the partisans and prisoners were often taken, so I would say that this is where the SAS men went. I don't know for sure, but it seems to make sense.'

There were no hairpins or switchbacks on this path, following as it did the bottom of the gulley down the great flanks of Altissimo. This was the last hurdle, the last moment when death could have taken them. Picking their way down the path in the pitch darkness, they made it to the valley floor beneath. These men, who had inflicted such heavy losses on the Germans without taking a single casualty through enemy action, who had created chaos and confusion, had finally evaded capture and surmounted every obstacle before them.

At 0400 on the morning of 15 February, dragging their feet the last few hundred metres as overwhelming exhaustion set in, they passed the first forward American platoon.

After an exfiltration lasting five days, at last the end was in sight. It had been a magnificent achievement.

Riccomini's party, who were due to head out on 11 February, had in fact delayed their departure to help Gordon Lett control another serious inter-partisan squabble. They then paused briefly en route to take out a German lorry, but finally made it safely to Allied lines five days after Walker Brown's party. For Riccomini personally, though, there was to be no peaceful post-war retirement. His first combat parachute jump had actually been when he landed in Rossano on 27 December – he was a relatively new member of the SAS – but having distinguished himself during Operation Galia, he subsequently joined Operation Tombola, another SAS operation in the Cusna Mountains. By the end of March 1945 he was dead, aged twenty-seven, killed during an attack at the Villa Rossi. Shortly before, when Galia ended, he'd written to his wife: 'The real thing is that I might not ever be able to settle down after all this . . . however, darling, remember that I do think of you very often, and that one day I will be home again.'

Lett himself remained at Rossano, continuing the fight, until mid-March 1945, when he was ordered to leave to take up other duties. He passed through Montereggio where the partisans and some of the International Battalion paraded in his honour, before taking a route that delivered him to the town of Barga ten days later. This remarkable man had achieved all he could – all anyone could – and his work in the Rossano Valley was finally complete.

In his post-operation report, Walker Brown uses unusually emotive language for such a formal document. One cannot help speculating that he wanted to communicate the achievements of his men to the military hierarchy, to pay tribute to their Herculean endurance and relentless bravery. Constrained – and doubtless frustrated – by military protocol, he notes in his summary that:

> The operation in the area inland from Spezia has been spectacular both in the results achieved against the enemy and

the manner in which the difficulties of terrain and winter warfare were surmounted.

It lasted for a period of nine weeks during which from reports at present available, it is known that the following casualties were inflicted on the enemy:

22 trucks and trailers destroyed, one truck damaged, a minimum of between 100 and 150 total casualties inflicted on the enemy during various actions which included attacks on German marching columns and on the town of Borgeto.

The skilful use of 3" mortar and Bren guns enabled large bodies of enemy to be engaged, and 59 hours marching without rest or rations over hills deep in snow gave the party sufficient mobility to shake off the German troops deployed for pursuit.

SAS casualties, according to information at present available, amount to six missing – now reported as POWs – out of a total of 33 deployed on the operation.

A full report will be issued when the whole party has been debriefed.

There is a jarring footnote to both Operation Galia and the feats of Lett's International Battalion. For reasons which remain a mystery, but which may have political undertones related to fear of Communism, the British Government blocked all recommendations for medals to Italian freedom fighters. Once again, it seems that the Italian partisans and civilians had paid the highest price, and received the least reward.

PART FOUR

The Crow's Flight
Slovenia

'Old men forget: yet all shall be forgot,
But he'll remember with advantages
What feats he did that day.'

William Shakespeare, *Henry V*

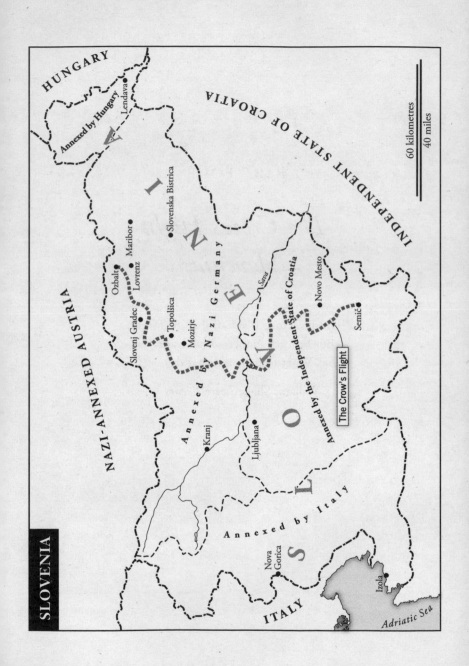

SLOVENIA

HUNGARY

Annexed by Hungary

Lendava

INDEPENDENT STATE OF CROATIA

NAZI-ANNEXED AUSTRIA

Ozbalt

Sloveni Gradec

Maribor

Lovrenz

Topolšica

Mozirje

Slovenska Bistrica

Annexed by Nazi Germany

Sava

Novo Mesto

Semič

Annexed by the Independent State of Croatia

The Crow's Flight

Kranj

Ljubljana

SLOVENIA

Annexed by Italy

Nova
Gorica

Izola

ITALY

Adriatic Sea

60 kilometres

40 miles

CHAPTER FOURTEEN

The Invasion of Yugoslavia

I arrived in Slovenia in April 2017 to follow the trail of one of the most notable escape stories of the entire Second World War. 'The Crow's Flight', as the escape became known, was a masterpiece of planning, logistics, endurance, fortitude and defiance in the face of overwhelming odds. It also brought together a rare combination of individuals who proved capable of pulling off an absurdly ambitious scheme – in particular an Australian POW called Ralph Churches, and a group of partisans who led 105 men a remarkable 250 kilometres to safety, across mountainous terrain and sometimes within 200 metres of the German army. It seemed to me that occasionally the fates conspire, and in the midst of some of the darkest days in Europe's history, wondrous things can happen.

I was met at Ljubljana airport by my two in-country guides – Svetlana Dramlić and Sasha Jovičić. The former was an olive-skinned, dark-haired young woman, who greeted me with a beaming smile and a warm welcome in near-perfect English. Slovenia lies at the bottleneck of Europe – hemmed in by the ragged Adriatic coastline and Italy to the west and Austria to the north – and as such travellers have passed through the country on their way west to the heartlands of Europe for millennia. Svetlana was the embodiment of the resultant fusion of Asian, Mediterranean and European cultures. Indeed, as recently as 2016 almost half a million refugees fleeing the barbaric conflict in Syria passed through the country, leaving their mark – however faint – on a culture that has become used to being a staging post of any exodus from the east.

Behind her stood Sasha, her husband, who gave a laconic half smile that made the rolled cigarette dangling from his lower lip twitch briefly before it sagged once again to smoulder just above his chin. He had a distinct air of sleepy bonhomie, one that belied his role as an expert logistician. For now, though, he gave a shrug, raised an eyebrow (a gesture in itself that seems to span continents) and hefted one of my bags onto his shoulder before heading to a waiting car. I took this as an invitation to follow, and hurried in his wake.

From Ljubljana, we would be driving nearly 120 kilometres north-east to the town of Maribor, the launch point for the escape. This provided a perfect chance to not only view the changing landscape from the comfort of the back seat, but also to conduct my first piece of impromptu research by chatting to Svetlana en route.

Any drive of any length in Slovenia will soon be overshadowed by mountains, and very swiftly the landscape rose in serried ranks before us, dominating our northern horizon. Several of the highest were lost in the clouds, their upper slopes white with snow, running in venous white trails into the vast tracts of forests that coated their flanks. It looked forbidding, a world far removed from the comfort of our car and the dark strip of tarmac on which we travelled.

'We're one of the most heavily forested countries in Europe,' Svetlana told me rather proudly as we began to drive through undulating green foothills. 'We're also one of the highest – the average altitude here is over 400 metres. We've got a lovely bit of coastline – only fifty kilometres of it, mind you – and some wonderful rivers and towns in the lowlands, but this is definitely a land of mountains.'

'Do you think that has made you tough as a people?' I said. 'That it spawned the partisans? Their relationship with the land around them was always said to be their great strength.'

She turned in her seat to face me, as if to emphasize her point.

'The partisans have always had a complicated relationship with the people of Slovenia,' she said, eliciting a grunt of acknowledgement from Sasha beside her. 'There are those who think they were absolute heroes who liberated our country. And those who think they were agents working for the Communists, who took advantage of the war to further their own ends. As ever with these things, it's very complex.'

'And what of the Crow's Flight?' I asked, slightly deflated. 'Is there a feeling of pride about that?'

She smiled broadly.

'Ah yes. We think it was amazing. There were so many ordinary Slovenians involved, as well as the partisans. It is something that is celebrated here, although it is strange that so few other nations seem to know about it.'

With that she turned back to the road, leaving me to ponder what she had said as I stared over the green plains to the mountains beyond. This had been the setting of an escape story of such immense ambition and scope, it seemed barely credible. What is undeniable is that it took place in a land with a complex past, going through a time of turmoil as the Second World War drew to a close. To understand the escape, and the people who made it possible, I knew that first I had to understand its cultural context. In late 1944, when the Crow's Flight took wing, it did so against a backdrop of deep political disorder, infighting and ethnic friction in a nation that trembled on the edge of oblivion.

Two hours after leaving the airport, as the dusk began to settle, we drew into the bustling heart of Maribor. This is Slovenia's second largest city, and miraculously retains some of its original Habsburg architecture. This is particularly notable when one considers the price it paid in the Second World War for being the industrial centre of the region, with an extensive network of railways and roads that were a natural focal point of the occupying German army's logistics effort. As a centre for armament manufacture, it became a priority target for the Allies in the latter stages of the war, and suffered twenty-nine separate large-scale bombing raids, which laid waste to 47 per cent of the city. No other major urban centre in what was then Yugoslavia suffered such extensive damage. I was particularly keen to visit Maribor, as this was not only the point from which the escape began, but also the site from which Hitler declared his victory in Yugoslavia in 1941, sounding the death knell for many thousands of its occupants.

Svetlana and Sasha dropped me off and I walked a few hundred metres to the main city square. It was a tranquil, picturesque setting with couples strolling arm in arm and old men sipping coffee in the evening light. It was virtually impossible to imagine the hell that was unleashed from not just here, but also the nation as a whole. What made it doubly poignant was that the moment of capitulation, the final acknowledgement of a devastating defeat, had taken place precisely where I was standing.

Before me stood Maribor City Hall, built in the sixteenth century, remodelled in the nineteenth, and then happily restored to its former glory several decades later. Its magnificent facade – a series of perfectly symmetrical windows beneath a roof of deep, claret red – has a central balcony, featuring a set of fluted stone columns in front of an impressive pair of double doors.

Adolf Hitler, on his only wartime visit to Yugoslavia, had once stood on that balcony. It was 26 April 1941, and his forces had won a surprisingly easy victory. This was the triumphant denouement of that invasion, the moment the Führer addressed a crowd largely mustered from the German-speaking sections of the city's population.

Because of its strategic significance, Yugoslavia had been doomed from the outset. The country had been born in the dying days of another devastating European conflict, the First World War. At the start of the war, the Habsburg Austro-Hungarian Empire stretched south into the Balkans and included present-day Slovenia and Croatia. The Turkish Ottoman Empire also controlled large parts of the Balkans until 1912, when the independent states of Serbia and Montenegro allied with Greece and Bulgaria to push the Turks out of the region. When the Austro-Hungarian Empire started to dissolve in 1918, the independent Kingdom of the Serbs, Croats and Slovenes was created. This was ratified by the Treaty of Trianon in 1920 and renamed Yugoslavia in 1929.

For centuries, the partner countries in this union – and the ethnic groups within them – had shared an uneasy relationship under the hegemonies of the Ottomans and Habsburgs. Each had a fierce sense of national pride, of identity and of cultural vision. Synthetic nations seldom prosper, and the situation was not helped by the fact that the new kingdom was ruled by a Serbian monarch – Peter I – who swiftly established Serbia as the key state, with the hierarchy of the police, the military and national politics all dominated by Serbs. Of the 165 generals in the Royal Yugoslav Army at the start of the Second World War, only four were not Serbian (a factor that was to have a crippling effect on the viability of the army when the Axis powers invaded). Tensions remain high even today between the nations that made up the former Yugoslavia, manifested in the brutality of the Balkan wars of the early nineties.

By 1939, Yugoslavia was ruled by a regent, Prince Paul, who hoped to remain neutral after war broke out but misjudged the ambitions of Mussolini and Hitler. He was coerced into signing the Tripartite Pact with Italy and Germany on 25 March 1941, fearing that if he did not accede to Hitler's demands the country would be attacked. This infuriated the mainly Serbian officer corps who launched a coup d'état on 27 March, deposing the regent and installing his cousin, the seventeen-year-old King Peter II, in his place.

This provided just the excuse Hitler needed. He swiftly issued Führer Directive 25 (the war would subsequently become known as 'Operation 25'), declaring Yugoslavia a hostile state. On 6 April the invasion of Yugoslavia commenced with a devastating air assault on Belgrade, effectively incapacitating the Yugoslav air force.

Operating from bases in Hungary, Romania and Bulgaria, the German forces then launched their invasion. Italy and Hungary joined the ground offensive on 11 April, with Italian forces advancing down the Dalmatian coast towards the major town of Ljubljana, encountering virtually no resistance en route. On 12 April, Ljubljana was taken.

The remarkably swift capitulation of the Royal Yugoslav Army has been a topic of much debate. In terms of their size alone, this was a formidable force, comprising thirty-three divisions and four air brigades. They were, however, badly led, with senior officers making the ill-judged decision to defend the borders of the nation as opposed to its many natural strong points. Clothing and footwear were in desperately short supply throughout, and much of the outdated heavy weaponry relied on horses to be moved. The schism between the Croatian and Serbian factions also led to unrest and even mutiny. In Zagreb on 10 April, the mainly Croat 4th and 7th Armies actually welcomed the German invasion. The result was a fractured, disjointed, ill-equipped force that stood little chance against a co-ordinated assault from an experienced enemy.

On 17 April – a mere eleven days after the invasion began – an armistice was signed. This was merely a formal declaration of a fait accompli, with local authorization for ceasefires already having been passed down from the Yugoslav High Command as early as 14 April. Nine days later, Hitler appeared on the balcony of Maribor City Hall to acknowledge the (well-rehearsed) adulation of a sizeable crowd.

An image was taken of the Führer at that moment, one I now held in my hand. I tried to position myself in exactly the same spot as the photographer seventy-six years before, to imagine what he had been thinking. As he listened to the speech amid the clamour and cheering, the flag waving and the marching bands, he would have undoubtedly heard Hitler utter the words that unleashed hell on the nation: 'Make these lands German again.' It was an open-ended charter for ethnic cleansing and widespread brutality. In the next few years, more than 80,000 Slovenians were deported, and 29,000 sent to concentration camps. It was from this balcony, now gilded in the evening light, that the occupation of Yugoslavia began.

Some northern areas were annexed by Hungary, and Macedonia was annexed by Bulgaria, but dominating the region were the occupying forces of Italy and Germany. Italy controlled South Slovenia and Montenegro, with Germany controlling North Slovenia and Serbia. Croatia was the only region that retained its own identity, although it was in effect a puppet state in vassalage to Germany. But even Hitler could not fully understand the complexity of the nation he had conquered, and the fierce, tribal spirit of its inhabitants. The war of Yugoslavia – which had thus far appeared to be a masterclass of German military might – was in fact only just beginning.

History shows us that the arrival of a powerful invading force can frequently unite an otherwise fractious and dissolved nation – Afghanistan being one of the most notable contemporary examples. Sadly, this was not the case for Yugoslavia after the invasion in 1941, and the various puppet states, tinpot monarchs and militias swiftly aligned themselves to the forces they saw as offering their best chance of power once the conflict was concluded. They also sought allies who would destroy the other political parties and ethnic groups who might oppose them.

As such, Croatia was run by Ante Pavelić, a Fascist whose military force – the Ustaša, or Croatian Revolutionary Movement – was pro-Muslim, pro-Catholic, but deeply anti-Semitic. The Ustaše were widely reviled throughout Yugoslavia, and were as feared as the SS. In Serbia, a resistance movement to the occupiers swiftly sprung up. The Chetniks, originally supported by the exiled Yugoslav Government, were under the command of Colonel Draža Mihailović, and had been recruited largely from the remnants of the Royal Yugoslav Army. They were openly anti-Muslim, but also conservative, monarchist and nationalist. Doubtless baffled by the fractious, ever-changing political landscape of the various resistance groups, the Allies initially supported the Chetniks until they discovered they were collaborating with the Germans. The Chetniks memorably described this as 'exploiting the enemy', but the Allies were not convinced and switched their support to the left-wing (usually Communist) partisans, who by 1943 were under the control of the Yugoslavian Communist Party's General Secretary, Tito.

Tito was a near mythical figure. He had been on the wanted list of the Royal Yugoslav Police before the war, and had risen swiftly to dominate the ranks of the partisans. As befits the nature of the organization – initially a guerrilla force, elusive and mysterious – for a long period there was only a hazy idea of who Tito actually was. Some thought that Tito stood for *Tanja Internacionalna Teroristicka Organizacija* (Secret International Terrorist Organization), some thought it a kind of rank, others said Tito was a beautiful, formidable young woman. The truth – as ever – was rather more prosaic. Members of the resistance had always taken cover names to disguise their true identity, and Josip Broz picked Tito as it was a common name in his home district.

It was with Tito that Brigadier Fitzroy Maclean – the SAS officer in charge of supporting partisan operations – had a conversation in 1943 that epitomized the intractable divisions in the region during the war.

> As we sat talking under the stars, I asked Tito whether now, two years after his original negotiations with Mihailović, there was any hope of reaching agreement with the Chetniks and thus forming a united front against the enemy. He replied immediately that there might be some hope if the Chetniks would stop fighting the partisans and start fighting the Germans and if those of them who had come to terms with the enemy could either be brought to heel or finally disowned. He did not, however, regard such a change of heart as any longer within the bounds of possibility.

Churchill had little time – both literally and figuratively – for such complex politics and fickle loyalties. He was, of course, famed for his ability to cut through red tape. He was said to walk into his office each morning and immediately move everything in his in-tray to his out-tray, reasoning that the important material would make its way back to him, and he took a characteristically straightforward stance on supporting the war effort in Yugoslavia. When briefing Maclean, he voiced his impatience with the complexity of the military and political picture on the ground by saying: 'Find out who is killing the most Germans, and help them kill more.' A distinctly Churchillian approach, but one that in itself created a dilemma – the most effective fighting force in the region was undoubtedly the partisans, but to support them was seen as effectively supporting a significant Communist force on the doorstep of Western Europe. However, his approach was 'whoever is the enemy of my enemy is my friend', a sentiment that was formally ratified at the Tehran Conference of 1943 when Stalin, Roosevelt and Churchill met and agreed, among other things, to offer equipment and military support to Tito's partisans.

Many of the romantic notions that surround the partisans relate to their appearance – a common perception is of a dashing, almost foppish group dressed in traditional mountain costume and draped with bandoliers of ammunition. The reality was that until the Allies began a concerted set of air drops to them late in the war, they begged, borrowed, and stole most of their clothing. The one recurring factor was a red star on every cap; a badge of honour and a powerful rallying symbol that persists in Slovenia to this day.

It is clear, then, that the logistical complexity of the Crow's Flight went far beyond difficult terrain and tenacious German pursuers. It took place against a backdrop of a war within a war – different ideologies, bitter historic enmities and heavily armed groups diametrically opposed to each other, all within the same nation. The escape was not only a masterpiece of nerve, logistics and planning, it was also a triumph of local co-operation along its entire meandering length. It is only when one knows this tempestuous history, and the depth of the feeling within each opposing faction, that the realization dawns of just how remarkable that co-operation was, and why it resonates within the nation to this day. At the same time, the Crow's Flight would not have come about at all without a genuine visionary from within the multinational group of POWs in Yugoslavia, someone with the necessary charisma and powers of persuasion to not only convince his fellow prisoners of the viability of the escape, but also to win over the partisans and hoodwink his German captors. To do so he had to master a new language, garner an in-depth understanding of local history and culture and implement a plan of Machiavellian complexity.

One might assume that such a figure would stem from the Oxbridge-educated officer class, or perhaps from the Special Forces community, well versed as they were in operations with local guerrilla groups and warring factions. One might not naturally associate such a role with an Australian lance corporal who had been taken prisoner without ever being under fire.

Ralph Churches was born in 1917, the youngest of eight children from a pioneer farming family in the Murray Mallee in South Australia. His life was uncompromisingly tough from the start, although he was bright enough to receive a scholarship to attend Adelaide High School. He graduated, and after a period working as a cobbler, managed to find a job as a clerk with the State Bank of South Australia.

Ralph joined the Australian Imperial Force 2/48th Battalion on 17 June, 1940. He had married his fiancée, Ronte, just two days before enlisting. They would not have a honeymoon until after the war, and she would not see him again for four years after he sailed for North Africa on 17 November 1940. He served in Egypt and Syria, before being seconded to Europe with the Australian and New Zealand Corps (the ANZACs). It is notable that his drawing skills and attention to detail quickly saw him singled out for intelligence work. However, this career was short-lived: in April 1941 his force was surrounded, and Churches – with six other men – rowed a boat for two weeks down the coast of Greece to escape capture. Despite this heroic effort, he was taken prisoner in May. This near-fanatical desire to escape, this deep sense of duty, was to be a characteristic of Churches throughout his subsequent incarceration. He ended up as a POW in southern Austria, where he managed to escape twice but didn't get far before he was caught, something he put down to a lack of detailed planning on his part. It was a valuable lesson learned – Churches had the emotional intelligence to understand that the best way to thwart your enemy is to inveigle your way into their systems, to become a trusted confidant. On his arrival at Stalag XVIII-D near Maribor – after a harrowing four-day rail journey from Austria in cattle wagons that nearly killed him – Churches immediately set to work. Carefully, meticulously, showing an extraordinary ability to play the long game, to wait, to watch, and to control those around him, he began to plot his escape.

CHAPTER FIFTEEN

Prison Camp at Maribor

The day after I arrived in Slovenia, Svetlana drove me to Melje on the outskirts of Maribor, the old site of Stalag XVIII-D. It was a beautiful day, with not a breath of wind and the sky an unblemished cornflower-blue. The heat was oppressive, and I wound down my window to cool the car, then quickly wound it up again as fine white dust raised by our passing barrelled in. My first glimpse of the site, through a rather grimy window, was of ranks of lorries – today it is a bustling goods yard, swiftly returned to its original use after the end of the war. The Germans, as an occupying army, were adept at taking over logistical centres for their own purposes, and it struck me that this was the perfect site for a prison camp. The movement of human traffic is – after all – no more than the movement of a series of packages, albeit ones that require basic provisions to be kept alive.

I was due to meet Ralph's son Neil Churches at the site, and he soon appeared, an avuncular figure in his late fifties, slightly out of breath and ruddy-cheeked as he strode up the hill.

'Nine thousand miles from Australia,' he said, 'and the last hundred yards are the hardest.'

Neil had worked in the theatre and in IT, but since the death of his father two years before, had dedicated himself to unearthing

247

the truth behind an event that had loomed so large in Ralph's life, and subsequently in his own. Neil had flown in from Melbourne to walk some of the route with me, and it was his suggestion that we explore the site of the prison camp first.

'It's important to me,' he said simply, as we strode towards the cluster of customs sheds and disused railway lines. 'It could help me explain why Dad was the way he was sometimes. We didn't have an easy relationship on occasion, and the more I learn about this escape the more that relationship makes sense. I'm also bloody proud of him, and want to make sure as many people as possible know the truth.'

The camp was entirely dominated by a large warehouse at its centre, with a few smaller buildings sitting in the gloom of its immense shadow. It was a somewhat dilapidated site, but the traces of the past remained strong. At the fringes of the main buildings lay small patches of waste ground, dusty and barren, with a herd of goats shuffling through one of the larger areas, anaesthetized by the heat of the day as they nosed optimistically through piles of rubbish in search of food. Overall, it presented a rather bleak scene, and despite the warmth of the day I felt something of a chill at the echoes of the past that remained – an industrial site that held the memories of another time and another purpose.

A network of disused railway lines ran through the site, feeding the satellite buildings, but all ultimately converging on the giant structure at its centre. As we walked, we stepped over the tracks still in place, being slowly reclaimed by lush grass or clogged with piles of litter – the detritus of a working goods yard. Neil paused, looking down at the rusting metal beneath his feet.

'They're poignant, these lines,' he said. 'Some of the worst atrocities of the war were perpetrated by moving large numbers of people in goods wagons along railway tracks. Dad sometimes talked about being moved here, the brutality of spending four days continuously in cattle wagons, the loss of dignity of being crammed in among so many other men. He was in bad shape when he got here – he had malaria, cholera and dysentery. Not unnaturally he wanted to get away as quickly as possible. Not to escape necessarily, but be part of a working party outside the wire. He worried that if he stayed here it could have killed him.'

We moved towards a weathered fence next to the small grassy field occupied by the herd of goats.

'This was the exercise yard,' said Neil. 'Doesn't look much now, but it was vital for the sanity of the prisoners. They had football matches here, boxing tournaments, the lot. It wasn't just a good way to maintain morale; it also meant, from a German perspective, that the men were less restless, and less inclined to escape.'

We leant on the fence, and I did my best to imagine several hundred Allied prisoners in the green space before me – a ragtag collection of nationalities and uniforms shouting in several languages, the men all the while attempting to reconcile themselves to years in captivity, to an uncertain future, to being totally at the mercy of men from another land, and to being far apart from loved ones. But the scene was too tranquil, too sedate, and I finally turned away to look at the building behind us.

Both Neil and I knew what this building was, and yet neither of us wanted to speak of it. This vast customs shed had once held 5,000 Russian prisoners of war. In contrast to the Allied prisoners, who were accommodated in barrack blocks and dormitories, the Russians were housed in the most brutal conditions imaginable – overcrowded, sleeping on the floor, beaten by their guards and ravaged by typhus that killed them in their droves. There was only one toilet, and food was a thin gruel. Local Slovenians risked their own safety to smuggle loaves of bread though the barred windows, but this simple gesture of humanity was not enough to stem the tide. The conditions within this building were said to be as bad as Dachau, Auschwitz and Mauthausen – this was a concentration camp in all but name.

What is particularly horrific is the thought of dying men, clustered against barred windows, watching fellow prisoners play sport, lounge in the sun and stroll around the prison camp. Through a simple accident of nationality, they had been deemed sub-human, and knew they would die in the darkness around them. Such psychological torture is beyond measure.

'Dad talked about that building,' said Neil quietly.

We had sought, and been given, permission to enter the warehouse. At the time, it had seemed a real coup, the chance to walk under the same fluted wooden archways where history had unfolded, albeit of a sinister kind. And yet now, in the sunlight of a glorious Slovenian day, neither of us wanted to take the next few steps.

'Come on, shall we go in?' I finally said to Neil, gesturing towards the warehouse. 'Have you ever been inside before?'

'No,' he said. 'When I've visited here in the past it's always been forbidden. Dad talked about having to move the dead bodies from there – it was a punishment for Allied prisoners – and he said that the moment you opened the door you vomited, the stench was so bad. It'll feel strange opening that same door all this years later.'

It might seem a fanciful notion, but they hold their memories, these buildings. As the heavy metal door crashed back, it revealed a cavernous space, a place full of shadows. The first breath was of stale air, lifeless and heavy, with the sliver of daylight through the door illuminating particles of dust that twisted and spun in the gentle eddy of our passing.

Some events are remembered by elaborate memorials, some by ceremonies, and some by simply leaving the remnants of them untouched. This shed at Maribor is just such a place – it is empty, yet full of the memory of the appalling human suffering that occurred within these four walls. To live, to work, to laugh in this building would be a travesty.

I moved slowly into the darkness, my steps hesitant, my progress hindered by the knowledge of what had happened here. When I glanced back I saw Neil had stopped in his tracks.

'Just give me a moment, would you?' he said.

I left him standing by the door and carried on into the main building, climbing an old set of rickety wooden stairs into another cavernous floor above. I heard Neil's footsteps behind me, and turned to see that he had joined me.

In a peculiar way, this was a beautiful building, precisely the sort of open space that would be converted into executive flats or open-plan offices in many other cities around the world. The wood of the pillars and beams was dried and twisted, each one grooved, scarred and channelled like an ancient olive tree. I looked at the base of the pillar beside me, and thought of a man who perhaps had lain with his cheek pressed against it, thinking of his children, his wife and his home, as the life ebbed out of him.

No official records exist of the numbers of Russian POWs who died in this shed at Maribor, but it was certainly hundreds, and possibly thousands. Over millennia, mankind has devised many ways of killing prisoners, but perhaps the most barbaric is to simply herd them into an overcrowded space, pull a heavy door shut, and leave them in the suffocating darkness.

What is undeniable is that removing bodies from the customs shed hardened Ralph Churches' resolve to escape. In later life, he spoke of his burning desire to 'put one over' on the Germans, and one can only conclude that such sentiments were born in the fetid darkness of the customs shed in Stalag XVIII-D.

*

The timing of his arrival at the prison camp was opportune, as beyond the wire there were tectonic changes taking place. Although the occupiers had initially been welcomed by parts of the Yugoslavian population, they had swiftly revealed their true colours. Slovenia found itself not only occupied and subdued, but threatened with complete cultural annihilation. In German-occupied northern Slovenia, the German language was imposed, street and town names were changed and Slovenian cultural organizations were banned. Mussolini was quick to endorse such a policy in southern Slovenia, noting, 'I would say we could easily sacrifice 500,000 barbaric Slavs for 50,000 Italians.'

The state capital, Ljubljana, was surrounded by watchtowers and ringed with barbed wire, creating effectively the largest concentration camp in Europe. It was made the capital of the new Italian region of Provincia di Luciana on 3 May 1941, with a new mayor – Leon Rupnik – who had been a general of the Royal Yugoslav Army. Ljubljana would remain a bastion for the occupying forces until the end of the war, a major hub from which anti-partisan operations were launched.

The result was resistance, a co-ordinated uprising of such defiance and ferocity that it compelled Colonel Peter Wilkinson – an SOE officer seconded to the partisans – to write that 'no similar popular uprising had been seen in Europe since Andreas Hofer led the Tyroleans against Napoleon.'

The Axis powers had implemented a standard occupation infrastructure after invading Yugoslavia. They appointed puppet leaders, making sure that they were closely aligned with their own political ideologies, and ruthlessly oppressed any sense of cultural identity. In doing so they had made a fundamental mistake. They pitted themselves against a Slovenian population that had not only been forging their own powerful sense of identity for centuries, but that had also grown up hunting and hiding in the thickly wooded mountains of their home state. In effect, these were people who had their own natural warrior caste. By attempting to subdue them through brutality, by treating them as subhuman, the occupying forces had instead stirred up a hornets' nest that would see the mobilization of one of the most effective guerrilla forces in military history.

The Liberation Front (*Osvobodilna Fronta*, or OF) came into being the day after Hitler had imperiously surveyed Maribor from the balcony in the town square. Created at a meeting of political and cultural figures at the house of the literary critic Boris Kidrič, it was drawn from a range of organizations – trade unions, student groups and Christian Socialists – and was notable in that large numbers of women joined, fighting alongside and on equal terms with the men. Through the length and breadth of Slovenia, the partisans were mobilizing.

Although the early stages of the uprising were courageous and spirited, they were also disorganized and sporadic. Predictably the response from the Axis powers was one of ferocious reprisals on a mass scale. Mussolini, on a visit to Gorizia, noted with typical vainglorious, venomous bombast that:

> This country has degenerated to the point where the poi-
> soned seeds should be exterminated by sword and fire . . .
> The local population sympathizes with the rebels and is
> supporting them. Before this process of disintegration
> becomes uncontrollable, we must exterminate it. We shall
> do as Julius Caesar did with the rebellious Gauls: he set fire
> to the villages, killed the entire male population, and took
> the women and children into slavery, far from home . . .

Treatment of captured partisans was brutal in the extreme, although this was readily reciprocated (the partisans did not take prisoners). One of the techniques used by the Germans when partisans were captured was to make them write a last letter to their loved ones on the eve of their execution. Ralph Churches gives an account of one such letter, written by two brothers – Albin and Marjan Milavic – on 26 December 1941. The words are made doubly poignant by the fact that their brother Ivan had already been killed in action only a month before:

> Dearest Parents,
> Our last greetings go to you dearest dad and mum and our brother France. Forgive us and may you be happy, give our love to the boss, the Kral boys and uncle. Marjan and I must die, today it'll all be over. Ivan has already died in action. Dearest parents, God be with you! A hug from Albin and Marjan

These letters were posted in public places, along with posters making it quite clear that any taking up of arms, or co-operation with the enemy, would result in a similar fate.

Ralph goes on to note that 1,590 Slovene hostages were executed in this manner, including eighty-two women.

Perhaps unsurprisingly, such tactics backfired dramatically, and the insurrection spread. The partisans grew in strength and confidence, launching bolder and bolder missions and even facing the Germans in pitched battles. In one such encounter, the Battle of Dražgoše in January 1942, 200 partisans fought 3,000 Germans. They eventually had to give ground, melting away into the hills around them, but this was the largest and fiercest resistance battle the Germans had faced anywhere in Europe. The Italians swiftly lost control of their regions, and in June 1942 the local Italian High Commissioner reported to Rome that he controlled only thirty-nine of a total of ninety-five municipalities.

Of the 1,936 settlements under his authority, he held sway in only thirty-six. He estimated that within these regions, he had control of only 30 per cent of the population, and 10 per cent of the territory. All of this took place against a backdrop of a concentrated Italian campaign against the Resistance, which lasted from June to November and resulted in thousands of arrests and executions, and the razing of whole villages.

Meanwhile, Ralph Churches had been developing his plans. The urge to slip the bonds of servitude, to run for the hills, must have been strong indeed, but Ralph knew that Maribor was a long way from any Allied-held territory – he writes in his book *One Hundred Miles as The Crow Flies* that 'Switzerland was 250 miles and Turkey 600 miles away.' As such, he decided to bide his time, and 'wait for something to turn up'.

As other ranks, the prisoners were contracted out for work by the Germans and might find themselves moved to satellite camps nearer their place of work. Often set up by the civilian contractor, these camps were less heavily guarded. In April 1942, Ralph found himself in a camp of about a hundred men working on rebuilding a road near the Austrian border and quickly realized that this offered a glimmer of hope, a chance to escape that simply wasn't available if he stayed in Stalag XVIII-D. But first, he needed to know his enemy, to learn their methods, their strengths and weaknesses.

And so, this son of a pioneer Australian farmer set himself the task of becoming fluent in German, and borrowed every book he could on the local culture and political scene. He had a real aptitude for languages, and was soon chatting amicably to his guards (albeit with a slight Austrian accent picked up from them). He became so fluent that after the war his wife sometimes struggled to get him to speak English.

His language skills brought him to the attention of the satellite work camp's commandant, and he was made a *Vertrauensmann* – which is best translated as 'right-hand man', or even 'trustworthy'. No sense of collaboration should be read into this – he had a plan, and this was simply one of the stepping stones.

What is remarkable about Churches was that his burning obsession to escape never wavered. Every action, every event, every thought was geared to ultimately making a getaway: 'From the moment of my capture, as a brash twenty-three-year-old, I was seized by a pride-dictated decision that somehow, some day, I would escape.'

Far from resenting the promotion of their comrade, the other POWs soon elected Churches as Camp Leader, making him their representative in all matters of negotiation with the prison camp authorities. In effect, he had become their commanding officer, a rallying figure in moments of duress, and often their sole source of authority and order. Les Laws, one of Churches' fellow escapees and himself a significant figure in the story that was about to unfold, remembers Ralph as a very popular man who was 'not afraid to stand up to the Germans if necessary'.

It seems that his initiative and ingenuity knew no bounds. The prisoners were allowed to receive Red Cross parcels, in which were cigarettes, coffee and chocolate. Appreciating the value of these as bargaining tools, all three being virtually unobtainable for the Austrian guards, Ralph stockpiled them. He was meticulous in his record-keeping, signing items in and out of stores and keeping a ledger of every exchange. Soon the guards regarded him as an ally, a source of gifts, and became more lenient in their treatment of not only him, but also the other prisoners.

Meanwhile, the first British mission to support the OF on the ground in Slovenia was established on 27 June 1943, effectively recognizing the Slovene partisans as an Allied army. When Italy bowed to the inevitable and withdrew from the Axis in September 1943, they left their areas of occupation in Yugoslavia unregulated. In the resultant power vacuum, supply runs and air drops intensified, and even though the Germans scrambled to occupy regions under threat, this proved a pivotal time for a previously ill-equipped guerrilla force.

The fall of Mussolini was a huge boost to the POWs too, although for many it signalled the imminent end to the war, and a reason to sit tight and wait for liberation. Churches remained entirely resolute in his plan to escape. After the satellite work camp was closed and the inmates transferred back to Maribor, he was excited to discover that some of the men would be shuttled daily to work on a railway line which ran parallel to the River Drava, at a location called Ozbalt. Their site of work was to be the south bank of the river, nineteen kilometres west of Maribor. Crucially, this placed them closer to the area of partisan operations, and what's more in a remote area abutted by thick forests. A perfect site for escape.

As we had walked the grounds of the main Stalag, I had asked Neil Churches about the systems his father had put in place at the camp to keep the guards firmly on his side. Neil had immediately laughed in delight.

'Oh, he was good,' he said, 'really good. He had it all worked out so well that when the Gestapo launched a search of the camp, the guards actually sent them deliberately to the wrong areas as they didn't want their supplies compromised. He really did run a slick operation.'

Such was Churches' influence that he even arranged for a grand piano to be purchased with funds generated by a whip-round of the inmates. Each man received four and a half

Reichsmarks camp pay under the Geneva Convention, and the resultant 1,000 Reichsmarks kitty was duly used to buy a splendid piano, which the Germans brought to the camp in the back of one of their trucks. It arrived in time for the 1943 Christmas show, a surreal spectacle indeed for the watching guards in their austere uniforms undergoing their own rather bleak festivities.

If Churches' easy camaraderie with the guards was notable, his relationship with the camp commandant was truly extraordinary.

The prison camps were generally placed under the charge of minor officials, or those retired from active service (often from the military Armageddon that was the Eastern Front). In the case of the Maribor camp, this was Commandant Johann Gross who arrived early in 1944.

'Dad has said that Johann was one of his best friends during the war,' said Neil. 'It got to the point that they were addressing each other not only by the familiar "Du" form in German – reserved only for confidants and good mates – but were actually using each other's first names. They became very close indeed.'

This relationship reaped real rewards for Churches, who was trusted enough to occasionally be left alone in the commandant's office (during one such occasion he stole a compass from the desk, something he kept until his dying day). It also allowed him to visit Maribor on unsupervised errands. During one visit, he was in a cafe and saw that some school children had left an atlas unattended on a table. He immediately ripped out the pages that carried the maps of Austria and Slovenia – again, a memento he kept for the rest of his life.

One of the recurring themes of the descriptions of Churches' actions throughout the war is his deep-rooted sense of humanity. Having stolen the pages, and in doing so placing himself in considerable jeopardy had he been spotted, he noted after the war that his main concern was that the school child who owned it would get into trouble. Such humanity would end up saving several lives during the course of the escape.

Such forays into Maribor also allowed Churches to carefully glean information about the progress of the war. He did so by reading local papers and by listening to the radio – even though the news came from Goebbels' Ministry of Propaganda, he was adept at filtering it for useful intelligence. He came to the conclusion that the local Slovenes would be worthy allies in his escape bid, not believing for a moment the Axis line that the partisans were of no more significance than 'lice on a dog'. He was also keenly aware of the state of heightened tensions in the town, manifested in a large Gestapo presence. This in turn made the locals very wary of contact from any prisoners – a classic German trap was to have an agent pose as an escapee, then betray any people who assisted him. In this sense, Churches' excellent German counted against him – few native Slovenians could believe that any Allied soldier could have mastered the language so effectively.

As the months passed, he painstakingly gathered intelligence, cultivated his relationship with the guards and commandant and bided his time. He describes his demeanour during this period as 'a cheerful if somewhat chuckle-headed British colonial'. It was the perfect cover – still waters run deep, and in Churches' case they covered his real intentions perfectly. His was a masterpiece of infiltration.

CHAPTER SIXTEEN

Failure is Not an Option

Neil and I stood with our backs to the station at Ozbalt, craning our necks up at the precipitous, heavily forested hill that loomed over us.

'I still can't believe they legged it up there,' said Neil thoughtfully, almost to himself, 'it simply doesn't look possible.'

'Well,' I said, my own gaze still fixed on the hill, 'we'll be walking up it ourselves shortly, so we'll soon find out.'

Neil smiled philosophically in acknowledgement, and began to trudge along the tracks, leaving the station behind him with barely a backward glance. It looked little more than a ruin, a sagging little building virtually unchanged from the days of the war. I peered through one of the grimy windows, making out the frame of a bed, a swivel chair and the skeleton of an old desk. Plainly the station was no longer in regular use – it seemed strange that this was the point that launched such an audacious escape bid, so incongruous a setting for something of such élan and scale.

I re-joined Neil some two hundred metres along the track, where he was standing peering intently into the undergrowth.

'Yep, I think it was here. Difficult to tell, but it looks about right.'

In front of us, on the other side of the tracks, was a path leading into the deep emerald shadows of the forest. It was almost certainly here that Ralph and six other prisoners had staged their initial escape, the prelude to the mass breakout to follow.

The events leading to this initial escape spoke volumes for not only Ralph, but the men that accompanied him. His closest conspirator was Les Laws, a fine pianist and jazz musician before the war, and himself in possession of a fiercely independent spirit. He had been a driver in the Royal Engineers when he too was captured in Greece. On the train journey to Maribor he had emptied a latrine bucket over a particularly bumptious German corporal. Laws was the ideal partner in crime for Churches, and as they shared a barrack room the two men had quickly become close confidants.

Churches had decided, after months of careful research and planning, that the summer of 1944 would be the best time to make his escape, when the weather would be better for travel. He had also realized that the only way to escape was to make contact with the partisans. Ozbalt was within a hundred kilometres of confirmed partisan activity, and he felt that the presence of the prisoners must surely be of interest to them. But he knew they took no prisoners, and were deeply suspicious of agents dressed in Allied uniforms. Churches was a stickler for dressing smartly, and habitually wore his characteristic Australian slouch hat so he could be readily identified. He had tried to impose similar standards on his fellow prisoners, and had largely been ignored, as they preferred to work in shorts and T-shirts in the summer heat. His rationale for smart dress was also an act of subtle defiance against his captors, showing that they had not completely subdued his spirit. He worried that his smart appearance would arouse the suspicions of the partisans, but did not want to compromise himself by setting a poor example to the men under his command.

Ralph had one other major disadvantage in that he did not as a rule accompany the working parties to Ozbalt. His role as Camp Leader made him exempt from such duties, and thus he faced a dilemma, how to gather information on what was potentially an escape site rich in possibilities – something he had waited two years for – without weakening his current position in camp.

The solution was twofold. Les Laws, using the excuse of needing to protect his musician's hands, had persuaded the guards to let him assume the duties of collecting water from a nearby farmhouse for the working parties. It wasn't long before he was undertaking these duties completely unsupervised. He slowly built a friendship with the woman who lived there, a mother of two small children whose husband was working away, sealing the relationship with gifts of chocolate and soap. Seeing that Les had a chance of contacting the partisans via the farmer's wife, Churches asked him if he wanted to work on the escape plan together. It turned out that Laws was also considering the possibility of escape, having made four unsuccessful attempts in the past. Les had already decided to talk to the woman about contacting the partisans, even though this placed both him and her at risk. If they had been compromised he would probably have been relocated to another camp, and she would have certainly been executed. Ralph and Les quickly agreed that co-operation was the best option if their escape plans were to be successful.

At the same time, Churches had gleaned yet more information about the locations of the partisans and the turning tide of the war. Much of this came from discussion with other *Vertrauensmänner* when they met to collect Red Cross parcels. It also came from the civilian population during Ralph's trips into Maribor, who were emboldened by the increased success of the partisans' military endeavours.

With the added success of the D-Day offensive in Normandy, which had started on 6 June, Churches decided that he would make his escape in August, and to this effect began to stockpile equipment. By that time, the Allied advance would – hopefully – be moving ever closer to Slovenia.

Seven decades later, Neil and I were standing in front of the section of undergrowth where his father had hidden this kit.

'Of course,' he said, turning to face me, 'Dad faced a real problem in that he had to essentially resign as Camp Leader and as a *Vertrauensmann* to be able to get to work at this site, and hide his escape kit away. That's how he ended up having such an extraordinary conversation with Commandant Johann Gross.'

Churches had approached the commandant not only to tender his own resignation as Camp Leader, but to urge him to apply for a transfer to another camp. In doing so, he knew he would spare Gross the punishment that would be meted out to whoever was overseeing the camp when the escape took place. This – yet again – shows Churches' deep sense of humanity. He took a huge risk in persuading Gross to apply for a transfer, implying as it did that a major event was about to take place in the camp. I said as much to Neil.

Once again, he chuckled at the story. 'Yeah, Dad mentioned that conversation. He said that Johann took an age to talk round, before finally the penny dropped. There was a rather touching moment when they shook hands and wished each other luck, before going their separate ways. Happily, the commandant who replaced Gross was apparently a complete bastard, so he basically got what he deserved after the escape took place.'

Churches was now free to join the working party at Ozbalt. In the interim, Laws had broached the subject of the partisans with the woman in the farmhouse. This had immediately borne fruit. As far as the other prisoners working on the railway were concerned, they had simply been joined by a civilian who was helping them out on the maintenance of the track. The new arrival earned the nicknames 'Cadger' and 'Flash Harry', as he was always scrounging cigarettes and had a somewhat louche manner. In fact, his name was Anton, and he was working under-cover for the OF.

Suddenly, the possibility of escape, for so long a distant chimera, became very real. Laws suggested at this point that they be joined in the escape by his good friend, Andy Hamilton. Churches in turn suggested that they be accompanied by Kit Carson, another close confidant. Hamilton and Carson shared a barrack room with Laws and Churches, and after further consultation they decided to take the four other men who shared the same accommodation.

This seemingly innocuous decision actually had huge implications. As a rule, Allied prisoners who escaped were returned to prison and then punished with varying levels of severity. This applied to individuals and small groups, but an escape of more than seven men constituted a mutiny. Mutiny was punishable by trial and firing squad. In agreeing to increase the size of their party from two to eight, Churches and Laws had effectively signed their own death warrants, should they be captured. This decision turned the escape from what might be viewed as something of a caper – an adherence to the duty to escape in the face of an understanding enemy – into a simple binary choice. Escape by all means, but there could be no option for failure. To be recaptured would mean execution; this was no longer a game, it was deadly serious.

And now, at the moment of truth, they faced a setback. The Germans launched a series of offensives against the partisans and won several victories. Intelligence that Churches gleaned from his contacts indicated that this might be the prelude to a strategic withdrawal by German forces – a final act of defiance and show of military might. If the Germans withdrew from Slovenia, it would mean the relocation of all the POWs. They had to get away now.

On Monday 28 August 1944, Churches, Laws and the rest of the escape group joined the main working party on their daily short train ride from Maribor to Ozbalt. The entire workforce numbered over eighty, and were accompanied as usual by several ageing Austrian guards and the civilian contractors who would guide them in their work.

As ever, Ralph had prepared impeccably. He wore his British battledress over the top of his work shorts, and also wore a warm sweater despite the late summer heat. In his rucksack he had a tin of bully beef, a block of chocolate and a packet of biscuits – this he would cache near the railway line for when the moment of escape came.

Laws had been informed by Anton that the partisans planned to take the village of Lovrenz, a mere ten kilometres from the working site in Ozbalt, and hold it for twenty-four hours. This was to be their chance – a brief window of opportunity to link up with a fighting force that would then spirit them away into the mountains.

Two days passed, with the working parties returning to camp as normal and no signal forthcoming that the partisan capture of Lovrenz was imminent. The escape group grew increasingly nervous. Finally, on the evening of the 29th, Laws was informed that the escape had to happen the next day, and was given a rendezvous point of an old chestnut tree close to the farmhouse.

On the 30th, the men travelled to work on the train – one of them was unable to join them as his working detail didn't allow him to travel on that particular day, a bitter blow indeed. This was the day of days for them, the culmination of months of planning, of carefully recruiting local contacts, of playing a delicate game of risk and reward with the camp commandant, the guards and the trust of their fellow prisoners. It could all be undone in one unguarded moment, one miscalculation. Standing at the site, looking at the railway line stretching in either direction, it must have been a moment of high adrenaline, of silently exchanged glances, of sweating palms and hammering hearts. There could be no more planning, no more meetings, no more research. The time for action was upon them.

At Ozbalt, they worked as normal before slipping away in the afternoon, one by one, on the pretence of having a smoke or taking a toilet break. Churches was nearly compromised at the very last minute when one of the guards saw him approaching his hidden rucksack, but – showing considerable coolness under intense pressure – he simply offered the guard three cigarettes from the stores, with a promise of more over the coming days. Satisfied, the guard ambled away.

Another member of the escape group had been unable to give his working party the slip, and had to watch in silent frustration as his compatriots slipped into the woods without him.

At the end of the day, the working party gathered their tools and trudged back to the waiting train. Six men were missing, but in the noise and confusion of the departure from the site, their absence was not noticed. Their escape had begun, and the clock was ticking. They had to make it to Lovrenz in time to meet the partisans, and put enough space between them and the camp as possible before the pursuit began.

Anton was waiting for the six escapees beneath the chestnut tree, and they quickly set out towards Lovrenz. Within seconds, the entire group had been swallowed by the forest. They could not have known that this was the start of an epic traverse of Slovenia, pursued by German forces outraged at the audacity of the escape. All they were focused on was reaching Lovrenz, and ten kilometres in Slovenia is quite unlike ten kilometres in the lowlands of Europe. Churches described their guide as being 'lean and tireless' – setting a trend for every partisan they would meet en route, the result of living in the mountains and years of fighting a war of constant movement. In the words of one partisan, 'if you could run fast, you would live. If you were slow, you would die.' Churches and his companions were receiving a swift, brutal test of what was required to operate with the partisans, a test they had no option of failing.

Neil and I were about to face a similar, rather sobering experience. We had decided to walk as much of the same route to Lovrenz as we possibly could, and the first section required us to scale the overgrown cutting towards the path in the woods.

Inspired by Ralph's story, and the stirring deeds that had taken place where we were standing, we threw ourselves at the bank. I tried to imagine Austrian guards eyeing me suspiciously, and quickly realized that they could have leant on their rifles and enjoyed one of Ralph's contraband cigarettes at their leisure before sauntering over and arresting me. My progress was slow, noisy and amusingly incompetent – the very antithesis of 'covert'. Neil, despite his splendid genes, was faring little better, and at one point needed me to place both my hands on his backside to shove him up and over a particularly steep section of the bank. We were thirty metres into the trek, and already the reality of moving through the Slovenian landscape had struck home.

Much of Slovenia is – even today – essentially a wilderness. Covering 20,000 square kilometres, it has a population of only two million, and is the third most forested nation in Europe. The dense, ancient woodland is home to boar, bear, wolf and lynx. In the dark recesses of ancient glades and quiet hollows are vipers and ticks, and the thick undergrowth makes movement nearly impossible without local knowledge. Today, a well-established network of paths criss-crosses much of the country, but even now there are regions that are virtually inaccessible. In 1944, huge swathes of the country would have been seen as death traps by the occupying forces, populated as they were by locals who knew the area as well as the backstreets and alleys of any home town.

Ralph, Les and the other escapees had entered a near-primal world. This played very much to the advantage of the partisans – difficult terrain to move over is easy terrain to hide in – but it must have been a hugely daunting environment to move through for men who were used to prison camp routine, poorly fed and ill-equipped.

Neil and I huffed and stumbled up the steep tracks leading to a series of false summits. Eventually, after several hours of hard trekking, we crested a rise to see the village of Lovrenz in the valley below – chocolate-box pretty and neatly laid out around three ancient churches.

Neil had plainly struggled on the trek, and as I watched him it dawned on me what an emotional weight he carried. Born the son of a war hero, one who – by Neil's own admission – was hard on his children as he worked through his own demons after the war, Neil had spent a great deal of his life trying to prove himself to (and then trying to defy) the powerful force of his father's personality. Now, at last walking in his footsteps physically, as opposed to psychologically, he was battling to replicate, to live up to, the deeds of Ralph. I could only begin to imagine the turmoil that generated within him.

But we had made it, not all of our baggage physical, and Neil turned to me as we surveyed Lovrenz for the first time.

'Of course, when Dad got here, he was suddenly in the midst

of the party of the century! That must have been a strange sensation for someone so used to operating covertly and subtly.'

Neil was right. When the group entered Lovrenz, they were immediately taken to the officers commanding the partisan group that had taken the village. For the rest of his life Ralph spoke of his admiration for the partisans, and for the huge debt of honour that he owed them. This first encounter made a significant impression.

Soon we were drinking slivovitz with two pleasant young men whose well made-over German uniforms and polished riding boots betokened their officer status. Double thin red stripes on their epaulettes suggested that they were lieutenants, and this turned out to be the case.

Les Laws was equally struck by the appearance of the partisans, who looked like characters from the popular romantic musical, *The Maid of the Mountains*, which was set in a bandit camp. What was particularly potent for all the men was the appearance of a number of women within their ranks – for men incarcerated for several years, this was plainly a most welcome sight. Churches writes:

Maybe it was the reaction to three years of the life monastic, but I don't recall seeing one girl partisan who did not look pretty and who did not wear her made-over uniform in comely fashion and well.

This may be construed by some as slightly sexist – the partisan women fighters were entirely formidable, and were given no special treatment by the men in that regard – however, under the circumstances, it is perhaps forgivable that Churches and his companions were somewhat giddy with the potent blend of liberty, exhaustion and the sudden proximity of several young women.

Soon there was another source of inebriation, of a more traditional variety.

By now, Neil and I were sitting in the incongruously named 'Ali Baba' cafe in Lovrenz village centre, enjoying a well-earned cup of coffee.

'Dad said that all they wanted to do was get him drunk!' he said. 'Every time he tried to talk about the escape route, about potential destinations, about logistics, they would nod and smile and say "Drink!" before pressing another glass of slivovitz into his hand.'

Slivovitz is a fiery local spirit – a kind of plum brandy – drunk in Slovenia with undimmed enthusiasm to this day. Being something of a stickler for military history, I thought it only correct that we order two glasses, which we dutifully downed before continuing our conversation in slightly huskier voices.

'It was really under the influence of the drink that Dad had the big idea. To his dying day he can't be sure whether he would have come up with it if he'd been sober, but the fact is that he decided to go back and spring everyone else.' Neil sat back proudly, shaking his head at the absurdity of it all.

It is worth noting that there is some dispute about exactly who came up with the concept of a mass escape. Les Laws wrote after the war that it was actually the day after the party that he approached the CO of the partisans to suggest returning for the other prisoners. But such confusion is understandable given that the escapees were three sheets to the wind, and emotionally and physically exhausted by their own exertions over the course of the day. There is the possibility that they both had the same thought at different moments of course, but in terms of the source of the idea, Neil was entirely adamant.

'It was definitely Dad,' he said. 'In fact, he had a furious argument with Les about going back. Les – probably quite reasonably – thought it was madness. Dad said he had to work really hard to bring him round to the concept.'

If Les was difficult to convince, then the partisans proved even harder to crack. It was not so much that they were against the idea – this would be a major coup for them, as well as providing a powerful bargaining chip to maintain the flow of supplies and support from the Allies – it was just that Churches' German was so perfect it placed him under immediate suspicion. Was he an infiltrator? Was he trying to lure the partisan force into a carefully laid trap?

Finally, it was agreed – they would return to the work site at dawn the next morning en masse, a fighting force of one hundred heavily armed partisans. But they would do so with Churches and Laws accompanying them – at the first hint of trouble, the first indication that the partisans had been betrayed, the two men would be immediately executed.

As I watched the sun set behind the mountains, and the general bonhomie of a warm Slovenian evening fuelled by slivovitz settled upon me, I reflected on that decision, perhaps one of the more remarkable gambles taken by any escaped POW in the whole of the Second World War.

As Ralph and his fellow escapees partied in Lovrenz they were, to all intents and purposes, home free. The fact that their original escape group of eight now numbered only six, due to the two men they had been forced to leave behind, meant that they no longer faced the threat of execution if captured. This was a situation they were about to change in the most dramatic fashion imaginable. They were now in the hands of an impressive local force, and had complete confidence in their protectors to guide them to safety. They also had no idea what had happened when the depleted workforce had returned to the prison camp, but could have reasonably expected that their absence would have been noticed and German forces dispatched to the railway site to retrieve them.

In fact, it had still not been noticed that they were gone – the sergeant responsible for roll call had spent the evening in Maribor with his girlfriend, and had not returned to the camp in time. For this mistake, he was sent to the Russian front.

Ralph also knew that if the escape attempt was compromised, if a battle ensued, then he would be shot by the partisans along with Les. Once again, he had made a decision that placed him in imminent peril, but had done so in order to save the remainder of the prisoners under his charge. It was the gamble of a lifetime.

The following morning, after a few hours' restless sleep and nursing pounding hangovers, Ralph and Les joined the partisan force on the trek back to the railway siding at Ozbalt. Immediately, Churches noted that this was a highly professional outfit, although he was surprised to see that two of the officers were on horseback. These same officers split the force into groups of ten men, who moved swiftly between areas of cover – a tactic that proved essential as a Fieseler Storch reconnaissance aircraft droned overhead. It was a cool, misty morning, and after a small group had carefully recced the position ahead, the bulk of the force arrived at Ozbalt and hid itself in the thick undergrowth overlooking the work site.

They waited in complete silence until – to Ralph's great relief – he heard the rattle of the train approaching. It was 8 a.m. on the morning of 31 August, and the largest successful operation to free Allied prisoners of the whole Second World War was about to begin. Success hung on a knife edge – how would the guards react? How would the prisoners themselves respond? Could the Germans have used this as an elaborate trap of their own? The partisans lay motionless behind their weapons, their two POW accomplices scanning the line beneath them desperately, hearts pounding, their own lives to be decided in the next few minutes.

The train stopped directly beneath them, and they watched the workforce alight and ready their tools for the day ahead. With a hiss and a clatter of pistons, the train began to move, gathering momentum as it commenced its journey back down the tracks. The moment it disappeared around the corner, a whistle was blown by the partisan commander and the operation began. A great shout went up, and the partisan force exploded from the undergrowth, brandishing their weapons and roaring instructions at the guards and the prisoners. Surprise was total, paralysing and devastatingly effective.

One of the working party was a Royal Engineer called D. W. Luckett, who had been captured in Crete in 1941. He writes in his own account of the ambush that a 'gang of the fiercest looking characters possible suddenly bobbed up from behind the small bushes which grew to within a few yards of the line, all were screaming as hard as they could, and brandishing Sten guns, which they pointed straight at us.'

There were eight guards with the workforce, and yet not a shot was fired. Terrified, they dropped their weapons and raised their hands. They in particular had been told of the ferocity of the partisans, and believed that they would be tortured and executed. However, they had an unlikely ally.

Churches had taken the precaution of wearing his distinctive slouch hat, knowing that it would be a rallying point for the prisoners and indeed the guards. D. W. Luckett writes that Churches was shouting, 'Come on, you jokers, get up here into the trees.'

I mentioned this moment to Neil.

'Yeah, that's the essence of what he was saying.' He smiled. 'But if you imagine him saying it in a slightly more forceful, Australian manner, then you'd be about right.'

Churches was also quick to enjoin the partisans not to shoot the guards, and indeed could be heard shouting at the guards themselves, telling them not to shoot back, knowing it would be their death sentence. Such was his relationship with the guards that, as they were bustled up the hill at gunpoint, one of them turned to Churches and said to him that he was a *'grosser Gauner'* – a great rogue – a term of affection as much as admonishment.

The prisoners had also scrambled into the woods, and were now being rounded up by the partisans so that a forced march could begin to get them as far away from the ambush site as possible. In total, there were seventy-nine prisoners in the group, as well as four civilian contractors and eight guards. Add to this the partisan force, and the size of the task becomes apparent. Facing the partisan commanders was a march of 250 kilometres across occupied territory, guiding a group of ill-equipped, unfit malnourished men through some of the most demanding terrain in Europe, under the noses of the German occupier who would deploy every means possible to find them. The first stage of what would be the largest mass escape of Allied prisoners in the Second World War was underway.

CHAPTER SEVENTEEN

A Traitor in their Midst

As their long march began, Churches was immediately struck by the military efficiency of the partisans. This was no ragtag collection of desperate patriots, but instead a well-drilled army, with a clear rank structure, established operating procedures and skills that would have graced any Special Forces unit. The latter had been honed in the previous three years of hit-and-run operations, and drew on the inherited knowledge of generations of woodsmen and hunters. The skills of these hunters remained the same, all that had changed was the quarry.

There were three main characters who would loom large for Churches over the course of the escape. They were 'Sveik' (real name France Gruen), 'Franchek' (Franjo Vesenjak), and 'Cholo' (Karel Cholnik).

Sveik led for much of the route and was a natural focal point for Churches. He was in fact a political commissar – every partisan group had one – but proved very swiftly to be a resolute, strong and highly capable military leader. Churches describes him as being taciturn to the point of impenetrability (it was twenty-seven years before he would learn his real name), but felt immediately that the group was in the right hands.

Franchek was a young partisan – only eighteen – allocated as an interpreter, and as such he barely left Churches' side for the majority of the route. Out front was Cholo, who had been a soldier in the Royal Yugoslav Army and was a tireless tracker, scout and guide.

Such clear rank structure was typical of the partisans by this point of the war, when they were a very well-established fighting force indeed. They had set up an extensive support network throughout the country, as well as endlessly refining their own operating protocols to make them undetectable to the enemy. No detail was left to chance. A process was invented to cool smoke from cooking fires so it wouldn't betray a position to the enemy. Training camps were established to pass on the skills of stalking, sniping and advanced field craft. As their confidence grew, and their supply chain became more established through Allied air drops, so did their infrastructure. There was a radio station, the poetically named Kricac (The Screamer), a newspaper called *The Slovenian Reporter* and even a rudimentary social welfare system. The Slovenian National Liberation Committee became the Slovenian National Liberation Council, effectively an underground government capable of producing its own currency. Several hundred schools were established, as well as hospitals – many of them in the forests that were terra incognita to the enemy. Photographic darkrooms were also set up, a crucial means of recording not only the atrocities perpetrated by the Axis powers, but also the activities of the partisans themselves. Over the course of the war, 150 photographers produced 100,000 photographs of the occupation.

Slovenia was facing the physical deportation and eradication of its population; but it was also facing cultural genocide. Deaths pro rata of artists and writers were extremely high – writing poetry was considered an act of resistance and was punishable by death. Through the covert work of the partisans, the OF published many volumes of poems during the occupation and even gave concerts and theatrical performances, thus keeping the ember of their own cultural identity alive.

It is important to note, however, that as the prisoners took their first steps into the mountains, the Germans – although losing the war – were still very much a strong presence in Slovenia. This was far from a vanquished enemy – in terms of munitions and numbers of troops they far outnumbered the partisans. Indeed late 1944 represented the height of German munitions manufacture in the Reich. A mass breakout at the heart of one of their districts was an act of defiance that had to be mercilessly destroyed, and the partisans moving the huge, unwieldy group of men away from Ozbalt knew perfectly well that they only had a few hours before the Germans launched their pursuit.

They were right to be concerned. Only an hour after the ambush, the air-raid sirens sounded in Maribor and every remaining POW was evacuated to Austria with only half an hour's notice. Much as this rankled with the men left behind, it transpired that it saved their lives. Stalag XVIII-D was accidentally bombed by the Allies shortly afterwards, sustaining heavy damage. Churches' and Laws' actions – albeit inadvertently– had saved the lives of those who were left behind as well as the main group of escapees.

The group marched hard for four hours straight, their initial route taking them up precipitous, heavily forested slopes and ever deeper into the heart of the mountains. This was a simple tactic from the partisans' point of view – to get the group into their area of operations. As such, any immediate German pursuit would be met on the partisans' own terms. During this period, they covered fourteen miles – taking them past Lovrenz and into the wilderness beyond – and by the end they were footsore, frightened and hungry.

One of the recurring themes of the escape – and indeed the operations of the partisans throughout the war – was the co-operation and support of the local population. Their collaboration may not have always been active, but the support for the escape was almost universal. To show the passage was clear, local people would hang white washing outside their houses en route. They also supplied food – and this in a nation stripped bare by war, where the vast majority struggled to survive. The first stopping point on the march was a small settlement where the prisoners were served soup at a large secluded farmstead. Most of them had left their pots and utensils for eating back at the ambush site and Churches suddenly found himself the centre of attention, as the group turned to him for guidance. Just how do you feed soup to a large group of hungry men without any spoons, cups or bowls?

Churches also knew the partisans would lead the group into the most inaccessible regions of the mountains in order to avoid the pursuing German forces. Looking round the escapees he saw exhausted men, most wearing shorts, T-shirts and ill-fitting boots. He suddenly realized just how ill equipped the group were for the rigours of the mountains.

He was under the most intense psychological pressure, and it is not at all surprising that Churches had a nervous breakdown shortly after his return to Australia at the end of the war. Touchingly, when I broached the subject with Neil, he noted that it happened only days after he embraced Ronte, his wife, on the station platform where she stood to greet him after four long years apart.

'I think sometimes that the true end of his journey,' he said, 'wasn't reaching safety, it wasn't being repatriated, it was actually putting his arms round his wife. He mentioned it a few times during the escape, apparently.'

The escapees were all there under his care, not only because he was a natural figure of authority and had been their Camp Leader, but also because it was he who had decided to go back and get them. He had persuaded the partisans to help them, and as such had placed all of their lives in danger – and indeed the lives of their families, as there certainly would have been widespread reprisals if they had been captured and identified. And by no means were all the prisoners happy to be there – several had wanted to see out the war in the relative comfort and security of the camp.

Churches finally sorted out the soup issue – the men borrowed the partisans' utensils after they had eaten. This created the added burden of every meal taking far too long, and would have to be addressed imminently. Later along the route, the group managed to beg, borrow and steal enough utensils to make this less of an issue, and were using a series of old tins, jars, pots and mugs. But at this early stage it presented a real problem. Keenly aware that even as they ate, truckloads of Germans would be deploying from Maribor – still only thirty kilometres away – the partisan commander ordered them to move before half the men had finished eating. Their route took them into even more forbidding and dense country, home turf for the partisans but what must have seemed like a deeply alien landscape for the escapees.

The Austrian guards and civilian contractors were turned free along the route, having been stripped of their weapons and uniforms. They shook Churches' hand as they left, thanking him for their freedom and indeed their lives. He learned after the war that they had all made it back to Maribor safely.

A measure of the intense mental strain all were under came in a short but tragic incident as they arrived at their final rendezvous, late into the evening. A deeply distressed partisan approached Churches, clutching a picture of his wife and two young daughters. He explained that he had joined the partisans very recently as the Gestapo had started to take an interest in him, and had just learned that in his absence his family had been sent to a concentration camp. Churches comforted him as best he could, but to little effect. Moments later, the sound of a single gunshot rang through the darkness – the man had placed the muzzle of his rifle in his mouth, and pulled the trigger.

There was nothing to be done but make the most of their present surroundings. They had reached a tiny settlement to the north-west of Slovenska Bistrica, where they were told they were to spend the night. Here a surprise awaited Churches. He had mentioned in passing to the partisan commanders in Lovrenz that there was a poorly defended outpost with eight British prisoners of war close to Ozbalt. He was amazed to see five partisans turn up with these eight prisoners in tow. Showing extraordinary chutzpah, the partisans had despatched a fighting patrol to release the men, who now joined Churches' party – swelling their number to nearly ninety. The other surprise was less agreeable. The partisan fighting patrol had initially made an error of navigation, and liberated ten Frenchmen from a similarly remote outpost, before realizing their error and returning for the British prisoners. If certain members of the main party were less than pleased to be on the run through wild country guided by what they regarded as a group of brigands and an insane Australian, the Frenchmen were positively incandescent. They had forged a very comfortable life for themselves indeed in their secluded haven, with girlfriends in the local village and an easy work routine. They set up a cacophony of mutinous disapproval from the moment they arrived, and did not let up until the end of the trek. As one ageing partisan noted long after the war, 'Ah, those Frenchmen. They kept going on strike!' It seems a distinctly Gallic solution to a somewhat unpalatable situation.

But, like the rest of the group, any other options they all had were now a distant memory. They were deep in the woods, with a large and motivated German force massing in their wake, and a long, long trek ahead over some of the wildest terrain in Europe. Success would need impeccable planning, near nationwide collaboration from a wary civilian population and a great deal of luck.

For me it was now time to say farewell to Neil, and jump ahead on the route to explore some of the more extreme environments through which the group moved during their trek. Svetlana had arranged for a local mountain guide – Herman Novak – to meet me at a mountain refuge in Klopni. This would give me a real impression of the highest terrain over which the group travelled, and would also lead me to their site of greatest peril, a single moment when the entire escape was placed in jeopardy. It was an event that would haunt Churches for the rest of his life, and I was keen to visit the site for myself.

My first challenge, though, was to keep up with Herman as he effortlessly moved along the initial stages of the route. We were over a kilometre up in the sky, an altitude of 1,300 metres, walking through dense woodland that was dusted with snow, following a twisting track that was leading us into the heart of the Steiner Alps.

Herman was a compact, jocular, lean figure, all big smiles and bounding strides. He was also – rather depressingly – sixty years old, which gave me pause for thought as I leant against a tree to catch my breath and rest my burning thighs. Years of squinting into the middle distance, towards the next ridge, the next peak, the next destination, had given him a network of crow's feet from the edge of each eye, deltas of experience and mountain wisdom. This, combined with the fact that he sported a rather splendid, piratical grey beard, gave him a somewhat buccaneering look. It came as no surprise when he mentioned that his uncle had been a partisan. But for an accident of time I could quite easily imagine him draped in bandoliers, creeping through the undergrowth in the soft light of dawn.

In following the path of the Crow's Flight as best we could through the mountains – and certainly retracing their steps at some points – we were addressing one of their fundamental challenges. It was not simply that they were being pushed to the limits of their endurance, it was that they were also so badly-equipped for cold weather.

Ralph had been right to have concerns about their pitifully inadequate clothing. For the first two nights of their exhausting route march into the mountains the men slept where they fell – curled up in outbuildings of remote farms, or sometimes simply catching a moment's rest on the forest floor. They had shivered and trembled through nights where the wind was cold and the air was thin, and it became obvious that they would succumb to exhaustion through lack of sleep long before the rigours of the long march broke them down.

The leader of the partisans – Sveik – had already split the entire group into sections of ten men, each with a partisan guide. Ralph recalls being in awe of the physical prowess of the partisans on the march, particularly the scouts: 'Super fit, covering two miles for every one mile the group walked. Utterly fearless, operating on their own, armed only with a Sten gun or a rifle.'

But despite these precautions, the danger of being caught was ever present. Throughout their entire trek, they were never more than fifteen kilometres away from German forces. Several times they had to pass within 200 metres of watchtowers or sentry positions.

Sveik therefore made the decision that they should march at night, and lay up during the day. In the modern armed forces, this is standard practice on any escape and evasion, but for these men it was a blessed relief. The heat of the day meant they at least had a chance of sleeping, and the darkness gave them cover to move – although it dramatically increased the risk of injury from slips and falls.

They had an added incentive, one that drove them ever onwards, past the point of exhaustion and ever deeper into the mountains. The partisans had taken custody of a traitor who was caught poisoning some soup destined for a large group of partisan fighters. He had been handed over to the group for transfer to another region, where – Ralph presumed – justice would be arbitrary, short and terminal.

A few days later, the traitor gave his captors the slip. The group knew that the nearest substantial German presence was at Slovenj Gradec, a mere twenty-five kilometres distant. For a fit man, travelling fast, that was two to three hours away. Undoubtedly this was where he was headed, and the partisans knew that before dawn their location would be swarming with Germans. The group had already halted to sleep, but found themselves roughly woken and force-marched for several hours, leaving them confused, physically spent and ever more debilitated. But it had probably saved their lives.

Unbeknownst to any of them, the Germans had reinforced key sections of the route they thought the group might take, trying to anticipate bottle necks and crossing points where they might be attacked and recaptured. One such crossing point lay dead ahead.

The entire group was about to walk into a trap.

During the course of the escape, the average distance covered was about fifteen kilometres a day – with the partisans doing twice that distance as they moved up and down the lines, cajoling, threatening and rallying the lines of weary escapees. This may not sound a great deal, but it is important to remember that this was no flat ramble – it was hard going through mountainous terrain clad in dense forest.

As I walked with Herman, I was keen to replicate the pace of the partisans, and so we leant into the steep hills, every exhalation fogging in the still air as we laboured each step, cresting green ridges before letting gravity propel us down the slopes. The scenery was breathtaking – the snow not only made the landscape a fantasy vista of laden conifers and alabaster slopes, it also deadened every sound. The only noise was the sawing of our breath and the occasional crack of a snow-laden breaking branch, a distant echo that resonated through the trees like a gunshot. We marched in companionable silence, stopping every now and then when a gap appeared in the trees, resting our hands on our sticks, and looking out at the glorious panoramas before us.

One would think that the escapees would have little time to ponder their surroundings, but Churches was profoundly moved by the beauty of the landscape around him. As a farmer's lad from Australia, he was overawed by the mountains of Slovenia, and – referring directly to the land through which he passed – noted in his memoirs a line from a Reginald Heber hymn:

Though every prospect pleases, and only Man is vile.

The line was particularly apt given his current situation, but he was very soon to learn just how vile a truly devious man can be – the traitor had, it seemed, done his work well.

For Herman and me, the end of our day's hiking was an innocuous-looking farmhouse sitting on a ridge, a few kilometres west of the tiny village of Topolšica. To one side was a rolling field, emerald-green with lush alpine grass. At the back of the farmhouse, the land dropped away sharply, a thickly wooded hill that led to a chuckling stream several hundred metres below it.

'Is this the site, Herman?' I asked, dropping my pack and slumping down on top of it. We had travelled about twelve kilometres, two short of the target distance, but still a good hike through snowy mountains on a brisk day.

'It is, Monty, yes. I think it's even the same house, perhaps just renovated a little since the war.'

Aside from the ubiquitous barking farm dog (a constant hazard for the group, effectively an alarm call that gave away their presence), I could scarcely imagine a more tranquil scene. It was here that the group had arranged to rendezvous with local supporters, to have some food, rest briefly and then move on.

The lead scout had flashed his torch into the darkness as the group huddled in silence in the woods around him. There was no response, so he flashed the torch again.

Clear as crystal, a voice resonated out of the night ahead.

'Wer ist da?' – 'Who's there?' – unmistakably German, and unmistakably a challenge.

Much has been made of the partisans' covert talents, their ability to move silently and vanish into the shadows, important skills when in virtually every fight they ever faced they were heavily outgunned, invariably outnumbered and faced the possibility of being outflanked, outmanoeuvred and massacred. The fact that they fought any pitched battles at all is testament to their courage and was also a powerfully defining hallmark of their war. The escapees were about to witness a vivid demonstration of such courage.

'Partisaaaaaans!' bellowed Sveik at the top of his voice, and at once all hell was let loose. D. W. Luckett describes what followed:

The silence of the night was shattered and made hideous by the stammer of several machine guns opening fire on us [. . .] the rounds zipping through the trees and bushes like hornets.

The partisans had seen men run in situations like this, and be cut down; they had seen men hide, and be taken prisoner. They knew their best chance of survival was to attack – uphill, charging through a killing zone, all the while bellowing their defiance and resolve. But this was more than just a mindless dash – the partisans had learned a few tricks of their own.

As they advanced, they immediately spread out and began firing short bursts before quickly moving again. This gave the impression of a force of some size. Their leader – presumably Cholo, although this has never been confirmed – began bellowing, 'Partisan Company One, Advance! Partisan Company Two, Advance! Partisan Company Three, Advance!' This mantra, continuously shouted during the firefight, gave every impression that a huge force was moving irresistibly up the hill towards the farmhouse.

If the response of the partisans was slick, ferocious and well drilled, the escapees could not have presented a greater contrast. This is not entirely unreasonable – this was a group of men who had not faced fire for many years (and some, like Churches, had never faced it at all). They had dropped to the ground, and were not moving at all. Franchek, one of the lead partisans, noted their frozen immobility.

'Go back! Run!' he roared at them.

The men scattered into the night, a helter-skelter dash into the sanctuary of the darkness around them. One can only begin to imagine what Churches and Laws experienced at this moment. They had asked all those involved to trust them, and as such they felt the lives of the many men under their supervision were their responsibility. During the last few days of brutal marching, they must have begun to feel the first flickers of hope that they could genuinely pull this off, and yet in a single moment of sound and fury, it had all gone spectacularly wrong.

One of the lead partisans had already been shot dead, and the prisoners were now scattering into the impenetrable night of the deep forest.

But the heroism of the partisan response had taken effect. It is not known how many Germans were holed up in the farmhouse – there is every chance that it was a small detachment. Plainly every outpost in the region was on high alert due to the information gleaned from the escaped traitor, but in this case the enemy numbers were not quite as catastrophic as they might have been. The firing gradually subsided, and the partisans immediately scattered into the woods to retrieve the sheltering prisoners. By dint of good luck, and a rare ability to quickly cover large tracts of ground at night, the partisans had soon rounded up all but six of the escapees. They could not wait for the missing men. Using a gulley next to the farmhouse, they moved the group on at great speed, knowing all the while that their entire operation had been compromised.

As fast as possible, they set out to put as much distance as possible between themselves and the German soldiers. Churches recalls the sound of gunfire in their wake, and surmised that the Germans had been lured into a series of running battles in pursuit of a will o' the wisp enemy who held a mighty prize. In *The Crow's Flight* he notes: 'The Germans might not bother to chase a small crew of escapers – but 100 – well, they certainly would! The partisans could therefore attack the German chasers.'

To a degree, the Germans were now playing directly into the hands of the partisans. As they entered their heartlands, the OF fighters could stage a series of hit-and-run ambushes, lurking in the undergrowth and attacking the German patrols who floundered in their wake. A series of small skirmishes was perfectly tailored to the partisans' modus operandi, and must have been a terrifying experience for their pursuers.

Finally, the group reached a safe point a few miles north of the township of Mozirje, a flight of about five kilometres that left them spent and deeply rattled. Churches had found it a shattering experience. To come so close to annihilation, having shepherded the group so far, was an intensely disturbing moment. He would not speak of the ambush after the war, perhaps fearing the mental demons it would unleash.

CHAPTER EIGHTEEN
A Final River to Cross

The group had been on the march for nearly a week, and the mutterings of discord that had been a feature throughout now reached a crescendo – perhaps fuelled by their close escape. Churches dealt with it in his customary, uncompromising manner, confronting the main agitators and informing them that they were free to leave at any time. He did note – fairly vigorously – that they had 'not pulled on uniforms to be Hitler's guests', and what he was offering them was a chance to 'get on with the duty they had solemnly sworn to do.'

The speech – one of several Churches made during the course of the escape – had the desired effect, although the rumblings of discontent never entirely ceased. Churches' approach was a masterpiece of man-management – his own steps never faltered, he made sure his turn-out was of the highest standards, and always wore his slouch hat so he could be easily recognized and approached at any time. Aware of the growing disquiet, he began to constantly move up and down the line of men and arranged for different groups of escapees to lead different sections of the trail, to keep them engaged and motivated.

By now, the group were within fifty kilometres of Ljubljana – the section of the escape that held the most threat of

289

compromise and capture. There were two major dangers in passing the city. The first was that the forests had thinned, and much of the route was now in open country that was of great strategic significance to the Germans. The second was that this remained a centre for German logistics, surrounded by roads that were constantly patrolled and heavy with traffic. The partisans' problem was that they had to pass reasonably close to the city, as a diversion would have added tens of kilometres onto their route, and they must by now have been well aware of the parlous state of the escapees. It was a huge gamble, but one that had to be taken.

Moving only at night, they flitted between areas of sparse cover, their progress punctuated by bursts of machine-gun fire and the staccato crackle of rifles in the distance. To cover their passage, the partisans were staging a series of hit-and-run raids as a diversionary tactic. For three consecutive nights, they moved in total silence, with all talking forbidden and all equipment muffled, a ghostly column of men twisting in a line that sometimes stretched for over a kilometre, being spirited through open country, hidden by a local population who risked horrific reprisals if discovered.

Their swift, stealthy movement over this dangerous ground reaped rewards, and soon they were entering more established partisan regions. Although they were not quite halfway through the entire trek, there was a surreal event that made them all abruptly aware that they were in more benign territory. While walking along an exposed dirt track in the afternoon – in itself a huge departure from their normal protocol, which had been based entirely on covert movement at night – Churches was asked by Franchek to form the men up in 'best parade ground style', as they were about to be inspected by a British officer!

They were duly marched into an open field and presented to a delegation of thirty men, one of whom was unmistakably a major in the British army. Churches stood his men at ease and saluted the major, who in response reached out and shook his hand warmly. Churches recalls their opening exchange:

'You surprise me, Corporal,' said the Major. 'I've always understood that Australians reserved their salutes for special people on special occasions.'

'Believe me, Major,' I replied. 'This particular occasion measures up on both counts.'

Churches also recalls that the major – whose name he remembers as Jones – informed him that they were nearly in safe territory. A leading partisan in the accompanying group – one Edvard Kardelj – also spoke to him, and expressed a similar sentiment.

Occupying Churches' mind at this juncture was one final, hugely intimidating obstacle, a prodigious natural barrier that stood between them and freedom. Having exchanged pleasantries with the major and his entourage – a meeting he later described as one of the most bizarre moments of the entire escape – the group bade their farewells and the march resumed. This impromptu parade had taken place in occupied territory, behind enemy lines, with German forces on high alert in the area. It is perhaps a measure of the partisans' confidence, and indeed their sense of showmanship, that they had arranged such a surreal parade for their allies – a flamboyant show of defiance, a vivid illustration of the transfer of power that was taking place.

One of Churches' final questions had been to Edvard.

'How on earth are we going to cross the Sava River?'

The Sava is the Danube's largest tributary, a wide, powerful body of water, completely exposed, with German guard posts and watchtowers every few kilometres along its length. It divided

Slovenia from east to west, lay a few days' travel distant, and there was no way it could be avoided. The Sava, in effect, represented a border, a final obstacle between the occupied territories to the north and the partisan-controlled regions to the south. The bridges were all heavily fortified – too well manned to be taken by the partisans with their light weaponry – and the water too deep to wade.

Edvard's response was noncommittal: 'That, I'm afraid, I cannot tell you.'

Two days after our mountain trek, Herman and I stood on the banks of the Sava. It rolled by lazily at our feet, languid and muscular, its power undeniable, following a path carved over many millennia. It was early morning, and behind us a quarry was just coming to life, with shouts of men arriving for work, a cough of a vehicle ignition and the first clatter of steel on stone.

Industry has always been drawn to large rivers as a means of transport and an unending supply of freshwater. Where industry goes, human habitation follows, and the scene around us reflected the scenario facing the group of escapees seven decades before. They would have to cross the Sava a mere twenty kilometres from Ljubljana in an area of intense industrial activity – a twisting, heavily patrolled corridor dotted with guard posts that at the time represented a zone of vital importance to the Germans and their last area of real power in Slovenia.

Herman and I had selected a site based on local topography and historical accounts – the latter drawn mainly from Ralph's book. I had a feeling that we were pretty much spot on. We discarded the points where steep banks and rapids would have made such a large-scale operation unfeasible. Where we stood, the banks sloped gently towards deep water, the river drifting past slowly, its surface burnished and still in the morning sun. There were no buildings as such along this stretch of river; just ranks of tress and low scrub. The lack of habitation would have been good for the escapees, but this spot had the disadvantage of being very exposed – with so little cover, upon arrival at the river the group would have had to move across at great speed to avoid discovery. The pressure on the partisans was intense – a seminal moment in the escape was upon them.

We had arranged to borrow a small wooden boat to make our own crossing. As we clambered aboard, each of us made the fundamental mistake of assuming that the other knew precisely what they were doing, and as such our crossing was a festival of clattering oars, loud splashing, a series of slow revolutions in the current accompanied by muttered oaths and bellowed commands. Hauling the boat up on the other bank a considerable time later, we sat and reflected on the partisans' plan in the light of our own faintly calamitous efforts – a plan that had somehow spirited over a hundred men across the Sava, without detection, under the very noses of an enemy who were on high alert for their arrival.

This was a phenomenal achievement, as there was every chance that – given the position of the ambush a few days before – the Germans would have anticipated several points of crossing. This could well have resulted in a firefight well beyond the capabilities of the smaller outpost the escapees had previously encountered, and would effectively end the escape bid as well as the lives of many involved.

'This crossing used everything the partisans had at their disposal, everything,' said Herman. 'You could say that they got lucky, but for me this was their greatest achievement.'

The German occupiers had already placed watchtowers every few kilometres – a fact Churches was keenly aware of, having been given a map by one of the partisan guides. On it the river meanders through the landscape, with German positions marked by swastika flags. These entirely dominate the major twists and turns of the Sava, and overlook long stretches of open ground along the banks.

On their last evening before approaching the Sava, the men were instructed to get a good night's sleep, as the next day would be a busy one. After a final route march to a location near the banks of the river, the men were ordered to lie low, stay quiet and await instructions.

Night fell and with it came the unmistakable clatter and snorting of a large number of horses approaching. The partisans had mobilized the local farming community, using a quirk of wartime agricultural necessity. The occupying forces had seconded many of the animals normally used to work the fields, and as such the farmers needed to drive their remaining horses across the river in order to work the fields on the far side. This tended to be done at night, to ensure that the animals were in place for work to begin early the next morning.

But this was not simply a case of using a convenient local distraction to move under cover. Virtually the entire local village had been mobilized. Small boys signalled the all-clear by throwing rocks into the river. A network of houses were made available for warming the escapees after the crossing, for supplying food and for treating any wounds that might be incurred. This was a true community effort, and magnificent deployment of local assets for one purpose alone – to spirit the Crow's Flight to safety.

At 10 p.m., the order was given, and the first of the men clambered into two boats – each holding six people – that would be rowed back and forth by local rivermen. The prisoners were to be handed over to another partisan group on the south side of the river, so this was a poignant moment for Churches, as he said farewell to Cholo, Sveik and Franchek, who had been with him from the start. They embraced warmly, just before Churches climbed into the boat, then they slipped away into the night. Churches would not see any of them again for nearly thirty years.

As the men began their crossing, the horses were split into two groups to be driven into the water 500 metres upstream and downstream of the group. It was a noisy and slow process, as some of the horses were reluctant and tried to make their own escape. Meanwhile, in the distance, there was the constant accompaniment of any major movement of the escapees – gunshots, as patrols of partisans attacked outlying German positions in order to draw their forces away from the river. Colonel Peter Wilkinson's much-vaunted Slovenian 'popular uprising' had reached its zenith on that warm September night, and every member of the escape group made it across within three hours. Having been one of the first to cross, Ralph waited anxiously on the riverbank to see for himself that all the men were safe.

Over the course of the war the partisans used similar techniques to spirit nearly 7,000 wounded fighters, civilian refugees and escaping Allied prisoners and SOE operatives to the safety of the opposite bank and the lowlands beyond. The Crow's Flight escape represents the largest ever group to make the crossing successfully, and was used as a template for later successful crossings with big groups.

Although in terms of distance the group was only just over halfway to their destination, they were now moving through the south-eastern region of Bela Krajina, close to the Croatian border. While there was still an undeniable risk of being attacked by German aircraft, they were finally out of the reach of enemy infantry. They now knew they were aiming for the town of Semič, in the hands of the Allies and with a substantial air strip alongside it. The ensuing march – much of it along metalled roads – played hell with their feet. They were in the final stages, achingly close to salvation, when morale dipped once again and the march ground to a halt.

Rounding up the men, Churches gave them what was to be one final, stirring address.

> 'You're bloody heroes, you've made history,' he said. 'We've done more than 150 miles in fourteen days, we're not going to jib at the last ten, are we? I'm buggered too, but I'm making it to Semič this afternoon. Please fellas, this last time, make it there with me.'

And finally, at 1700 hours on Wednesday, 13 September 1944, led by a small, indefatigable Australian in a battered slouch hat, the largest successful escape group of the Second World War marched into Semič, into the hands of the Allied forces, and out of danger.

Herman and I had said our goodbyes in Semič at the end of our own trek. He had epitomized so many qualities that I associate with the partisans – seemingly limitless stamina, a certain style, and an easy familiarity with the mountains and forests. But mainly there was a defiant pride in who he was, a powerful sense of his own identity and the lineage he represented. I was sad to say farewell.

But for me, there was one final piece of business to attend to. Svetlana had left a message on my phone to say that she had found one of the surviving partisans who had moved with the group, and what's more, one who had been in the ambush at Topolišca. This was truly momentous news – here was living history, a man who had charged up that deadly forested hill in the darkness, who had searched the undergrowth for the escapees afterwards, and who had marched alongside that twisting column of desperate men.

I had contacted Neil, who fortuitously was still in the country, and asked him to meet me that afternoon at Otok, the site just outside Semič from where the group was finally airlifted to Bari in Italy. I had also arranged to meet Svetlana and the partisan there.

Driving the last few kilometres across the gently undulating arable land that abuts the site of the temporary air strip – long gone now, although the screen of trees that Churches mentions lining the end of the strip still remains – the first thing I saw was the Dakota that now stands as a monument to the escape. It was silhouetted on the horizon, snub nose pointing skywards, for all the world like it was readying for flight. As I pulled up alongside it, Neil was there to greet me, and shook my hand warmly before we settled down at a conveniently placed picnic bench to catch up on my journey and for him to describe his further investigations concerning Ralph.

We did not have a great deal of time to chat, as in the middle distance I saw Svetlana's car approaching. Neil was just describing the final night when the group had left Otok (there had been two postponed starts, and as only six of the group had ever flown before, this was a momentous experience for all of them), when I stopped him in mid-sentence.

'Look,' I said, 'I hope you don't mind me saying, Neil, but I think you honour your dad by the work that you're doing. We've found a partisan who was involved in the ambush that night, and he's come here to meet you.'

Neil looked thunderstruck, and wordlessly turned to look at the car as it drew to a halt in the parking space opposite us.

Alosz Voler stepped out and walked slowly in our direction. He looked remarkably sprightly for a ninety-two-year-old, even more so when one considers the life he had led.

As a Slovenian of fighting age, Alosz had originally been con-scripted into the German army, and found himself readying for the invasion of Normandy in the summer of 1944, manning the defences for the battle to come. A mere three weeks before the invasion took place, he had somehow managed to negotiate a short period of leave – highly unusual at a time of such heightened tensions – and had used it to return home. He immediately de-serted and joined up with his local partisan brigade. He may have only been a callow nineteen-year-old, but he was a fully trained (and equipped) soldier and was quickly involved in partisan oper-ations. One of his first was to escort a large group of prisoners – the Crow's Flight. He moved with the group for three days and two nights, and Svetlana had told me that he recalled many details very clearly – one was of an Australian with a distinct slouch hat.

Alosz walked slowly up to us and grasped Neil's proffered hand in both of his – twisted and arthritic, but still steady and strong. He smiled, and spoke in Slovenian directly to him.

'He says,' offered Svetlana in translation, 'that you look just like your father.'

Neil nodded and smiled, the two of them still clasping each other's hands long after the moment of greeting had passed.

I left them alone, animatedly exchanging stories and memories of Ralph, of the ambush, of the great march and of the war. Look-ing back at them as they sat in the shadow of the Dakota's wing, it seemed entirely fitting that this setting should be the site of such a reunion. They sat beneath a symbol of flight, of hope, of escape, a frail old man brought to life by the mirage of an ally from distant days defying the occupiers of his country. And Neil opposite him – still carrying the legacy of his father, learning more about the man he plainly idolized, and continuing his journey.

*

Upon my return to England, Neil emailed me a link to some footage from the Australian War Film Archive. In it I saw a man talking to directly the camera, his gaze unflinching, his words clear, the power of his personality apparent even through the filter of the lens. The interview was shot in 2003, when Ralph would have been eighty-five years of age, and yet he still bridles and bristles, ramrod-straight and word-perfect.

In it he is describing his treatment when he arrived back safely in Italy, to be met by an incredulous hierarchy from the regular army. Les and Ralph were debriefed by what he described as 'a caricaturist's dream of a model of a modern major general' – in fact a colonel from the Intelligence Corps. Ralph relates how he had to launch a staunch defence of the partisans, who were still regarded by many as nothing more than a militia. The interview concluded with the following exchange, a tale Ralph recounts with a distinct twinkle in his eye.

He walked to a big wall map. It was a map of Slovenia and surrounds. And he had pinpointed every POW camp, working camp. He said, 'Hmm. Only a hundred mile as the crow flies. If these partisans are so clever why aren't more of our fellows going up?'

Les joined me protesting, 'Sir, we were able to go to the partisans. The German security is very tight. We were in a position to go to the partisans and they got us out.'

'Mm. I still say, a hundred mile as the crow flies. I can't understand why more of our fellows aren't doing it.'

And I did my block. I said, 'Maybe, sir, it's because they're not bloody crows.'

He bridled a bit and he went 'Humph. Oh, of course, you're the Australian, aren't you?'

A fitting tribute perhaps, to this redoubtable, remarkable little man who ploughed such a memorable path in the face of overwhelming odds, and swept so many along with him in his wake.

SELECTED BIBLIOGRAPHY
AND SOURCES

BOOKS

Dan Billany, *The Cage* (Longman: London, 1949)

——, *The Trap* (Faber: London, 1986 repr.)

Barbara Bond, *Great Escapes* (Times/HarperCollins: Glasgow, 2015)

Vincent Brome, *The Way Back* (The Companion Book Club, Odhams: Watford, 1958)

Ralph Churches, *A Hundred Miles As The Crow Flies* (privately printed: Adelaide, 1986)

Matthew Cooper, *The German Army, 1933–1945* (Macdonald and Jane's: London, 1978)

Virginia Cowles, *The Phantom Major – The Story of David Stirling and the SAS Regiment* (William Collins: London, 1958)

Alfred John Evans, *The Escaping Club* (Fonthill: Oxford, 2012 repr.)

Lisa Fittko, *Mein Weg über die Pyrenäen* (dtv; Munich, 2013 repr.)

M. R. D. Foot, *SOE in France 1940–44* (HMSO: London, 1968 revised edn.)

M. R. D. Foot and J. M. Langley, *MI9* (Bodley Head: London, 1979)

John Esmond Fox, *Spaghetti and Barbed Wire* (Higham Press: Alfreton, 1995 repr.)

Anton Gill, *The Great Escape* (Review/Hodder Headline: London, 2002)

Richard Grunberger: *A Social History of the Third Reich* (Weidenfeld & Nicolson: London, 1971)

Robert Hann, *SAS – Operation Galia* (Impress: Exeter, 2009)

B. H. Liddell Hart, *The Other Side of the Hill* (Macmillan: London, 1973 repr.)

Peter Scott Janes (ed. Keith Janes), *Conscript Heroes* (Paul Mould: Boston, Lincs., 2006)

Donald I. Jones, *Escape from Sulmona* (Vantage: New York, 1980)

Anthony Kemp, *The SAS at War* (Murray: London, 2000)

Uys Krige: *The Way Out* (Maskew Miller: Cape Town, 1955)

Brian Lett, *SAS in Tuscany* (Pen and Sword: Barnsley, 2011)

Gordon Lett, *Rossano: An Adventure of the Italian Resistance* (Hodder & Stoughton: London, 1955)

Fitzroy Maclean: *Eastern Approaches* (Penguin: London, 2009, repr.)

Eric Newby, *Love and War in the Apennines* (Hodder and Stoughton: London, 1971)

L. H. Nouveau, *Des Capitaines par Milliers* (Calmann-Levy: Paris, 1958)

Mona Ozouf, *De Révolution en République* (Quarto/Gallimard: Paris, 2015)

Jože Pirjevec, Božo Repe (eds.), *Resistance, Suffering, Hope – The Slovene Partisan Movement, 1941–1945* (National Committee of the Union of Societies of Combatants of the Slovene National Liberation Struggle: Ljubljana, 2008)

FILMS
Le Chagrin et la Pitié, (Marcel Ophuls: France, 1969)

WEBSITES
Acknowledgments to various bulletins of the Escape Lines
    Memorial Society, and its website:
    www.ww2escapelines.co.uk
Acknowledgements to the *Conscript Heroes* website:
    www.conscript-heroes.com

ACKNOWLEDGEMENTS

It really is difficult to know where to begin in terms of thanking everyone involved in making this book a reality, but in the spirit of Ralph Churches I shall do my best! Thanks to Anton Gill – your unflagging enthusiasm for this project, and the high quality of your research and advice, made this book a joy to work on. Thanks to everyone at Seadog Productions – what drive, what dedication, and what vision to make an initial idea such vivid reality. Special mentions to Lib, Tom, Rich, Suze, Katy, Sally, Sonic, Stu, George, Sally and Linda. Thanks to Rob Coldstream and Alf Laurie at Channel 4. Thanks also to my foreign mountain guides – you are a credit to your profession. You walk in the footsteps, and maintain the finest traditions, of your forebears. Thanks to Herman, Svetlana, Consuello and Joel – your assistance and knowledge was invaluable. Thanks to all at Macmillan – Ingrid Connell, you have the patience of a saint, and as ever thanks to Julian Alexander for acting as the honest broker throughout.

And thank you – beyond measure – to every veteran, survivor, resistance fighter, local, and partisan who shared so many of their experiences with me. In the process you showed me how important simply doing the right thing can be. It has been a privilege to be able to tell your stories. And finally, thanks to Tam for – as ever – putting up with my pacing and muttering as the book took shape, and to Isla and Molly for assisting with uncommissioned crayon illustrations. The three of you make me realize why it's worth doing anything to get back home.

PICTURE ACKNOWLEDGEMENTS

We would like to express our gratitude to those who generously allowed us to use photographs from their private collections.

Page 1 (top) © United Archives GmbH/Alamy

Page 1 (bottom), page 2 and page 3 (top) © Patrick Guérrise

Page 3 bottom left © Imperial War Museums (HU55451)

Page 4 and page 5 (top) © Michèle Agniel

Page 6 and page 7 (bottom right) © Len Harley

Page 7 (centre and bottom left) © Bruno Spinosa

Page 9 (top left) © John Redhead

Page 9 (bottom) and page 10 © Robert Hann. More information on Operation Galia can be found in the highly acclaimed *SAS Operation Galia* by Robert Hann, which describes his father's experiences as an SAS paratrooper in Operation Galia and won the Impress Prize for New Writers. http://www.hannbooks.com/index.php/sas-operation-galia

Page 12 (top) © Universal History Archive IG via Getty Images

Page 12 (bottom) and page 16 (top left) © The National Liberation Museum Maribor

Page 13 (bottom), page 14 (top left and bottom), page 15 (top), page 16 (centre and bottom) © Neil Churches. More information on the Crow's Flight can be found in *A Hundred Miles as the Crow Flies* by Ralph Churches, a gripping first-hand account of one of the great escapes of the Second World War by an extraordinary man who, after escaping a POW camp with six others, went back for his mates – all 90 of them! www. ahundredmilesasthecrowflies.com, Facebook: Ahundredmilesasthecrowflies, Twitter: @100CrowMiles

Page 14 (top right) © Pat Palmer

The following are © Seadog TV & Film Productions Ltd: page 3 (bottom right); page 5 (bottom), page 7 (top), page 8, page 9 (top right), page 11, page 13 (top), page 15 (centre and bottom)

extracts reading groups
competitions books new
books discounts extracts
competitions events
books new extracts
events books reading groups
extracts new
books interviews events
discounts books
new books events
events new events
discounts extracts discounts
www.panmacmillan.com
extracts events reading groups
competitions books extracts new